THE
GLOBAL
CODE

THE GLOBAL CODE

HOW A NEW CULTURE OF UNIVERSAL VALUES IS RESHAPING BUSINESS AND MARKETING

DR. CLOTAIRE RAPAILLE

St. Martin's Press
New York

Author's note: Names of certain individuals have been changed. Many of their quotes come from Imprinting Groups conducted over the years.

www.stmartins.com

Library of Congress Cataloging-in-Publication Data

Rapaille, Clotaire.
   The global code : how a new culture of universal values is reshaping business, marketing and how we live and communicate / Clotaire Rapaille.
      pages   cm
   Includes bibliographical references and index.
   ISBN 978-1-137-27971-2 (alk. paper)
   1. Culture diffusion. 2. Culture and globalization. 3. Cosmopolitanism—Economic aspects. 4. Values—Economic aspects. I. Title.
   GN365.R37   2015
   306—dc23

2015011877

ISBN 978-1-137-27971-2 (hardcover)
ISBN 978-1-4668-7934-8 (e-book)

Our books may be purchased in bulk for promotional, educational, or business use. Please contact your local bookseller or the Macmillan Corporate and Premium Sales Department at (800) 221-7945, extension 5442, or by e-mail at MacmillanSpecialMarkets@macmillan.com.

Design by Letra Libre, Inc.

First edition: September 2015

10 9 8 7 6 5 4 3 2 1

"The real voyage of discovery consists not in seeking new landscapes but in having new eyes."

—Marcel Proust

CONTENTS

PREFACE

Discovery is my life. I've dedicated my entire career to uncovering hidden meanings and invisible dimensions and to decoding the unconscious cultural archetypes that drive us. My goal has always been awareness and helping people to look at the world around them with new eyes. Every discovery is exciting to me, and each teaches me something new. Every now and then, though, I make a discovery so big that it changes my life.

That's what happened when I discovered the Global Code.

For decades now, I have been operating with the understanding that the way each of us looks at our most important archetypes—love, health, and money, for instance—is guided by unconscious messages that are distinctive to the culture in which we were raised. This was the core idea behind my international bestseller, *The Culture Code.* A few years ago, though, I noticed something happening in my discovery sessions: while there continued to be codes distinctive to a particular culture, there were indications of additional strong unconscious messages that were consistent in all the places I studied. For example, when I did the discovery of the code for flying, I came away with unique codes for each culture—but at the same time, I came away with another code, a common code, that appeared regularly regardless of location.

This was something new, something I hadn't noticed in all the years I'd been doing discovery work. Once I uncovered it, though, it became evident in every international discovery that I did. In hindsight, it made perfect sense. We are now so completely connected globally that our culture of origin is only part of the story. We have gotten to the point where a global unconscious is beginning to influence us in very meaningful ways.

The implications of this are enormous. Just as the Culture Code for a particular archetype unlocks a culture's thinking about that archetype, the Global Code unlocks how we all think about that archetype. It does not, however, override the Culture Code. Instead, it works in concert with the Culture Code. Therefore, if you are interacting at a global level (and nearly all of us are at this point), you need both if you want to navigate the world successfully. This is true at a business level (Why are clinics located in hotels in major international cities such a good idea?) and at a social level (Why are Americans so often off-code when they try to promote tolerance around the planet?).

I have now completed enough global discovery sessions that I am ready to share what I have uncovered. I call it the Global Code. This book will address many of the archetypes that most concern us on a global level—things like survival, health and beauty, education, pleasure, adaptation, and change—and will juxtapose the Global Code against the Culture Codes I have discovered.

I will address what the codes mean for the world, and analyze on-code and off-code behavior in a variety of cultures. The structure of the book will be similar to that of *The Culture Code,* with an opening chapter addressing my discovery of the existence of Global Codes, and then 12 chapters focusing on key archetypes. As with *The Culture Code,* this book is filled with stories from my discovery sessions and with vivid examples of the codes in action.

My goal with *The Global Code* is the same as my goal with *The Culture Code:* awareness, enlightenment, and entertainment. I hope you will come away from this book with a powerful new perspective on how our newly connected yet divided world is affecting all of us. I also hope that you will take great pleasure in the reading experience. This book is thought provoking, controversial at times, not always politically correct, and always filled with my unique way of looking at the world.

As with *The Culture Code,* while I think *The Global Code* will be meaningful to anyone interested in human behavior, the book has its greatest practical application in the business community. Frankly, anyone doing business outside their own borders is taking a huge risk if they are doing so without a clear sense of the global mind-set about their product or service. In many ways, this is true even if your customers are only domestic. What the Global Code is teaching us is that these codes influence everyone everywhere. I also believe that this planet needs new pilots and that our common enemies are so powerful that we need a global action plan. This plan can only be successful if it is "on-code," which means that it respects the Global Code.

So there I was, going around the world many times a year, like a satellite looking at planet Earth. I quickly became very frustrated with all the available explanations of where the world was going. For me, they were journalistic theories and tourist comments. But none of them gave me the new insights I was starving for. I realized that nobody had accumulated the material necessary to decode the Global Mind. But I had, and I was going to be given the opportunity to do more.

Several of my clients were concerned by globalization. Is this the way of the future? How should we prepare ourselves for it? At the same time, an antiglobalization movement emerged and realized that the dangers of globalization are more important than the benefits. The global reaction and the global tension taught me that a "global mind" had started to express itself. The combination of new technologies, new travel possibilities and 24-hour breaking news had transformed the way we think and the way we operate. This is when I realized that we were facing the emergence of a new global consciousness and, even more important, of a new global unconscious.

My mission became clear. I had to decode this global collective unconscious. This book that you are going to read is the journal of this journey. It will take you around the world to places like China, India, Brazil, France and Russia, but also to Denver, Kansas City and inner-city Washington, D.C. It is a fascinating journey and I would like to share it with you. Let's see how it all started when I was a child.

INTRODUCTION

THE GLOBAL CODE

As a child I was interned at a Jesuit boarding school, where I was allowed to leave only three times a year. Yet I dreamed constantly about being free to discover the world. I wanted to get out. I wanted to travel. I was only 10 years old, but I had maps, itineraries and heroes whom I wanted to emulate. Marco Polo, Magellan, Alexander the Great—you name it. I was ready.

Like a stranded prisoner, I sent messages in bottles. I had pen pals around the world, from Cambodia to Cape Town, from Moscow to Mexico. I was so excited to receive their letters with those beautiful stamps. Opening the letters was like breathing fresh air from Africa, Asia or America. If I closed my eyes, I could actually imagine being there.

My first real taste of travel was at 18, when I hitchhiked to Scandinavia. From Paris I went to Belgium, Holland, Denmark, Sweden, Norway and back. I slept in youth hostels and made many friends along the way. When I was 20, I won a scholarship to go to Japan. In Japan, I learned how to speak some Japanese, write ideograms (kanji) and practice kendo. In 1964, when I was 23 years old, I drove my little Citroën Deux Chevaux (two-cylinder car) from Paris to India and back. The journey took me through Yugoslavia, Greece, Turkey, Iran, Afghanistan, Pakistan, India, Iraq, Syria, Jordan and Lebanon. This took four months in total.

The feeling of crossing the Bosphorus and entering the Asian continent was overwhelming. Arriving in Tehran and camping at the French embassy in the wake of De Gaulle's state visit and feasting on the leftover gourmet food and wine that remained from a dinner party that had been hosted there was indescribable. I crossed Afghanistan and discovered the valley with the Buddhas of Bamiyan (unfortunately later destroyed by the Taliban), slept on top of the big colorful trucks in Pakistan, enjoyed Sikh temples and experienced both the beauty and the horror of India.

In 1965, I was sent as a cultural attaché to the French embassy in Nicaragua. This was a paradigm shift for me. Now for the first time, I was not just traveling. I had a function, a job and a house in another culture. At that time, nobody wanted to go to Nicaragua. It was perceived as being at the end of the world, but I loved it.

I had recently graduated from Sciences Po in Paris and was still working on my doctorate. I arrived in my three-piece suit to introduce myself to my new boss, the ambassador. I will always remember our first conversation. "Rapaille, sit," he ordered. "Here is some advice you should follow if you want to survive here in Nicaragua. Every other week there is a revolution, and every other week there is an earthquake. When there is a revolution, you run into your house, and when there is an earthquake you run out of your house. Don't get the two confused, because if you do, you will die. Here is my first present to you." And he proceeded to place a .45 caliber handgun in my palm. "Tuck this behind your back, never arrive at the embassy at the same time or using the same itinerary, be discreet and you'll be safe," he instructed. "Thank you, Your Excellency," I said, to which he immediately responded, "And please call me Raoul, we are not at the Quai d'Orsay."

Of course I had taken my little Citroën Deux Chevaux with me, and it became incredibly useful for exploring Central America. I could not help it; I had to explore and discover these new countries. I drove from Managua to San Salvador, Guatemala, Honduras, Costa Rica and Panama. Everybody was looking at my little car as if I had built it myself; luckily, it generated a lot of sympathy, as it was not one of those big pretentious American cars. In 1969, I went to Brazil and spent several months studying witch doctors in the Amazon. I was living with a local indigenous tribe, eating their food, sleeping in hammocks, crossing piranha-infested rivers and catching every possible tropical disease you can imagine!

By 1968, I had moved back to France and was following the global student uprising, which began in Berkeley, California. Paris in May 1968 was another planet: "il est interdit, d'interdire" (it is forbidden to forbid). Everybody was in the streets for a truly general strike: "L'imagination au pouvoir!" (Give power to imagination). Very quickly, however, order was restored, ending a period that might have been one of the last expressions of French creativity. After that, France became too rigid for me, and it gave me the feeling that I had to move again.

My life destiny was imprinted at an early age. I was an explorer. I was here to discover hidden continents, deep within the global collective unconscious, which stretched beyond the geographical boundaries set by mapmakers. I was born in France, and one of my heroes was Jean-François Champollion, the young scientist who went to Egypt with Napoleon Bonaparte. He was the first to decipher the hieroglyphic inscriptions that had remained a mystery for centuries. He became my role model. I was not going to go around the world just to take pictures and accumulate "souvenirs"—I wanted to decipher hieroglyphics. I wanted to go deeper into the collective unconscious. I wanted to understand what nobody else could understand. I wanted to see what nobody else was able to see. I was already on my quest for the Global Mind. That was my mission. I spent the next 40 years exploring cultures on six continents. Many of the Fortune 100 companies became my clients. Their executives all became deeply involved in my passionate mission, which was to bring to consciousness the hidden forces behind people's behavior.

From China to Brazil, Germany to Mexico, and nation by nation, I built a network and a company that covered most of the world, with affiliates and representatives in 12 countries. This book is a journey, a captain's log from the exploration of the global mind. It is a discovery of the next evolutionary stage of global society. Darwin wrote about the evolution of species, but we can apply the same principles to societies. Can we see a pattern in this evolution? Are we going to see some societies and cultures disappear like the dinosaurs? Are we going to see others growing and developing, like *Homo sapiens*? Are humans going to self-destruct by not taking care of our only home, this planet? Or are we going to transform ourselves into a superior species?

Earlier I mentioned my interest in globalization. Of course, when everybody began speaking about it, I was asked by some of my clients (P&G, Boeing and others) to discover the hidden code behind globalization. People started reacting against globalization, as witnessed by the rise of anti-globalization political movements. People were afraid to see their everyday lives so drastically modified by new trends. They were afraid of losing their jobs to people in India and Bangladesh. They were afraid of losing their lifestyles. So one of the questions was, Can we find a generalized model that will apply to the world, or are we condemned to keep discovering tensions, oppositions, and a multitude of explanations, most of them contradictory?

After 1989, and with the fall of the Berlin Wall, many authors started talking about a new world order. Key texts appeared, like *The End of History and the Last Man* by Francis Fukuyama, *The World Is Flat* by Thomas Friedman and *The Clash of Civilizations* by Samuel Huntington. At the same time, the world saw an incredible resurgence of wars and violence. People began calling it the New World *Disorder*. Were we moving toward global order and governance, or were we heading toward global chaos?

The first decade of the twenty-first-century was defined by 9/11 and the ensuing wars in Iraq and Afghanistan. Those events further fractured the world order. The Arab Spring was even worse, as Arab states started disappearing and tribal warfare became the norm. Voltaire's Age of Reason became like an old dream that never materialized, and I started feeling nostalgic for the future envisioned by the philosophers who wrote *L'Encyclopédie*.

So where are we going? What are the tools that we need to decode our future? On the one hand, some people see the world as flat, but on the other, people see it as a multitude of divergent spheres. As a result, we see many countries and many cultures regressing to medieval times, tribal warfare or pre–Cold War sentiment. Is global capitalism the solution? On the surface, it seems it has taken hundreds of millions out of poverty. At the same time, the Internet, new technology and the advent of 24-hour media seem to have created more anxiety and frustration than ever. Secular attitudes are challenged by a resurgence of religious extremism. For example, Turkey is forgetting nationalist secular hero Mustafa Kemal Atatürk.

Democracy is out of breath and collapsing in many parts of the world. So I tried to find new literature or theories that could help me understand where we are headed, but I could not find any. Is the world global or local? Are we moving forward or backward? Do we have the universal values and universal truths we need to build a global community? Or must we simply accept that the world is multipolar, with different centers and worldviews that must each be seen through their own lenses?

Are we witnessing the end of the Western value system, the end of Western-style democracy and tolerance? The resurgence of fascism, and the rise of extreme right-wing political parties in Europe and Russia, as well as the spread of Islamic terror do not portend a rosy future.

Maybe the whole notion of progress should be reconsidered. Is it progress to have more money and less meaning? Should we be full of food and empty of ideas and meaning at the same time? Would we rather have less money and more meaning? Or is "meaning" an emotional illusion? Is education the solution? Or is it dangerous to know too much?

Then several clients asked me to study the "Millennials." This is the generation of people who were born with cell phones in their hands. You know, the ones who allegedly do not know how to write, only text. My team and I traveled to 16 cities around the world to try to decode their new mind, their new priorities, their hopes and anxieties. For the first time in my life I came across a new Global Tribe, one using the same tools, the same symbols, and the same rituals, all imposed by their cell phones. Is this the new global philosophy?

This book is an attempt to put all of the pieces of the puzzle together.

Many writers have already explored the global brain—that is, the interconnectedness of billions of cell phone users. But not so many have explored the possibility that this fantastic "brain" might be empty. It may simply be made up of billions of connections without anything to say. The fact that you have a brain does not mean that you have a mind. The brain is made of neurological connections and the mind is how we use and shape those connections. The brain itself has no identity; that being said we can explain and decode the American Mind or the Chinese Mind—this refers to the way Americans or Chinese use and shape their brains. So let's see if this new technology has created a new Global Mind.

THE GLOBAL CODE HYPOTHESIS

Is there anything like a global code—that is, an unconscious structure common to all the inhabitants of this planet that resonates with them at a deep emotional level? Or are we doomed to keep fighting and killing each other because we cannot agree on a global code?

Anybody who has traveled the world can see the unique elements of each culture, as well as the commonalities. Sushi is not couscous, but at the same time, people everywhere get married, build houses and raise children. Most of them also have cell phones, use the Internet, and share the same dreams of moving up and creating a better world for their children.

My hypothesis is that we can observe a global code in the making. This code is created by a Global Tribe of multicultural individuals who permanently benchmark the best practices of the world and share them with each other. It will become—and is already becoming—the standard aspired to by people everywhere.

WARNING

In most parts of the world, you cannot buy a product without being given a long list of warnings of the risk of side effects. So I think that before you continue reading this book, it is only fair that I provide you, the reader, with a warning label of my own that you may or may not choose to heed.

You might disagree with some of the codes. They might make you uncomfortable, and you might choose to reject them rather than challenge yourself and your vision of the world. I went through the same process, and it was sometimes painful to have to give up some of my old ways of thinking. This work is not a journalistic overview or armchair psychology. It is the result of more than 40 years of hard work, collecting thousands of handwritten stories that reflect the most powerful memories, both older and more recent, of thousands of people around the world.

This book also aims to give you new tools to deal with your changing world, and you might find it hard at times to give up old "wisdom" (see the section on recalculating in Chapter 8, page 170) or to consider every new moment of your life as the starting point of your new personal GPS.

You may suspect that the Global Tribe consists solely of disconnected rich people. You would be wrong. Money might be more of a danger than a blessing. What the Global Tribe has, regardless of wealth, is an *attitude*, and what they are creating is our future.

If you have the same attitude, you are a member of the tribe, and an active participant in the creation of the Global Code.

DISCOVERING THE GLOBAL MIND

Sometimes the answer hides in plain sight. Sometimes, the "leapfrog event"—the thing that fundamentally changes the way all of us think of something or use something—is so stunningly obvious that we don't even notice it. It's like ET in the closet full of toys—clearly different, yet somehow blending in.

A few years ago, Boeing hired me to discover the Culture Code for flying in a number of countries. They were getting ready to build the next generation of airplane, and they wanted to make sure that they were giving customers what they genuinely wanted. Boeing conducted a series of regular focus groups with frequent flyers, asking them what they wanted in an airplane.

The results were not surprising. The discussion proceeded exactly as anyone with even a glancing familiarity with the airline industry would have predicted. Participants expressed that they wanted more legroom at their seats, more space to move around, quality service from the flight attendants, a wide choice of entertainment, and other luxuries and amenities. Based on the early stages of these traditional marketing focus groups, Boeing concluded that people all over the world would be thrilled if the planes they flew in more closely resembled their living rooms.

But I don't believe what people say. Why? Because what people say they want and what they really want are often two very different things.

I'm not suggesting that people lie. I just think they are genuinely unaware of what's important to them at the deepest level. I talked about this at length in my book *The Culture Code*. What really matters to people—the code to what products and services truly resonate with them—is usually stored in the unconscious, and it takes quite a bit of work to uncover.

I suggested to Boeing that they forget about the classic focus-group results and instead try an imprinting session, which is what I do.

We invited frequent flyers from around the world to participate in a three-hour session. We held these sessions in New York, San Francisco, Hong Kong, Shanghai, Rio, Seoul, Tokyo, Dubai, Istanbul, London, Paris, Berlin and Singapore. The discovery was amazing. What the participants wanted was something else entirely.

Each imprinting session involves around 20 to 25 participants. It is divided into three phases, each one focused on a different part of the brain—the cortex, the limbic and the reptilian. I shall explain this in further detail below. The first phase is "cortex." During this hour, we explore the "conscious" element of the brain. We collect clichés and stereotypes, and we usually don't learn anything new. The purpose of this phase is a "wash-out," to purge the brain. People usually tell us what they think we want to hear.

If you know anything about what I do, then you know that our conversations don't stay simple for long. After an hour or so talking about the topic at hand, we have a break and then move to the second part of the brain, the limbic. Here we are in a world of complex, sometimes contradictory emotions. Mothers around the world will tell me that they want their children to grow, and, at the same time, that they don't want their children to grow. They want their children to become independent and to leave, but at the same time they don't want them to leave. They want their children to go to school, but the mothers all cry on the first day.

To discover what underlies these tensions, I ask people to explore "latent structures." This is like looking at the other side of the coin. It is the Mr. Hyde to Dr. Jekyll. During this hour, we encourage participants to tell stories about seemingly unrelated words and concepts. I get them to imagine they are talking to a five-year-old alien from another planet. The one basic rule is that they have to start the story with "once upon a time," just as if they were telling a bedtime story to help a child fall asleep.

The participants don't really understand what we're asking them to do, but they usually comply. By beginning each story with "once upon a time," we help them to reconnect with childhood memories and disconnect the cortex. Think about a situation where you go to see your banker to find out how much money you have in your account, and he starts the conversation by saying, "Once upon a time . . ." If that happens, you know you are in trouble. This is not the kind of mental thought process that you want your banker to have. The participants are usually, in this phase, very confused. They do not understand what we are doing, as this process is very different from the kind of focus groups they are used to.

After the second break, we explain to the participants that we are going to conduct a relaxation exercise to help them remember their first "imprint," or memory, related to the subject at hand. In order to do so, we ask them to lie down on the floor and follow our instructions. We dim the lights, play a little relaxing music, and tell them that it's OK if they fall asleep. The goal is to re-create the same mental state they're in when they wake up in the morning. Usually for five to ten minutes after waking, we can still remember our dreams. But if we don't write them down or record them somehow, they evaporate. This is because the cortex always arrives late to work in the morning. When we wake up from a nightmare, we are still sweating (reptilian) and frightened (emotional, limbic). By re-creating this mind-set, we disconnect the cortex and help the participants access very old, usually forgotten memories.

After a half hour of relaxation, we guide them back in time to their first imprint. They know that whatever they write after the relaxation exercise is going to be completely anonymous. This makes a big difference and allows them to be honest with themselves. They don't have to pretend; they just have to remember.

At the end of the experience, we give the participants a pad and a pen and ask them to write down everything that they remember about the subject we're studying. When we analyze these handwritten stories, we are often surprised by their depth and variety. We call this "third brain" the reptilian brain. This part of the brain is mainly associated with survival and reproduction; it is not influenced by culture. In contrast to the limbic and cortex brains, which are acquired at later stages in a child's development, we are born with the reptilian. Nobody has to teach us to breathe.

The process of understanding this is a powerful tool for anybody looking to discover what people have in common beyond culture.

In our sessions, people around the world recounted stories of their experiences and memories about traveling in airplanes, and most of these stories were about much more than the time spent in the air. For them, the trip started when they left home and ended when they arrived back home. Airlines, in contrast, see their business as beginning at the departure gate and ending at the arrival gate. Most of the participants' horror stories were about the airport and how badly they were treated.

There were the stories of standing in huge lines to check into a "high-security prison" where they were "humiliated by ex-cons." Soon came the stories of delay upon delay for reasons that were neither discernible nor explained by the airlines; stories of missed connections; stories of waiting for luggage forever; and stories of people not knowing if they were ever going to make their flights.

But we also read stories about the ideal situation, the dream. These stories were told by people who had been lucky enough to fly on private jets. They said that this was the ideal. But at the same time, these stories did not include anything that they told us that they wanted in the first hour of the session. Private jets have very little legroom, no food, no entertainment and no service. They did not care. Why? Because what they *really* wanted was not to have to go to the airport.

Certainly, these people weren't getting most of the things they'd mentioned wanting earlier. Sometimes there isn't even a bathroom. Yet story after story about this experience was glowing. Why? Nearby airfields, no security, no need to get to the airport hours early, no problems with luggage and so on.

As is always the case, the code for flying was different depending on the culture I was studying. The French, for example, equate flying with poetry. The phrase "etre dans les nuages," which translates as "being up in the clouds," refers to the majestic beauty and poetry of flying.

It should be noted that the name of Antoine de Saint-Exupéry, a career pilot, came up regularly in my French sessions; Saint-Exupéry is, of course, far better known for his poetic work, *The Little Prince*. It was also interesting to me that so many French participants mentioned the Concorde, even though few could have afforded to fly on it and the plane itself had been grounded for nearly a decade at that point. Again, they spoke of the beauty and elegance of the plane, ignoring the rather considerable failings of the enterprise. To the French, flying is poetry in the sky.

In Japan, on the other hand, participants focused on something else entirely. There they spent so little time telling stories about the actual transportation part of the experience that a casual listener might think they were talking about hotels or restaurants. The Japanese spoke nearly exclusively about the services on the plane—the hospitality of the flight attendants, the food and drink served, how the pilot spoke over the intercom. To the Japanese, flying is about hospitality. It is about the way you are treated while you are in the air, not about the process of moving from one destination to another.

These were decidedly different codes, with foundations in decidedly different cultures. Something else emerged during this discovery, though, that opened my eyes to an expanded field of study. No matter where I was—the United States, China, Turkey or France—there were considerable similarities in the foundations of the stories people told. This was something I hadn't seen, or at least hadn't been conscious of, in the hundreds of other discoveries I'd done before. Something new was happening—over and above the Culture Code—that defined the unconscious experience for the entire culturally diverse group of people who had participated. There was a code that unlocked the unconscious wants of all air travelers, everywhere. As I said before, the most important part was that none of them wanted to contend with an airport.

The implications of this discovery for the airline industry are profound. In response, Boeing recently took a step toward being more "on-code" with their creation of the Dreamliner 787. Instead of building an enormous plane like the Airbus A380, which can land only at huge airports (therefore requiring more people to transfer to get to their ultimate destinations and therefore more airport time), they went with a next-generation plane that could land at all commercial airports. This reduced the need for connections and limited the airport experience.

Meanwhile, the conversation is under way about the next steps in air travel. The technology already exists for vertical takeoff and landing. The technology also exists to make planes virtually silent. These advances make it unnecessary to build airports far from cities. It's conceivable that in the not-too-distant future, you'll go up your office building's elevator to a "drop zone" on the roof, rather than taking a long, expensive cab ride to go on a business trip. In case you think this is far-fetched, you have to remember that in the early 1900s, cars were available to only a very limited elite and very few people gave them any chance to survive.

We believe that in the same way cars changed the world, new technology will change the way we relate to time and space. This kind of on-code approach will be embraced all over the world. The work I've done confirms this. Unfortunately, this is probably going to be sobering news to leaders in India, China and the Middle East, who are investing billions to build huge airports and massive highways to take people there. Such planning is decidedly off-code.

This discovery about air travel once again confirmed the effectiveness of my methodology and the fact that overlying every Culture Code is something equally critical. There is a common reptilian element that needs to be discovered and that can't be achieved by simply asking questions or by conducting traditional focus groups. Action based on simply believing what people tell you is an increasingly risky endeavor. Anyone interacting with the rest of the world—and at this point, that's most of us—without awareness of these unconscious codes is both walking through a minefield and missing out on huge opportunities.

THE THREE-BRAIN THEORY OR TRIUNE BRAIN MODEL

When I study a particular product, phenomenon or concept, I always turn to the three brains in order to discover a code. I use the theory of the three brains as a guide to scrape away the surface and get down to the root of why we do what we do. They are inherent to my method for defining the Global Codes and I will be mentioning them in each of the following chapters.

During the second half of the twentieth century, neuroscientist Paul D. MacLean developed the Triune Brain model, the theory stating that all human beings have three brain levels: the reptilian, the limbic and the cortex. The reptilian brain dominates our basic instinctual needs, the four F's if you will: feed, fight, flee and fornicate. All species in the animal kingdom possess the reptilian brain.

Then we have the limbic brain, which controls our emotions. It's the part of our brain that motivates us to accomplish our reptilian needs. The limbic brain makes us feel jealous so that we can be competitive and strive for the best, feel love and a sense of belonging so that we develop social ties that help us survive, and feel anger when someone takes advantage of us so that we may better protect ourselves against people with ill intentions.

Finally, we have the cortex brain, which gives us logic and reason. It is the part of the brain that is unique to humans and other mammals—it is not found in reptiles and fish, for instance. It controls our more abstract and complex thought processes like long-term planning and being able to imagine possible solutions to a problem. With our cortex, we are able to play out different scenarios in our heads, to think about sacrificing short-term pleasures for long-term gains, and to foresee obstacles that may arise from decisions and actions we take today.

A POSTCARD FROM THE CITIZENS OF THE WORLD

I'm going to propose a hypothesis in this book: there is a small group of people who are shaping, structuring and promoting a new set of values. These people are constantly benchmarking the best ways the planet offers to do pretty much anything and sharing their experiences with the rest of their peer group. I call them the *Global Tribe*.

The Global Tribe is permanently creating Global Codes, and in doing so, shaping our aspirational future and a new universal unconscious.

If you don't believe that, you're probably reading the wrong book. But if you're reading this on a plane, you might just be one of them—a member of this tribe. Let's explore some elements of their identity before we dedicate an entire chapter to a closer examination of tribe members and their hierarchy.

In the chapters to come, I'll take you deeper into the psychological and sociological underpinnings of my work and the reasons why my discovery process is so uncannily accurate and successful. For now, let me just say that I'm able to crack codes because I'm able to work in a completely distinctive fashion, digging up the unconscious meanings we assign to every element of our world. The codes are like keys to opening these reference systems, which were imprinted at an early age. Carl Jung called these unconscious structures archetypes. Following Adolf Bastian, I was one of the first to say that, between Jungian universal archetypes and Freud's individual unconscious, a unique and individual unconscious exists in another dimension—what I call the third unconscious. This third unconscious is made up of cultural archetypes. For decades now, I have believed that these unconscious structures are primarily produced by the culture in which one is raised. I still believe that, but it's now clear to me that as the world has become more connected there has emerged another level of meaning that comes not from a specific culture but rather from the input generated by an integration of cultures. This integration has been facilitated by the "magic"—and speed—of the connecting technology used by the Global Tribe.

This tribe represents a new kind of citizen of the world. This person has a strong sense of connection to his "village of origin," but he or she might live on or travel frequently to multiple continents. One place might serve as the best place to hold on to one's money and pay minimal taxes. One might be the best base for a business. Another might feed the desire for Old World charm and luxury, while another might offer the ultimate in technology and convenience. These places are likely to be dramatically different from one another, but they share at least one trait: they are situated close to a major international airport.

This person, of course, has the best and most efficient communication devices available to connect him or her to anywhere in the world at any time of any day. To this person, access to everything at all times is paramount.

Because of their travels, members of the tribe have a strong sense of and nimble knowledge of the best of everything—the best cars, the best hotels, the best medical care, the best everything. They know where to find it, and they won't accept less for the sake of convenience.

To these people, political ideology is just about meaningless. In fact, while they might have multiple homes, there's a very good chance that they won't have citizenship in any of the countries in which they reside. They live where they live because they appreciate the advantages that such places offer, not because they connect to a certain social sensibility. At the same time, they take pride in their roots and consider the place where they were raised to be their one true home, even if they get there very infrequently.

I call these citizens of the world "hubbers," because they tend to live in cities that are airport hubs, which grants them easy access to everywhere. They are the human embodiment of the Global Code, because they literally live and operate all over the world, and in so doing they have established a personal culture woven together from the best of what the planet has to offer. In many ways, they are the viral agents spreading global culture to the rest of the planet. They are the Global Tribe, and they constantly create the Global Codes. We could say that they are global leaders or global influencers.

I recently did sessions in several parts of the world to discover the Culture Code for security. As usual, the codes ranged from culture to culture. In Japan, the code was *control;* while in America, the code was *shotgun.* This is chilling to consider in light of recent events such as the Newtown massacre. When we went to Germany, we discovered that the code was *discipline.* This should not be in any way surprising—three different cultures, three different codes.

However, I also did several sessions exclusively with hubbers, in places they frequent such as Singapore, Macau and Dubai. What was fascinating was the strong consistency of the stories from location to location.

"What I like about being a Singaporean is that there are rules," said one participant, a 45-year-old male banker. "Everybody respects them, no surprise. It might look a little bit boring, but everybody is predictable. I worked in Switzerland before. I feel as comfortable in Singapore as in Zurich."

"A lot of people live in uncertainty, uncertainty is the big danger," said another participant. "In Africa you might work hard, but never be rewarded. It is important to know what to expect. It's hard to invest when you don't know how much you'll be taxed. Dubai is the best place to do business or to invest. Everything is consistent, decided by Al Maktoum. We do not have to worry about the next election."

"I like Hong Kong," someone else wrote. "Great night life, exciting, but with Beijing having the power, I don't know, not sure. There are less taxes in Hong Kong than in Macau, but I like Macau better, more predictable. Hong Kong? You never know what they might decide in Beijing. They could have another Mao."

These responses came from three different locations, but they are representative of the kind of stories I heard repeatedly from hubbers. Security, for them, wasn't about being protected from physical harm or theft. It wasn't about having power over others. It was about knowing what to expect. The hubber code for security is *predictability*. We will see that this is a strong component of the Global Code.

This, of course, makes sense when you look at the world through the hubber lens. Hubbers are people who experience multiple legal systems and law enforcement organizations. Because they travel extensively, they experience wider swings in their sense of security than those who live in one environment most of the time. Therefore, for the hubbers, feeling secure is about being able to anticipate what conditions are going to be. If they know what to expect—even if it's a certain level of danger—they're fine.

A SIDE OF ANXIETY WITH YOUR ORDER

As someone who spent his childhood in France during the German occupation and who has been studying Germany professionally for four decades, I am not at all surprised that the German economy has managed to survive and even thrive during a once-in-a-generation global financial crisis. Many years ago, I discovered the German Culture Code, which is *order*. This is of course evident in everything from the premium Germans put on engineering to the way they relatively smoothly assimilated the East and West after the fall of the Berlin Wall. It is even communicated by the numerous buildings in Munich that bear signs reading "no children allowed" and "no pets allowed." Children and pets are, by their very nature, disorderly, chaotic and unpredictable—and therefore not desired in many German spaces, such as restaurants, hotels or condominium apartments (or *Wohngemeinschaft*).

This sense of order has allowed Germany to absorb even the kind of financial hit the eurozone took in the early 2010s. While Greece crumbles, France argues itself into inaction, and Catalonia talks about seceding from Spain, Germany seeks to dissipate economic chaos quickly and efficiently. Rather than playing dangerous games of chicken with each other, unions and management choose to negotiate instead. Unions and management serve on committees together within corporations, and they operate with cooperation as a foremost principle. Germans work together as a unit perhaps better than any culture I've ever seen, and because of this, their sum is always greater than their parts. Using organization, co-operation, and teamwork to navigate through a worldwide crisis is decidedly on-code for Germany. However, there was something evident in the way Germany has handled this particular crisis that went beyond their Culture Code.

What I saw this time was an approach to handling crisis that I recognized from many hubber cultures—the productive use of anxiety. In Singapore, for example, there is an ever-present anxiety with regard to failure. In Singapore businesspeople express more concern about avoiding failure than anywhere else I've worked. This practically starts in the womb. I've done numerous discoveries in Singapore over the years, and regardless of the topic, I consistently get stories from participants about their mothers telling them that they were unwilling to accept failure in their children—even if this has absolutely nothing to do with the questions we're asking. The upshot of this is that Singaporeans expend a great deal of psychic energy rejecting the notion of failure as a possible outcome. There's obviously some value to this, as Singapore's economy is one of the strongest per capita in the entire world. As we will see later on, the code for Singapore is *kiasu* (fear of losing or failure).

Consciously or not, Germany adopted this approach when contending with the European economic crisis. It was clear in the way management and labor worked together, in the way Angela Merkel conducted herself with other European heads of state and in the way the German government provided wage subsidies to many companies to keep the middle-class employed and help them navigate the downturn successfully. In every case, Germany productively used the natural anxiety of its citizenry to act decisively in the face of failure.

What's notable is how well this adoption of a global survival technique meshed with the German code of *order*. Germany chose to deal with its anxiety in a typically German way, building a system to counteract the anxiety. When unemployment threatened to tick upward, the wage subsidies were put in place in a strategic fashion to offer incentives for companies to hire the unemployed. The government did this in a systematic manner, considering multiple options before putting this program in place. This doesn't mean that Germany has skated past the disastrous European economy, but by using energizing levels of anxiety in concert with its culturally ingrained sense of order, it has done significantly better than its eurozone counterparts.

The Global Tribe is aware of these differences between Germany, France, Japan, Singapore and others. Countries today act as laboratories, where they can experiment, select, sometimes improve, connect and promote their latest results. Together, they are creating the Global Mind.

THE LABORATORY OF THE GLOBAL MIND

Many centuries ago, the great city-states like Athens, Venice and Florence, and later Vienna, were the cultural and economic drivers of the world. Their independence gave them the freedom to innovate and experiment, while their relatively dense populations ensured that a large number of people would be affected by their examples.

All these years later, the city-state still serves as a laboratory for the emerging global culture. City-states like Singapore, Dubai and Hong Kong function in very similar ways to their forebears, as do places like London, New York and Zurich (even though these are not technically city-states). And much like the city-states of old, these municipalities are spreading culture outward. In this case, though, what the municipalities are spreading is an amalgam of the cultures that have produced them.

I've done several discoveries in these city-states. In Dubai, for example, I discovered the code for comfort. What I learned will sound familiar to anyone who has just read the previous pages:

"I feel safe in all aspects of life," said a man in his thirties who moved to Dubai from India.

"I can walk safely on the road without being robbed," said a woman, also originally from India. "I can wear my jewelry without fear."

"The rules and regulations are good," said a man from Serbia. "The food is healthy and the hospitals are clean."

Consistently throughout the sessions, I received story after story about the quality of the systems in Dubai, the value of reliability, and the solace that participants took in knowing that there were clear rules and regulations to follow. The overwhelming majority of the people who took part in this discovery came from somewhere else and chose Dubai as a place to live. A strong contributor to this decision was their knowledge that things worked in a predictable fashion there. The Culture Code for comfort in Dubai is *predictable order*.

It's understandable that this code echoes the code for Germany. As is true of so many of the emerging city-states, Dubai's population has seen dramatic growth in recent years. In the past two decades, its population has tripled, overwhelmingly from an influx of immigrants. Because of this, it is essentially starting its culture from scratch, and the way new cultures develop is by drawing on the best practices of other cultures. It makes sense that Dubai would create a system for comfort that was reminiscent of Germany, as I would venture to suggest that Germans are as systematic about their comfort as any people in the world.

To underscore this point, I did the same discovery in Singapore and came away with a very similar code. Certainly, these aren't the first cultures to arise from immigrants. As Americans, we're very familiar with other examples. However, these are the first cultures to emerge in our new globalized world. Because of this, they are the first to be able to cherry-pick their approach to the world from every other existing culture. What's fascinating is the reverberation that this is causing. City-states are benchmarking other cultures to create their own cultures, while at the same time showing what a culture built from these benchmarks looks like. The fact that these city-states are tremendously successful, both socially and commercially, is no accident.

THREE SIGNS POINTING IN THE SAME DIRECTION

Hubbers are emerging as affluent, visible and influential citizens of the world. Germany is thriving in the face of economic doom by combining a central element of its own culture with a central element of world culture. City-states are serving as a landing spot for the world's best ideas. Each of these situations points to an individual shift worthy of our attention. Taken together, though, they also speak to the rise of something that has been possible only in the last couple of decades but that will affect us for centuries hence. I believe all of these signs indicate that the heightened level of global connection we have experienced in the recent past has led to the emergence of a Global Mind—an unconscious driver that runs in tandem with our cultural mind and influences the way we perceive the essential archetypes in our world.

As hubbers shuttle between their homes spreading their blend of cultures, as gleaming new city-states rise from the best of what the world has to offer and as mature cultures stay young and vital by adopting what has succeeded elsewhere, these phenomena subtly influence how all of us think and conduct ourselves and how all of us will be able to succeed. When you add to this mix that the vast majority of us have at least some contact with cultures outside of our borders on a daily basis—something that was far less true even twenty years ago—it becomes clear that we're all thinking differently now.

However, most of this thinking is still going on at the unconscious level. As has always been true of our culturally influenced thinking about various archetypes, this globally affected sensibility needs special methods in order to be examined. It needs to be decoded.

Let's go back to the Global Code we looked at early in this chapter. We know that the Japanese equate flying with premium service. We also know that the Global Mind thinks, "no airports" when it imagines a pleasurable flying experience. What does this mean for Japanese airlines or for other airlines offering flights in and out of Japan? As I mentioned before, there are some big technological changes on the horizon that will address this. In the short-term, though, it would seem that the airlines should take a service-forward approach to making the airport experience as unobtrusive as possible. Maybe it would be by increasing staffing to get passengers through security faster and by getting luggage off of planes more expediently. Maybe it would be by offering snacks at the gate and at the baggage claim. Whatever makes Japanese flyers especially conscious of the quality of the service and as unaware of the airport experience as possible would be the most on-code approach both culturally and globally.

Why does any of this matter to you? Well, if you're like most people in developed countries, you're dealing with the rest of the world all the time. People halfway around the planet are your customers, your colleagues, your partners, your contacts and your Twitter followers. If you're interacting outside of your national borders, then you really need to understand the unconscious global messages associated with your communication. In reality though, even if you aren't interacting outside of your national borders, you need to be aware of these messages because they are influencing your neighbors and even you.

At this point we can see that predictability and order are key elements of the Global Code we are starting to discover. Today we can see many forces in action. Some of these forces are moving toward chaos and random killing and are very unpredictable. The Global Tribe is reinforcing the opposite, and choosing places characterized by order and predictability, like Switzerland. By voting with their feet, Global Tribe members are creating the Global Code.

LEARNING TO SPEAK CULTURE

Movement is the natural motion of life. In my book *Move Up,* I emphasize the impact mobility has had on our development as a species, as societies, and as individuals. From the moment our ancestors crawled out of the ocean, grew legs, stood on four feet and then on two, we have constantly been moving. It's not only essential for survival; it's essential for success.

Lack of movement suggests complacency, or worse, handicap. For this reason, in a professional sense, we say "I want to climb up the professional ladder," "There's no opportunity to move up at my job so I'm going to find something else," or "I'm going to step up to the plate to get that promotion." We're not satisfied with staying still—we want to constantly move and seek new opportunities, and so does the Global Tribe.

An essential characteristic of this unique group of individuals is that they can never stay put in one single place—they need to constantly be on the move—traveling, flying, driving, walking and running. They are in Europe one week and in Asia the next. They live by the beach in winter, work in cosmopolitan cities in the spring, visit the countryside in summer, and live somewhere completely different in the fall. Their agendas are filled with flight schedules and hotel arrangements. For the Global Tribe, borders and frontiers are imaginary. They freely move from one place to another. In our global, interconnected world today, borders are a thing of the past; I daresay they are even regressive. The fewer barriers we have, the better off we are.

Countries that isolate themselves, like North Korea, are basically planning their own demise. How can a society progress without input from the outside world? With such diversity across the globe, there are endless ways of doing things, of governing, building infrastructure and advancing in education and science. When we close ourselves off, we are closing ourselves off to new opportunities.

Japan's modernization at the end of the nineteenth century was largely due to the Meiji Restoration, during which foreign relations became a new priority for the country. Japan was aware of the growing Westernization of the rest of the globe and wisely wanted to be a part of it. They embarked on "learning missions" and sent nationals around the globe to learn from other cultures.

For three years, 48 members traveled through Europe and the United States on Japan's largest mission, the Iwakura mission, whereby members were encouraged to learn about modern judicial, governmental, educational and penal systems, as well as the West's way of doing business, developing industries and exporting and importing goods. Japan recognized the importance of mobility and opening up its borders to a world of knowledge.

Top managers around the globe know the benefits of freedom of mobility. Today, if companies want to grow, they need to think beyond their own set of walls, their own borders. The most competitive companies today are the ones that are going global, gaining turf in new countries or forming alliances and mergers with companies in other countries. If they want to compete in this globalized world, they need to think beyond the confines of their own countries.

However, companies that are going global face a great challenge when it comes to *speaking culture.* Conducting business in Australia is different from conducting business in New Zealand. Even when the language is the same, it's about having to understand the way meetings are carried out, how deals are formed, how casual or formal work attire should be, how to address superiors, and so on. Many companies struggle when confronting these cultural hurdles.

So who do companies come to for advice about how to ease this transition into the global? Members of the Global Tribe, of course. Individuals who speak culture with ease, have traveled a lot, know several languages, have experience working and living in different countries, and know how to adapt to cultural change with ease. This is why consulting companies have offices in cities all over the globe, and their employees are carefully selected individuals who have this globalized experience and knowledge.

"The world is a book and those who do not travel read only one page."

—Augustine of Hippo

In order to acquire this kind of knowledge, the Global Tribe has a passion for travel. You can imagine that with such a lifestyle comes great and varied experience. Each country, each culture, has its own rituals and ways of doing things, and when you travel you build a warehouse of knowledge.

In Spain, dinner starts at 10:00 p.m., initiated with several cocktails and drinks; the food isn't served until around 11:30 p.m., and the feasting can go on for hours. In Australia, you can be sure that a local would look at you strangely if you proposed a dinner outing at 10:00 p.m. when the custom is to begin around 6:00 p.m. or 7:00 p.m. at the latest. In Moscow, you tip your waiter if you were incredibly impressed with the service, but in Montreal you'd better expect a vulgar reaction if you forget to tip a dollar or two for every drink you order at the bar. In Italy, if a man looks at a woman from top to bottom and whistles at her it is perceived as a compliment, while in the United States it is perceived as wrong and even harassment.

When I travel to France, I love to attend dinner parties with my wife. She dresses up and looks fantastic. While we're at the party, we split up so as to mingle with other guests, just like other couples do. If I see another man flirting with my wife, I don't take any offense. In fact, I am flattered because he thinks my wife is fabulous just like I do, whereas if no one hits on her I feel pretty offended and think to myself, "Why isn't anyone after her, she looks beautiful, doesn't anyone want to seduce her?" This is part of French culture, where flirting is just part of the game. If we were in the United States, however, it would be absolutely vulgar to flirt with the wife of another man. Not reading the cultural signs could get you punched in the face!

From so much traveling, the Global Tribe begins to build a mental inventory of the different ways of living life. Differences from one culture to another become more apparent and stay imprinted in their minds. They learn quickly that flirting and courtship vary greatly from city to city and country to country. They pick up on which topics of conversation warrant nasty looks and which ones stimulate socializing. Their minds, being the warehouses that they are, become aware of these cultural differences and store them for future reference.

This is an essential part of survival—being able to read a culture and pick up the rules very quickly. For someone who has never traveled abroad, you can imagine that picking up social cues in a new cultural environment would be much more of a challenge. The Global Tribe not only speaks several languages, they speak several cultures.

PLANET EARTH IS THE ONLY SPACESHIP WITHOUT A PILOT

Many years ago, I had the pleasure of meeting an astronaut from NASA who has been on several missions to the moon. It's not every day that you get the chance to talk to someone who has traveled to outer space so I took the opportunity to ask him, "What was it like? Going all the way up there!" He responded, "You know, from up there our planet looks so small, so insignificant compared to our huge universe. I looked at it and thought to myself, 'Wow, that's home! That is my home, it's a lonely planet in this huge solar system, in this huge galaxy in our huge universe, and it's our only place we can call home. I better take care of it.'" His answer made me emotional. I knew exactly what he meant; we need to start taking care of our planet, our home.

Our world is changing so fast. The exponential rate of change we have experienced in the last century is incredible. In just one hundred years we have managed to fly in the sky, put a man on the moon, speed across the land in vehicles, develop weapons of mass destruction, and connect with loved ones thousands of miles away with just a click of a button. Our ancestors would have never dreamed of such a world.

But we were not prepared for this, and such change comes with a price: increased poverty, diseases, climate change, waste, and so on. The rapidly changing job market is a good indicator of how our world is evolving. Just over 20 years ago the Internet didn't exist. Today, this invisible network dominates our reality, and many jobs rely on it. More and more professions are becoming obsolete while new ones are arising. Those who can learn quickly and adapt will move forward, and those who cannot will be left behind.

What we need today is more predictability and consistency. City-states are more adaptable to change; the smaller the society, the easier it is to understand its members' needs and to change. One challenge many cities face is traffic congestion, and more and more places are implementing changes to face this problem, like bicycle-sharing services such as the Vélib' in Paris, Citi Bike in New York City, Ecobici in Mexico City and You-Bike in Taiwan. This is an adaptation to a problem cities are much better equipped to deal with than entire countries.

The future is moving toward the autonomy of cities and the rise of city-states. Istanbul would probably be better off as an independent city-state rather than being subject to the rules and laws of an entire country. Istanbul is so modern—some even say European—that it should have the freedom to function as an independent city and more easily satisfy the needs of its European-like constituents rather than the needs of the nation as a whole.

When we centralize the world with one dominating bureaucracy we are moving backward. Our new world should be managed by more mayors and fewer presidents. Reducing crime in the United States as a whole is a difficult feat; but when Rudy Giuliani implemented the "Broken Windows" approach in New York City, the method proved to be effective. The city's police were encouraged to crack down on minor offenses, which sent a message to the general population that no crime would go unpunished and that social order was a high priority. The results speak for themselves and were clearly visible.

When the mayor of a city implements a new approach, the results are tangible and it's easy to see if they work or don't work. Whereas, when a president implements some kind of change, it is much harder to apply to the entire country and measure the results.

Every spaceship has a pilot. Granted every pilot needs a well-functioning ship, which requires the expertise of engineers, mechanics and manufacturers; a place to take off and a place to land; flight attendants to establish order and so on. However, it is the pilot who has undergone many hours of training, has experience flying to many destinations and knows how to fly under varying weather conditions. It is the pilot who takes the passengers where they need to go. The pilot can identify poor weather conditions and steer the passengers clear of danger. Today, our spaceship has no pilot. Who will guide the world's future, taking us all where we want to go and should go? The Global Tribe will.

The Global Tribe is made up of that small network of individuals who find it hard to call one place home. They have frequent flyer plans with many airlines, travel light, speak several languages, have more than one passport, and have friends scattered around the world who are much like themselves. They have a weekend home, vacation home, summer home and winter home. They enjoy good wine and exotic food, have small closets with carefully selected and tailored clothing, have one-of-a-kind furniture pieces or classic antiques, shelves cluttered with books, and walls adorned with unique art pieces they have collected over the years or have inherited. They don't follow trends—they make them.

This new species of human making up the Global Tribe will be the one to define this spaceship's direction. Because of their lifestyle, they are constantly benchmarking, analyzing, comparing and judging to see what works and what doesn't work.

We have seen throughout history that civilizations need model citizens. The Greeks and Romans had gods they looked up to and gossiped about, who helped them understand their environment and the human condition. They were role models and models of a perfection that they could only dream of obtaining.

In today's globalized world, our models, the Global Tribe, are real people who set the trends, give us new perspectives, orient us and direct us toward a new worldview. They are the ones who will define a new reference system for the world. That is, they will define the Global Code.

In the following chapters we will analyze the Global Tribe, who they are, and the characteristics, behaviors, and rituals that make them unique to the rest of society. We want to find out what makes them the appropriate models for society, the ones who are defining the Global Codes that the rest of us want to mimic.

The following chapters will cover the various Global Codes I have identified based on my analysis of the Global Tribe. How do they perceive pleasure, technology, luxury, networking, change and adaptation? Which Global Codes are they creating and how will these codes impact our future? I want to understand why the Global Tribe is not into the selfie and what drives them to pursue higher education and why they are reverting to more classical forms of cultural expression rather than exclusively using those of new technology.

If I want to explore these subjects, it is because I am frustrated. However, this is not negative—I don't want to be comfortable. I don't want us to be comfortable because when we are comfortable we don't want to change things. There is always an opportunity to improve, to better ourselves and the world that we live in. So frustration is essential to success. In order to strive for success, we need to set the bar high. We need lofty goals, aspirations, models for us to look up to and strive to reach. This is our first step. The second step is feeling frustrated. I need to feel the emotion of being frustrated because I have not yet reached my goal. The last step is action—we need to take action, to move, in order to get to where we want to go. This is what I want to achieve with the Global Code. I am identifying the codes because I believe that in this globalized world we need a model, we need a reference system, we need a pilot. Let's see how the Global Tribe is working and moving us in this direction.

This group of individuals is defining the Global Code—benchmarking the world, choosing the best practices and creating the aspirations of everyone else. They are the "code leaders," the global influencers. To understand the Global Tribe, we have used several different approaches, including anthropological observation, ethnological participation, symbolic and symbiotic analysis, and code discoveries through imprinting sessions.

In the beginning, I was just another anthropologist studying an unfamiliar group, the same way I studied witch doctors in Brazil and Central America or Bedouins in the Middle East. As with any tribe, it was important to discover the hierarchy. It is the hierarchy that creates the structure of a tribe, and this Global Tribe is no different. Several opportunities helped me to dismiss old misconceptions about them and get to the deeper truth.

Let's start with some observations, before we plumb the depths of the unconscious imprinted structure.

The concept of the Global Tribe is new because its members are defined by their positions, their attitudes and their perpetual movement. They are not defined by fame or money, even if they sometimes have both. Whereas the majority of the Global Tribe may be working, traveling businesspeople, it is nevertheless the top of its pyramid that sets the standard for the rest.

In the past, they were called the "jet set," but this definition no longer fits the members of today's Global Tribe. *Glomads,* or global nomads, is closer to the mark. Their defining feature is that they travel all of the time. Another expression that I heard used in Barbados, while working for Royal Bank, was "platinum gypsies." "Platinum" meant that at the time, they had three platinum credit cards and were gypsies living out of a suitcase and going from one hub to another. As we will see, I am still not satisfied with any of these definitions, not least because the platinum card has since been replaced by the "black card."

They are constantly circling the globe with their families. Their children are the new generation of Third Culture Kids, or "TCKs." The metaphor of the satellite is key here. They have "replenishment stations" where they meet other members of the tribe, exchange information, organize events and parties, and plan their next move. These places are hubs, as we have seen before, and their visitors are the "hubbers."

So let me take you through my journey of discovery. We'll start first by exploring the Global Tribe.

PART ONE

THE GLOBAL TRIBE

ONE

WHO THEY ARE

THE GLOBAL TRIBE HIERARCHY

To study any tribe, an anthropologist must first settle on a definition—a set of criteria to determine who is a member of the tribe and who is not. It is also important to find out how you can become a member. Is it by birth, merit, force, initiation or location? It is also important to consider how you might be excluded or rejected.

We will start with the hierarchy as it is perceived by its members, but also by the outside world.

As we went around the world exploring and observing the Global Tribe, we also discovered how nonmembers, who may aspire to join, perceive them. The hierarchy rapidly became clear, and followed a centuries-old pattern. We can even use the same words used in ancient and traditional societies, since the hierarchy is so similar in structure to those older orders.

The tribe has different layers—at the top of the tribe you have the Court.

Around this Court you have the second layer—the Courtesans. The Courtesans are the "wannabes." They strive to become members of the Court and many would go to any length to do so. In the modern day, the Courtesans are social climbers.

Courtesans are constantly looking for favors, they want to be invited, young women want to "marry money," men want to be connected at the

top. Courtesans try to please the Court without revealing their true intentions. Their number one mission is to be noticed, to come out from behind
the veil of anonymity. They go where the Court goes—to the same schools,
universities, polo matches and charity events. Kate Middleton married a
prince, the dream of any Courtesan.

Courtesans attend every event possible, sleep with who they need to
sleep with, flatter who they need to flatter, and please who they need to
please. They are eager to have photographs taken with members of the
Court in order to be associated with the Court in social magazines. They
are the groupies at rock concerts. They don't have the same influence or
class as the Court, so they search for a Court member they can latch onto
in hopes that their fame will rub off onto them.

The third layer consists of the Suppliers, who have something to sell.
They are closely followed by the Aspirants, who want to climb the social
ladder. We should also consider the Symbolic Creators—the artists, thinkers, writers, and philosophers who provide the symbolic expression of the
tribe. Finally, we have the Third Culture Individuals (TCIs), who might
not belong in the Court or Courtesan category but who by their attitude,
lifestyle and continuous movement represent the bulk of the group and are
also an important aspect of the Global Tribe.

What we have here is a large group of individuals who might appear
to be very different from each other. Some have money; some might have
credentials but no money, like the Russian aristocrats who left Russia after
the Bolshevik Revolution. What they have in common, however, is a set
of goals, criteria and a reference system that makes them part of the tribe.

Today, because they can, people watch the Global Tribe like never
before—how they dress, which restaurants they go to, what kinds of cars
they buy. Of course, there are different levels of expectations or aspirations.
You might be attracted by their lifestyle, but you might also feel that you
might not be accepted. As when considering buying an expensive car, some
people might need to feel that they can afford it psychologically. When we
speak about joining the tribe, you need to give to yourself permission to
join.

Am I ready? Do I belong? Are they going to accept me? Is it my place?
In this process, the "aspirants" look at the tribe and realize that it has its
own stratification, its own hierarchy. How will I be received if I want to

join? Which level should I try for? It is the same feeling that some people have expressed when they have to choose a university. Of course they want to go to Harvard, Yale or Berkeley, but can they get in?

THE COURT

The Global Tribe follows a similar hierarchical structure to that of a kingdom. Let's start at the center, with the Court. They are untouchable, symbolic figures of fame, success and money. Bill Gates is the new Rothschild; the founders of Facebook, the new Ivy League of financial success, joining the Lauder Family, the Koch brothers and many others. This doesn't always mean that they have the right style or that they deserve their stripes.

Of course, charitable giving is the ultimate marker of arrival. Now that you've proven your ability to make money, you have to show your ability to give it back (see, for example, the Bill Gates Foundation). Observing the various hubs and city-states where tribe members live is a fascinating way to decode the Court. Everybody knows who they are, but few people actually know them personally. Some of them are as old as they are rich. Others have just arrived, and might feel young and still relatively poor. As they say in Palm Beach, "When you move to Palm Beach, you realize you've never been so young and so poor."

The members of the Court determine what is *in* and what is not. They choose which music, sports, fashion and recreational activities are acceptable at that time. These people are the members of the Global Tribe.

In order to differentiate themselves from the rest of the population, they define a set of behavioral standards and forms of etiquette. They create rules of refinement—how to address one another, how to address others in the hierarchy, how to dress appropriately for different occasions, which activity is acceptable for particular times of the day and seasons of the year, and so on. It's extremely important for them to follow the rules in order to preserve their membership and status within this in-group. Someone who fails to follow the rules set by the Court is clearly indicating to everyone else that they are not part of the club.

Every royal system across the globe has a court. From Japan to China, Egypt to Spain, each court has a similar function, but the complexity of the structure varies from culture to culture. Rulers have always recognized how essential the court has been for their survival. Where a king may not have been able to trust his own brother for fear he would murder him in his sleep and take over the throne, the king knew he could trust the court. They were his eyes and ears, his spies.

A king needed people he could trust, people who could maintain order and keep the populace in check. The best way to do this was by defining the culture the ruler wanted to foster. The court would act as his creative ambassadors, preserving and fostering the king's influence across the kingdom through culture and the arts.

The influence of the court was great. Where the king could not act, the court could step in. They had good taste and knew the latest trends. They guided culture much in the same way I believe the Global Tribe is guiding today's global culture, today's Global Codes.

THE COURTESANS

The Courtesans live close to the Court. They are usually younger and want to be invited into the Court. They want to marry the daughters of the Court, or marry the prince. Kate Middleton is the model. So is Lady Grantham of *Downton Abbey,* the classic archetype of the rich American woman marrying someone with a big title. In order to have a chance, Courtesans sometimes emulate the manners and style of the Court—that is, British for manners, and French for style. The global success of *Downton Abbey* is the ultimate proof that people all around the world—including Asia, Africa and South America—need a clear hierarchy, with a virtuous leader at the top. Some widows, even very rich ones, don't qualify. They are just trophy wives who married an old man for his money. Anna Nicole Smith is a perfect example. She would have never made it. The way for rich widows to qualify is to dress with style (Chanel, not Versace), dedicate their lives to charity, choose a "walker" (younger, but not too young) and soon remarry. Of course, involvement in charity is the best qualifier. The Charity Index Directory is the best example. How you choose which one you are going to dedicate your time and money to is key.

I remember being in the Palm Beach mansion of Robert de Balkany, where he was playing polo during the Season. I met his mother-in-law, the "Queen of Savoy," while she was having a drink by the pool. She was a very charming old lady. As we spoke, she asked me, "What are you into?" I did not quite understand the meaning of the question. Then she added, "I am into drugs. Hard drugs." "Wow," I thought to myself, as I looked at her suspiciously in a moment of hesitation. I wasn't quite sure what she meant. Then she continued: "And you, what are you into?"

She ended my embarrassment when she started explaining what she meant.

"My foundation helps thousands of young drug addicts go through rehabilitation programs and get an education. Dependency and addiction are terrible things, but I believe that we can help people overcome their addictions. What about you, what are you into?" she asked again. This is when I realized that I needed a cause (we will see later which one I chose).

She obviously was not a Courtesan. She did not care about maintaining an image or impressing anyone, and she sounded very dedicated to her mission. "I have a fundraiser next week in Gstaad, a nice party. You should try to come," she said.

The contrast was obvious. The younger women who want to have their pictures taken with the queen and always want to be seated next to her were the local Courtesans.

Many magazines dedicate themselves to helping promote the Courtesans. Many of these magazines do not have text and only show photos. A magazine editor confided in me: "People don't read the text. They just want two things, their picture and their name to appear." Members of the Court, however, don't want their photos to be taken. There are too many risks now with the Internet, but the Courtesans will not hesitate to pay big money to buy full pages, or even the front cover to make sure that their pictures are seen and that they appear in the magazine.

THE SUPPLIERS

The number one Suppliers are the real estate brokers. Of course, there are members of the Global Tribe who have many houses. The Suppliers like to deal with the tribe because members of the tribe buy and sell homes all the time. They are also very predictable in what and where they are going to buy. That is why you see advertisements in Aspen for homes in Newport, or in Palm Beach for homes in the Hamptons.

After real estate we have the luxury brands. All of them—Cartier, Royal Salute, Chanel, Rolls-Royce, Rolex, Bentley, and so on—organize parties, dinners or special events for the tribe. Naturally, the Court is very difficult to attract, as its members usually have personal buyers and are already oversolicited.

Around the Suppliers you have all of the individuals who work with goods and services that are of interest to members of the tribe. They are always trying to sell something. They never just want to have a drink with you for pleasure—they are always selling.

THE SYMBOLIC CREATORS:
THE ARCHITECTS OF A NEW WORLD ORDER

Do you want to be a follower or a leader? In business, all the clients I have ever worked with always tell me they want to be "the leaders in their industry"; they never tell me they want to "get by," "be alright" or "do OK." We all want to be the best that we can be—that's survival of the fittest. But in order to be the best, we need to understand what's going on in the present day. The world has changed, and there is one particular group of people that I believe are the models we should be following—this is the Global Tribe.

All of our previously held notions of nation, borders and nationalism are breaking down. In our globalized world, there is less of a need for the nation. The economist Robert Reich agrees with me, and in his award-winning book *The Work of Nations,* he touches on an important topic I want to address that relates to the Global Tribe—the age-old sociological concept of social stratification.

Society naturally follows a hierarchical order with a set group of leaders at the top giving orders to the lower levels of society. This varies from community to community and society to society, but in every culture there exist both formal and informal leaders that the rest follow. In feudal times we had the lords at the top, then members of the court, the clergy, and at the bottom we had farmers and people who worked the land.

Today, the world economy is going through a drastic transformation that is impacting the way we have traditionally perceived social stratification. Reich argues that the group of people we once had at the bottom—farmers and other manual laborers—will slowly be completely eradicated by machinery and high technology. China has already taken over most of our production with factories of not only people but also machines creating the vast majority of food and products we consume around the world. Individuals with routine jobs, such as assembly-line work, are much less competitive in today's global economy and are at a greater disadvantage than skilled labor.

Today's world economy places a greater value on those highly skilled, experienced and educated individuals who contribute something unique to the economy. Companies are now looking for the best of the best for even the most menial of jobs like secretarial or janitorial work. If we take the example of Google, the hiring process is so lengthy and elaborate because the company wants to ensure it is truly hiring the best person out there. We are shifting our priorities from quantity and volume to quality and value.

As Robert Reich in *The Work of Nations* puts it, "Those citizens best positioned to thrive in a world market are tempted to slip the bonds of national allegiance, and by so doing disengage themselves from their less favored fellows." He is talking about members of the Global Tribe. Many powerful multinational companies, such as Google, create puzzling obstacles for potential employees in order to pinpoint the candidate best at problem solving.

We can all see our world economy changing. The job market is not what it used to be. We are seeing more people lose their jobs to cheaper labor abroad (as with the car manufacturing industry leaving Detroit and moving to Mexico), companies hiring more skilled workers abroad rather than locally (as is the case with the hiring of computer technicians and developers in India) and more companies entering into international mergers and acquisitions, creating monster-sized global corporations (like the transatlantic union between Germany's Mercedes-Benz and America's Chrysler). We are going global.

The people of the Global Tribe are the pilots of the future because they are in tune with the new world economy. They are the creators of value. Creating value is important because it is what lasts longer than volume; it is quality, not quantity. Napoleon knew the importance of value over volume when he rewarded his best soldiers and commanders with medals and honors rather than financial prizes or raises. Napoleon did this because the honor of receiving a medal, of being valued, lasts longer and stays ingrained in the soldier's mind, whereas a monetary reward doesn't last long and the soldier is quick to forget the leader's appreciation.

> *"We don't have a money problem, we have a creating value problem."*
>
> —Kurt Frankenburg

The new world citizen Reich is talking about is a member of the Global Tribe. They are people who appreciate our global, interconnected world and reject notions of nation that are limiting and closed off. They don't see problems, they see possibilities. They don't view failure as a setback; rather, they see it as an opportunity to learn and improve. George Washington's military setbacks during the Revolutionary War made him understand that he might not be able to overwhelm the enemy in every battle, but learning from his losses and mistakes, he was eventually able to win the war.

Members of the Global Tribe are different from everyone else because they expose themselves to new sensations, experiences and states of mind. People who are closed off to leaving their hometown are people who are closing themselves off to new experiences. Members of the Global Tribe call the world their "home base," not any city or country. They are able to be comfortable anywhere and adapt quickly to new cultures.

A creative person is someone who sees beyond limitations, beyond borders and boundaries, and thinks in a "timeless" sense. What I mean by this is that creative people see beyond the here and now and think more in terms of what can be possible at all times and anywhere.

Oscar Niemeyer was a Brazilian architect who saw beyond the here and now. Though his work may be categorized as modern, it was actually classical because it was timeless. His inspiration was derived from the natural environment and the natural shapes and curves we see all around us, not from artificial constructs. He was motivated by the shapes of the waves and mountains, real elements in our environment that have always been here and always will be.

Coco Chanel changed the face of fashion, and her legacy has persisted throughout the decades. What made her work so iconic was its classical and minimalist nature. From the little black dress to the tweed jacket, Chanel's look became a standard in women's wardrobes around the world. Chanel told *Harper's Bazaar* in an interview that "simplicity is the keynote of all true elegance."

Actress and style icon Audrey Hepburn, who epitomized class, swore by Chanel's little black dress.

The Global Tribe is made up of people like Niemeyer and Chanel, people who stuck to the classics, saw beyond the local, and created value where there was none. Like Coco Chanel, who designed clothing not just for Parisian women but also for modern women around the world, the Global Tribe is creating value for the entire globe. They are creating Global Codes like the "little black dress" that the rest of our world will follow. We have entered a new era in history in which we are beginning to assess and define the global trends.

The Global Codes transcend time and place, and more importantly, they are distinguishable from the Culture Codes I have spent much of my work analyzing. Every culture has its own set of codes, its own ways of perceiving archetypes. The Global Codes are just as real and important to us as the Culture Codes.

Before I share with you the Global Codes I have identified, I need to paint a very accurate picture of the Global Tribe. I cannot put the cart before the horse. You will see that it is the Global Tribe that has helped me identify the Global Codes because the members of the tribe are less attached to any sense of place and time. They are more attached to everywhere and "every when."

Throughout his life, Louis XIII surrounded himself with artists, writers, architects, decorators, designers, scientists and philosophers. These creative people captured and crystallized a certain time period while commoditizing French notions of style and elegance, which reached their apex at Versailles in the time of Louis XIV and *L'Encyclopedie.* Similarly, Queen Victoria came to embody an entire era, and we still refer to the Victorian style today. Back then, the monarchy patronized artists of all kinds; for example, Voltaire was invited to the courts of the king of Prussia and the tsar of Russia. Today, artistic and symbolic creators have to find other means of survival. The times when the king would grant you a "rent," or commission to create, are over. Luckily, commercial capitalism offers plenty of opportunities as well. The art and luxury markets, which provide the symbols sought out by the Global Tribe, are both booming. We will see that the Global Tribe decides what is in or out and has created a fascinating code for the future of luxury.

THIRD CULTURE INDIVIDUALS

The Third Culture Kid (TCKs, 3CK) is a term that has been used to describe children of the Global Tribe. Their parents originated in one culture, but now live in another. Their children were born in a third culture. As their parents keep moving, they might even now live in a fourth culture. These parents are sometimes in the military, and their children are sometimes referred to as military brats. These kids are a good example of people who fit the profile of the Global Tribe not because of money but rather because of their mobility and exposure to several cultures. Third Culture Individuals, or TCIs, spend an average of 7 years abroad while growing up.

TCIs can also come from nonmilitary government jobs like the diplomatic corps. Of these individuals, 44 percent have lived in at least four countries. Eighty-five percent of missionary kids spend more than 10 years in foreign countries. The children of parents working in business are also more likely to live in multiple countries.

Like their parents, TCKs have expanded worldviews, which means that they are able to look at and evaluate what they experience in more than one way. They benchmark worldviews and cultures. Research has shown that they are more tolerant, more open and more flexible than monocultural individuals.[1]

Many of the most intense conflicts in the world today are intercultural. French resentment over Muslim immigration from North Africa and German animosity toward Turkish immigrants are examples of a monocultural group of people afraid of losing their cultural dominance, and therefore fighting back as hard as they can. Yet the time for such fights is long past. The leaders of the next new world must be third culture natives. They are the children of the Global Tribe. They are beyond cultures, sexism and racism, beyond borders and nationalities and beyond religions and ideologies.

We have Doctors Without Borders—now we need real leaders without borders. The new technology philosophy, which I call *technosophy,* teaches us that borders are obsolete, that there's no room for ideology in the global economy, and that our intelligence should be used to fight common enemies. This planet is our home, our only home. Human beings are our family, our unique family. It is time to accept our differences, to recognize them as strengths, to use them as assets and to pull together. We are at a turning point in human history—we can destroy our home and our human family, or we can move to another level, another league, following in the steps of our Third Culture Kids, listening to our Third Culture Individuals, and following in the steps of the Global Tribe.

We have seen that the Global Tribe has different levels. Of course, these are more symbolic than real, but these different levels still have the capacity to inspire the masses.

When we include all the different subgroups—Courtesans, Suppliers, Aspirants, Social Climbers, Symbolic Creators and Third Culture Individuals—we are looking at something entirely new. They are not the elite, not the jet set, not the rich and famous—they could be all or none of these. Some of the Third Culture Kids are just middle-class kids without a fixed home or a fixed culture to refer to.

This is the amalgam of subgroups that I call the Global Tribe. What the members of the tribe have in common is that they live in hubs, travel all the time, benchmark the world, and in doing so, create the Global Code.

THE ASPIRANTS

The next layer of the tribe is comprised of the Aspirants. These are all of the people who have enough money to try to become part of the tribe, but aren't quite there yet. They need to feel that they have a chance. They need to change their own perception of who they are and think of themselves as being able, or having "permission" to buy a Bentley, to fly private jets and to join the Metropolitan Club in New York. They are not sure they know all the rules, and they are afraid of making a mistake.

They are the ones of whom the executives of Rolls-Royce in America say, "they need 'permission to buy.'" Their number one fear is that they will not be invited. Their number two fear is that they will be rejected and never be invited again. The rules are very clear: if you speak to the Court, don't try to sell anything. Don't speak about work or money, aside from the money you want to raise for your foundation or for your favorite charity.

The lifestyle of the Court, or even of the Courtesans, is not for everybody. The Global Tribe is a minority, but their role is to set the standard. Hundreds of millions of Chinese and Indians are now moving in this direction. Incomes have, of course, soared at the top, and the rich have become richer. There have also been huge gains for the middle classes in China and India. Income growth in emerging nations has produced huge gains in human welfare. This has lifted hundreds of millions of people out of desperate poverty, giving them a chance for a better life. But because of the global connection provided by technology, this "better life" is more and more defined by the Global Tribe.

The Global Tribe drives their aspirations. Every teenager in the world today wants to have a cell phone. They all know Apple and Facebook, they all have blue jeans, and they all text all the time. They follow their favorite celebrities, know their lifestyles, and dream that one day they will be one of them.

Of course, not everybody will become a celebrity. Not everybody will become rich and fly private jets, but the Global Tribe inspires the dream. It guides what people are looking at and what they are looking for. This is the desire on which global brands play so skillfully. For a few dollars you can buy a little piece of the pie, the feeling that you are one of them.

The Aspirants are not at the Bentley level yet. They drive a BMW. They work, and this is a big handicap. They need to learn how to speak about art, opera, symphony, preservation, dog shelters and fighting cancer, not work. It is not enough to be successful in your business; you must learn the symbols and rituals of the tribe.

But more than anything, you have to move, and keep moving. The more sedentary you are, the fewer chances you have to join the tribe.

The magic number, three? How many homes have you lived in (even if you do not own them)? How many countries? How many languages do you speak? How many clubs do you belong to? How many diplomas do you have? How many cars do you have? How many companies? If the answer to these questions is "only one," then you are too sedentary, too stuck in the ground. If the answer is "two," then you have started flying, but you are not quite there yet. If the answer is "three or more," you are on the threshold of the Global Tribe.

ALTO—ANTHROPOLOGICAL LUXURY TRIBE OBSERVATORY

In 2013, I established the Anthropological Luxury Tribe Observatory (ALTO), an institution that observes the Luxury Tribe (which sometimes includes members of the Global Tribe) for anthropological and ethnographical purposes. As a psychologist, I'm interested in people's psyches, their unconscious. The purpose of ALTO is deciphering what drives people's behavior. I am perfectly aware that there are two sides to the coin: on the one hand we are individuals with primitive drives, emotions and desires, but on the other hand we are also social animals. We live in a social world we cannot escape even if we wanted to. Therefore, in order to understand the direction our future is taking, I need to delve deep into the social, put on my anthropologist cap, and get to the root of our behavioral interactions.

ALTO specifically focuses on the Luxury Tribe. Similar to the way the anthropologist Bronislaw Malinowski lived with the people from Papua New Guinea and took note of their behaviors, ALTO studies members of the Luxury Tribe around the world. You cannot simply ask someone a direct question to get the real answer—in anthropology, we believe that the best way to understand a group of people is to become one with them, to integrate ourselves within the community, and to behave just like a member of the tribe.

Together with Havas Luxe, Assouline and The Luxury Marketing Council, we decided to join forces and create ALTO. It allows us to follow the Global Tribe around the world, observing them as carefully as if we were early anthropologists studying a remote tribe in the Amazon. This of course can be done only with the permission of the tribe. After all, "by invitation only" is their motto. You don't just decide to join the tribe; you have to be invited. You have to understand their symbols in order to show you are one of them.

I have intentionally immersed myself in different social groups and organizations around the world to understand how this unique group of individuals makes choices. Why do they travel to one place but not another?

Why do they buy the products of one brand but not another? Why is one person a part of the tribe but another is not? ALTO helps me find answers to these puzzles.

In order for anthropologists to truly understand a tribe, we need to become one with the tribe—to live, eat and breathe like a local. In order to understand this Global Tribe I am so fascinated with, I make sure to participate in as many gatherings as possible where I can find this unique group.

Like the ornithologist who studies birds and tracks their migration patterns, we must also travel with the Global Tribe as they move to warm places in the winter and milder places in the summer. I've found them at cultural events like the Rose Ball in Monaco, Art Basel in Switzerland, the Cannes Film Festival in France, and the Old Masters auction in London. I can also find the Global Tribe at sporting events like the Hamptons Classic Horse Show, the Wimbledon Championships, or Formula One in Monaco, Singapore and Dubai. I've even seen other places trying to re-create these prestigious events, like Art Basel in Miami and Formula One in China. Not only do members of the tribe travel to the same places; they also travel together for specific events and certain seasons.

It's also important for me to travel with the Global Tribe. I need to be in Palm Beach, the Hamptons, Newport, Aspen, Gstaad, St. Moritz, Monaco, Nice, Venice and Baton. They travel to different places in different seasons and for different events. It is not just the Court or the Courtesans, but also the Suppliers and the Symbolic Creators who travel. From the Cannes Lions International Festival of Creativity to the International Consumer Electronics Show in Las Vegas, the same group of creators and suppliers often travels together. Here is what one of them had to say:

> At CES, we end up seeing people that we also see in New York, and it can be sort of silly, but we travel in packs, and because everyone is in the same place at the same time, good things tend to happen.
> —Matt Seiler, global chief executive of IPG Mediabrands

In 2014, I was invited by Mediavest to speak at the Cannes Lions Festival. I was just coming back from China, where we had conducted a fascinating discovery on toothpaste for Colgate. As I was walking in the street, I heard people calling my name. I turned around, and to my surprise, the whole China Code Discovery team was also attending. They were Chinese brand managers and advertising creative directors.

American executives from New York were also at the Cannes Lions Festival. They had all worked with me in China, and I was so happy to see them again in France. In China, we had discovered what I called "words to use" and "words to lose"—what you should always say and what you should never say when you speak about toothpaste. In one part of China we had discovered that some people were brushing their teeth before eating. Yes, before! Why?

The response was stunning—they wanted to clean their mouths and stimulate their gustatory papillae in order to better enjoy their food. The consequences were obvious—they do not want toothpaste with a strong flavor such as mint or vanilla. These became no-no words. But words like "preparing your mouth" and "stimulating your taste buds" became a must. The importance of knowing the "words to use" and "words to lose" when formulating a communication strategy should never be underestimated.

MEETING THEM

Let me give you some real-life examples of four modern hubbers.

Paulo is Brazilian and he lives in Rio with his three children and his French wife. He is not super-rich; he has to work to feed his family. But he presents most of the characteristics of the Global Tribe.

He speaks three languages and has lived and experienced at least three cultures. The first is the Brazilian culture into which he was born. The second is the French culture, where his wife and in-laws come from, and the third is the American culture, which he experienced when he studied in Berkeley.

Paulo is also "hyper-connected," always socializing on Facebook, Twitter, Instagram, etc. He's up to speed on all of the new gadgets, and has an impressive global network of other tribe members. He is into extreme sports and recently drove a motorcycle from Rio to Tierra del Fuego in Argentina—an event which he shared with his network via social media and email.

But what's more significant than Paulo's travel, sports or money is his attitude. He feels just as American as he does Brazilian. He's comfortable engaging with new cultures and adapts easily to local customs. He is mobile and in possession of a mobile mind-set. He benchmarks everything from the latest smartphone to the best mountain bikes to the latest kite-surfing equipment.

Jeffrey bears two nationalities, American and French; he is another good example of the Global Tribe member. He has an American father and a French mother. He has lived in both France and the United States, but also in Canada, where he studied at McGill University in Montreal, and in Mexico City, where he worked for three years. His network of friends is impressive. When he travels, he rarely needs to go to a hotel, because he always has the possibility of staying with a friend or family member. His family has homes in New Mexico, Colorado and France. He is fluent in French, Spanish and English, and also understands German. He is not a jet-setter, and has to work hard, but his attitude and abilities make him a member of the Global Tribe.

He once told me a story about meeting some friends in a Japanese restaurant in Lower Manhattan:

I was called up by my friend Akim, a friend of mine from Geneva whose parents are Afghan and Spanish, who told me that he was visiting New York on business and that we should meet for dinner. Akim completed his Masters at U. Penn., but before that was studying at UCL in London, which is where he currently lives. His cousin Massud had made reservations at this great Japanese restaurant, and another friend of his named Anders was going to join us. When I got there, we introduced ourselves and established everyone's connection to our common friend, Akim. It turned out that Anders was a Norwegian national, who had grown up in London and completed the same Master's degree at U. Penn. with Akim, he was currently working as an expat in New York. Massud, on the other hand, had grown up from Afghan parents who were exiled during the Soviet-Afghan war and stayed in Japan, where they had been working for the Afghan Embassy. Massud grew up in Tokyo and speaks fluent Japanese, he currently lives and works in NYC. Needless to say, he ordered a wide selection of Japanese delicacies that we had never even known existed! I was amazed—between the three of us, we represented at least 7 nationalities!

My good friend Alejandro is Jewish and Mexican. He studied at the University of California, Berkeley, where he obtained a doctorate in economics. He currently lives in San Francisco. He sent his children to school in Switzerland, as he believed that it would provide a richer and safer learning environment for them than Mexico. He feels at home in Latin America, as well as in Europe and the United States, and he has developed an incredible network of leading thinkers, businessmen and politicians. As a member of the Global Tribe, he likes to have other members stay with him when they visit Mexico City or San Francisco, where he has homes.

Every year, he organizes a large conference where he invites great thinkers from Oxford, Harvard, Berkeley and similar high-caliber institutions to present their challenging ideas. His motto is "Don't always believe what you think." He is a proponent of debating "dangerous ideas." Recently, he organized a historic confrontation between Deepak Chopra and Richard Dawkins, in which they discussed the following questions: Does the universe have a purpose? Is religion good or bad for humanity? Are science and spirituality inextricably linked?

Neeraj is Indian; he is married to a Pakistani woman, and they spend most of their time living in Singapore. He studied at Georgetown University, where he still has an apartment by the university. He also has a home in London, and of course an apartment in Singapore. He speaks Hindi, English, Malay and Mandarin Chinese. He lives in a hub because he saw it as the most strategic place for his nomadic lifestyle. He travels all of the time, lecturing and promoting his books.

When a French company that produces spirits asked me to discover the code for alcohol in China I met my first "gypsy" family. The brand manager was born in France but was sent to China to live and work. I met him during a project for a whiskey brand and he commissioned me to discover the unconscious codes for alcohol and whiskey in China and figure out how this brand could own these codes.

"How do you like living in China?" I asked him. His answer was, "It's great, this is a great moment to be here. My family and I are enjoying it. It is like learning another culture." "Have you made friends?" I asked. "Oh yes! Many are Chinese citizens, but we also have a lot of expat friends." Those expats, just like him, were Platinum Gypsies. "One good friend of mine is Australian, but he works for HSBC in Shanghai. Before that he worked in Singapore. His children are good friends with mine, and my wife gets along well with his," he continued.

The next time I met Jean-Paul, he was in New York City, where he had been promoted to head of a new brand of vodka for the United States. "How do you like New York?" I inquired. "I love it!" he said enthusiastically. "It's a great city! There's a big French community here, and our children are going to the Lycée Français." "And what about your Australian friends?" I asked. "They were sent to London, but they are going to visit us next month, we're planning on hosting a party for them!" came the response. I then asked him if he missed China. "It was a great learning experience, and I'm sure I will be back. I feel like Europe, Asia and America are now all part of my DNA. I don't know where I'm going to be next. Is it of concern to me? Not at all, it is a personal learning and growing experience," he concluded.

International companies like Pernod Ricard need executives with multicultural experience. During a recent meeting with top executives at Novartis, we realized that six different nationalities were present in the group. Of course, to work together people of different nationalities need a common language, which is English, but they also need to share some of the same values and principles. We found that clichés and stereotypes were a serious handicap to the group's productivity. We integrated the concept of Culture Codes in order to create a common awareness among the participants. Immediately the executives in the group were able to use their knowledge of the various pros and cons of each culture to the advantage of the team.

"We have experience working together, so we create a common language based on our evaluation of various cultures," one executive told me. "Is it like benchmarking cultures?" I asked. "Yes, exactly," he said. "We know the Japanese might be better at long-term planning, while the Americans might be better at short-term action and results. The Japanese like to miniaturize everything, the Americans to make everything big. It is also important to know where the best places are for your children to grow up, where to take the best vacations, where to invest your money. We know and we share it with each other; if we move, we share our contacts. It doesn't matter where we are—we are still together. When we arrive in a new place, we immediately connect with friends who live there, or with friends of friends." What he meant was that, as a member of the Global Tribe, you are always connected with the other members.

Indeed, this is a unique group of people. They may have their own place of origin where they were born and perhaps spent the first five years of their lives, but soon they have several new cultural imprints and they learn a few languages as well as new customs and protocols. They develop a cultural IQ, if you will.

Jean-Paul's children can compare French food to Chinese and American food; they have friends from all three of those countries. They have a network of connections and the technology to keep it alive—technology that I did not have when I was a child stuck in my boarding school in Normandy, dreaming of discovering the world.

What I saw in Jean-Paul's family was the ability to adapt and develop a cultural intelligence far beyond that of the sedentary masses.

Through these examples, we can see that the members of the Global Tribe fit many of the following criteria:

- They are mobile; they travel all the time.
- They respect the rule of threes—they have at least three homes (or three hubs they call home, even if they don't own a home there), speak at least three languages, are familiar with at least three different cultures, have lived in at least three different countries or continents.
- They live in a hub or a large city with airports.
- They are not attached to a specific nationality.
- They are hyper-connected and have an impressive network of friends.
- Most of the time when they are away from one of their hubs, they stay with friends, rather than in hotels.

As I became aware of the presence of these modern gypsies, I noticed a recurring pattern—they migrate together. (One of the heads of marketing at Richemont, who was well versed in the tribe, called them the "migratory ducks" (*canards migrateurs*). So I decided to follow their migration. Where do they go? When and where and why?

RULES AND RITUALS

After studying the Global Tribe for many years, I've discovered the details that make them unique. I want to outline these in this book before we begin to discover the Global Codes. If you want to be a member of the Global Tribe, you need to act like one. You need to be able to quickly pick up on the rules of engagement and participate in the rituals in an adequate fashion. Rule-breakers stand out instantly and are quickly rejected from the club.

BY INVITATION ONLY

The first rule I've identified is "by invitation only." Parties and social gatherings are simply an excuse for getting together and connecting with the network. Charity events, fundraisers, sporting events, birthdays and concerts are all excuses to stay relevant within the Global Tribe scene. At these events, members can meet new people from the tribe and find a place to connect.

However, not everyone can attend. What makes any tribe unique is that it needs to establish a clear divide between the in-crowd and out-crowd. So for many of their get-togethers, you need to be personally and formally invited. Unless the invitation says otherwise, you are encouraged to come solo and avoid bringing a stranger to the group. People who aren't invited know their place and don't just show up.

Nevertheless, those not part of the Global Tribe—potential new members or Courtesans—can try to find someone within the group who can nominate them as a guest worth inviting. There is a clear selection principle when it comes to inviting a new guest to the parties. Other members discuss who to invite and evaluate whether you are "one of our kind."

Once you are invited, you must behave appropriately and be respectful to the host by arriving on time. It's important, however, to pay close attention to the social rules and cultural context because in some societies arriving on time may be considered even more offensive than arriving early or late. In France and Italy, for instance, you always try to arrive 30 minutes to an hour late in order to give the hostess time for any last-minute preparations. Likewise, you must also pay attention to the cues indicating when it's time to leave. You don't want to overstay your welcome. If you start seeing other guests departing, then it's your turn as well.

A day or two after the event you should send a handwritten letter to the host expressing your praise and thanks. Members of the Global Tribe always keep personalized stationery with their full name at the top. However, as a sign of goodwill and friendship, you're encouraged to cross out your printed name and handwrite your nickname. A handwritten note shows your appreciation and intentions to foster the relationship, and crossing out your full name breaks down the formality and adds a personal touch.

Remember, the Court of the Global Tribe can be joined by invitation only. This is one of the most powerful concepts of the tribe. One does not simply decide to join the Court; rather, one hopes to be invited. In order to be invited, you need to send the subtle signals that identify you as a potential member. Who you know is, of course, key, but so is how you dress, what you drink, what kind of car you drive and your zip code. The Court will determine whether you will be accepted into the tribe and where you might fit in the tribal hierarchy—and of course your way of giving back through your dedication to charity.

CHARITY

Contributing to charitable causes demonstrates two things: you have higher intentions to make a positive impact on the world, and you also have the means to do so. You have enough wealth that you even have some left over to share it around. Money isn't the goal; it is the proof.

But the Global Tribe doesn't donate blindly—they give to causes that reflect their values and passions. They are likely to give back to academic institutions, scientific research, environmental organizations, the arts, local social causes, and international groups fighting poverty. They write checks to Harvard University, the Sierra Club, Doctors Without Borders, Save the Children and so on. The types of fundraising events you attend reflect your priorities and communicate this to the rest of the Global Tribe.

Raising money for charity is a sign of nobility for members of the tribe. If you're dedicated to rescuing little dogs, feeding starving children in Africa, raising money for cancer research, or preserving national heritage, then you are at the top. The Palm Beach Chamber Music Society, for example, organizes concerts in the Hamptons (during the summer) to raise money for children who want to learn music but can't afford it. One of the most popular balls is the Doggy Ball, which raises money to rescue animals who have been abandoned or treated badly. However, just because you are ready to part with your money doesn't mean you'll necessarily be invited.

THE MAGIC NUMBER

As noted earlier, the Global Tribe's magic number is the number three. Members of the tribe have at least three homes, three passports and three credit cards. They speak at least three languages, donate to at least three charities, have three cars and even have three or more ex-wives. The number three implies diversity, not sticking to one, not even to two. Three is the tribe's number of choice.

When I spoke in Barbados about the Platinum Gypsies, a representative of my client, Royal Bank, told me that this group of people always have at least three of everything, They have three platinum cards (which now might be three black cards) or are members of three platinum airline clubs. They are members of several privileged clubs that offer concierge services, including concierge medicine. They have experienced at least three different cultures and they have a minimum of three different houses (or places they call home, even if they don't own the property). They have more than three cars, and they almost never have the time to drive them. Many social directories ask you to identify your various homes, the name of your boat, and the brand of your aircraft, as well as the various clubs you belong to.

THEY ARE TRENDSETTERS

Today, very few members of the tribe have inherited their money. Most of them had to work very hard to get to where they are. Some of them are still very young and very active. In Tuxedo Park, New York, where some of them live during the summer, I spoke to Robert, a good friend of ours who created an Internet company. He used to live in France, where he was involved in real estate; he then moved to China and now he is back in the United States. His company is an online marketplace where dealers can sell rare and antique items. He bought three houses and 80 acres of land in Tuxedo Park, and he is now buying offices in the town of Tuxedo.

Victor is a new resident of Tuxedo Park; he made his money in stem-cell research and has a foundation that promotes projects that combine art and science. He travels around the world to promote his foundation. "I was going to buy a chateau in France," he said. "I found several, one was very nice and had been completely remodeled and restored by a British gentleman who bought it for $10 million USD and invested an additional $10 million to fix it. After all, how much time are you going to spend in France? I have so many homes already, and my foundation is in Chelsea, NY. I better find a chateau-style mansion in Tuxedo Park which is less than an hour outside of Manhattan."

By choosing Tuxedo Park over the Hamptons or Newport, the tribe creates a trend. They will attract new residents, influence the price of properties, and create a new narrative around these places.

SPENDING MONEY

The Global Tribe typically does not go grocery shopping, as they usually do not cook. They have other priorities. How you spend your money is a big indicator of whether or not you belong to the Global Tribe. The term "nouveau riche," for instance, will likely connote "former poor" to members of the tribe, and it does not have a positive connotation. The Global Tribe believes that being rich is an attitude, not a bank account. Many very wealthy people don't belong to the Global Tribe, and they never will. Simply put, they have a lot of money but the wrong attitude.

I remember organizing a meeting at the Burj Al Arab hotel in Dubai. I was presenting the results of the work we had carried out to discover the code for city-states. We had the code for Dubai, Hong Kong, Macau and Singapore. The hotel that hosted the event was a good example of what I was just talking about: lots of money but the wrong attitude.

I had rented a two-floor suite to receive my clients and present the results. Both of the teams from Richemont and Georgetown University that had participated in the study were there. The suite was so over-the-top that it completely lacked taste. There was too much gold, too much extravagance and ridiculously ostentatious draperies. As Coco Chanel said, "Fashion passes, style remains."

On another occasion, I was going to give a speech in Istanbul at a conference. My travel agent at the time recommended that I stay at the Four Seasons Hotel, right on the Bosphorus, because it had a beautiful view and good service. I then exchanged some emails with my friend Neeraj, who splits his time between Singapore, London and Washington. He is a good friend and definitely a member of the Global Tribe. When I told him about my travel plans, he advised, "Don't go to the Four Seasons . . . you cannot open the windows and they do not have a balcony. Go to the Kempinski right next door, you will have a beautiful view. You can enjoy a *raki* on the balcony as you watch the boats go by on the Bosphorus." Needless to say, I took his advice.

Members of the Global Tribe benchmark and permanently update one another on the best places to go and on what to do and not to do. Palm Beach is one of the Global Tribe's Meccas, along with Aspen, Gstaad, the Hamptons and Monaco. The Chinese like Singapore, Macau and Hong Kong. The Hindus like London. Australians go to Bali. Today tribe members might go to Miami for Art Basel, to Venice for the film festival or to Dubai for shopping.

In Palm Beach, there is a daily newspaper called the *Shiny Sheet,* where the week's agenda is published. What is happening and where? Of course, when you get close to the end of the season in Palm Beach, the *Shiny Sheet* tells you what is happening in the Hamptons and in Saratoga, Newport, Baden-Baden, Monaco and so on. Just by reading the agenda and the future agenda you know where these migratory ducks are going to be. They migrate in flocks. The same people who have a big house on Palm Beach Island also have another big house in Southampton, where the tribe will get together again.

The tribe doesn't stay at hotels—when someone asks the question "Where are you staying?" they mean, "With whom are you staying? Who are your friends from Palm Beach, the Hamptons or Newport who have invited you to stay with them?" If you don't have any friends, something is wrong with you. When you are friends with members of the Global Tribe, you become part of an interconnected group of people who want you to stay with them. The only problem may be choosing who you are going to stay with so as to not offend anybody. Andrew from Palm Beach: "I have so many friends from the Hamptons. Last year I stayed with the Browns, and this year I would like to stay with the Robertses, but I don't want to offend the Browns, so I have a big dilemma."

Spending your money becomes being focused on buying the right present for the friends you are going to visit and on buying the right clothes, as you always need to be aware of the dress code where you are going. It requires a lot of attention to be always properly dressed—never too formal, never too casual. Oscar Wilde used to say: "If I am occasionally a little overdressed, I make up for it by being always immensely overeducated." If the tribe members lack Oscar's "overeducation," they will try to make up for it by giving extravagant amounts of money to charity.

FUNDING THE ARTS

Members of the Global Tribe are the makers, takers and givers of wealth. As I mentioned before, being a part of the Global Tribe is not only about money; it's a mind-set. However, it's true that most of the Global Tribe members have larger bank accounts than everyone else because they are constantly reinventing themselves and looking for new sources of income. So for them charity is an important part of their lifestyle. Whether it's time or money, it's harder to be generous if you are poor.

If we go back to the metaphor of the historical court of a monarch, the royal family sponsored artists, musicians and writers through a pension or a fixed salary. Throughout history and all over the globe we have seen courts establish in-house workshops for a variety of fine-arts disciplines. These workshops helped the royal court foster the preferred style and cultural trends. By investing in the arts, the court controlled their influence and capitalized on creativity.

Ludwig II of Bavaria took great interest in the arts and in building Bavaria's reputation as Europe's new cultural capital. When Ludwig II came across the work of composer Richard Wagner, he was instantly charmed and summoned Wagner to his court. Ludwig II became Wagner's principal patron.

Ludwig II went to such lengths to keep Wagner content that he settled Wagner's debts, brought him to Munich, gave him an attractive pension and sponsored his famous operas *Tristan und Isolde, Die Meistersinger* and *Der Ring des Nibelungen.* The rest of the court became suspicious of Wagner's controlling influence on Ludwig II and pushed the king to banish Wagner from the court. After Wagner was exiled, Ludwig even set Wagner up with a comfortable home in Switzerland and donated a great sum of money to the opera house Wagner was building in Bayreuth.

Though it is rumored that Ludwig II's intentions were more romantic than professional, royal courts have always made it a priority to invest heavily in the arts. Members of the Global Tribe share this same interest and make an effort to contribute heavily to the fine arts and to various foundations that foster the kind of culture they favor.

"Money is better than poverty, if only for financial reasons."

—Woody Allen

THEY SET THE STANDARD

The masses look to the Global Tribe as the model for how to move up. They want to be like them; they want to join the tribe. It is often difficult for them to do so, even if they have the money. The difficulties might come from cultural or political factors. Generally, in India, for instance, culture dictates that individuals stay in the caste into which they are born. In Russia, culture focuses on a destiny of suffering. This creates a high degree of frustration. Because of the technology we all have access to today, there are no longer any secrets. Everybody can see how the Global Tribe lives.

But the fact that they travel all of the time gives members of the tribe a different perspective from that of monocultural individuals. They move en masse and follow the same agenda. Let's see what that agenda is.

A NEW REFERENCE SYSTEM

"Don't solve problems, make them obsolete."

Members of the Global Tribe are experts at benchmarking. They are exposed to so much variety that they unconsciously, or consciously, compare everything they see and experience—different products, behaviors, social rules and attitudes. With such knowledge they are able to mix and match aspects of different cultures to make a hybrid culture.

The best-quality products and services are hybrids. Boeing had the vision of the Global Tribe when they designed the 787 Dreamliner. The aircraft's great design and functionality is largely due to the contribution of people in 28 countries collaborating in its production—the wings are made in Japan, the engines in England and it's assembled in the United States.

The Global Tribe is constantly moving, traveling, meeting new people, trying new things and starting new projects. Their sense of identity is not tied down to a particular country or job. Their identity is the Global Tribe—it's belonging to the tribe.

The tribe is deeply concerned about quality and high content. Its members prefer surrounding themselves with other interesting people who have traveled, acquired crazy stories, tried bizarre food, played extreme sports and listened to obscure music. The more diverse and exotic the person is, the more attractive that person becomes. In turn, the Global Tribe defines itself based on its members' connections and this rich diversity. They view themselves as a different kind—a different species if you will.

This new species is the one who will create a new reference system. The members of the new species are the ones who speak the global language, the Global Code. This new reference system is the hybrid of all the great things different cultures have to offer. It's a new phase of social evolution.

The reference system that the tribe is creating is an open one. Kings and queens have dubbed individuals as knights for centuries, usually people who have served the throne or shown great bravery defending the kingdom. Today, however, even musicians and artists are knighted, including Sean Connery and Paul McCartney. That's a system that is open to change and modernity.

Imagination is more important than knowledge. For knowledge is limited to all we now know and understand, while imagination embraces the entire world, and all there ever will be to know and understand.

—Albert Einstein

The Global Tribe and the new reference system it is creating will not solve problems; rather, they will make them obsolete. Gay marriage, for instance, will no longer have space on the table for debate, not because it's not important, but rather because it is obvious that homosexuals should have the same rights as everyone else. Canada's former Prime Minister Pierre Trudeau had the right idea when he said that "there's no place for the state in the bedroom."

THE AGENDA

The tribe has a clear agenda. Its members follow the flock, the group, the Court. The agenda is sometimes dictated by the climate (most of the clubs are closed in Palm Beach for the summer), or by special events (Art Basel in Miami, the Cannes festival, Fashion Week in Paris, Old Masters in London). They migrate because all the others are also migrating. It has become an unconscious behavior, something that they do without knowing exactly why, without even needing to know why. It is instinctive behavior. So if nobody goes to St. Moritz anymore because of the rude and noisy Russian nouveaux riches, then you don't go. Word spreads quickly, and the Global Tribe can "recalculate" easily, using their tribal GPS. (We will explore this notion later on.) The tribe is very flexible because its members travel light. Let's look a little more deeply at that concept.

THE ISLAND MENTALITY

The Global Tribe lives on an island, both literally and symbolically. Palm Beach is an island with three drawbridges; Manhattan and Singapore are also islands. These places are insulated by waterways, and if we think back to the medieval concept of a moat and drawbridge, these places are able to isolate themselves in times of crisis and danger.

There is a symbolic dimension to having to cross water to get to the other side. It is like a purification ritual. You also have an island mentality, where having limited space means that the price of land will always go up. There's a premium placed on separation from the rest of the world. In Palm Beach, when you take a bridge to exit the island they say that you are "going to America." The Hamptons are also on an island, Long Island. London and Paris are symbolic islands: *L'isle de la cité*. (I explain this concept in detail in Chapter 3.)

Singapore, Hong Kong and Macau are also all islands. The Global Tribe migrates from island to island, meeting each other again and again, repeating the same rituals. These places are all going "up" and "away." "Up," as rich people become even richer. And "away," as they get more and more disconnected from the rest of the world, both literally and symbolically.

As we've all heard, the middle class is disappearing. It is as if they are drowning between the island and the continent. They are either joining the Global Tribe, or staying within the anonymity of the large continent. They become the No Content, Occupy, Anonymous, billions of cell phone people, all alone together, who see the island receding a little more every day.

GUCCI, NOT DELI

The Global Tribe moves from one place to another and repeats this process again and again. And whenever they land on a new "island," it transforms for them. These places change to cater to the needs of the Global Tribe. The rent for stores and apartments becomes more and more expensive. Very quickly, even supermarkets and delis close, to be replaced by Ralph Lauren, Gucci or Cartier stores. In Vail village, it is impossible to buy a salad that's not on a restaurant menu. If you want to go shopping for food, you need to cross the highway.

PROPER ATTIRE

When you meet someone for the first time, the way you dress and present yourself is everything—it's your business card. So the dress code is another essential rule the Global Tribe pays close attention to.

Prince William and Kate Middleton's wedding in 2011 was one of the most-watched events on television, and yet what probably stood out most was the guests' attire, especially the women's hats. In England, those elaborately decorated and one-of-a-kind hats we've seen in social magazines symbolize status and class. They are indicators to the rest of the tribe that a person is part of the group.

Members of the Global Tribe make it a point to be dressed appropriately for every occasion. This means not being overdressed or underdressed.

You'd never want to show up at one of those posh English events not wearing a hat when everyone else is, or worse, wearing a hat when no one else is. You would stand out like a sore thumb, sending a message to everyone else that you are "not one of our kind."

It's important to know what attire is appropriate for which event. Often, the best way to know this is by referring to photos of similar events or by asking an insider what he or she recommends as most suitable. In some cases, the host or venue will explicitly state in the invitation whether it's a suit-and-tie event or a black-tie event. But most of the time, members of the Global Tribe already know what is appropriate and what is not because they've been to so many similar events in the past. In summer you want to wear light shades, whites and pastel colors, while in winter you should stick to more somber and dark shades.

Women are lucky in the sense that they have more flexibility with their wardrobe and have more options to choose from. Men are often limited to pants, shirt, tie and jacket, with little room for variation and creative self-expression. Women, on the other hand, can wear a dress, skirt or pants, depending on the event, and have more patterns, colors and styles to choose from. However, the downside to dressing up for women is the taboo of wearing the same outfit twice.

FREEDOM THROUGH AWARENESS:
GREATER EXPERIENCE MEANS GREATER CHOICE

The nomadic lifestyle of the Global Tribe forces its members to be good social readers. They must quickly pick up on social cues and rules if they have any hope of surviving within a new culture. Their experiences and travels make them fluent in the language of culture.

Their mental warehouse of international experiences makes them more aware of the differences between one culture and another. I am arguing that this is a good thing because with awareness comes great freedom. The more aware we are of our options, choices and opportunities, the more freedom we have to take the best path.

If you were born and raised within a ten-mile radius and never left the nest, your cosmos would be very small. Your world of references and experiences would be small. You would have little knowledge of different ways of living life and different opportunities at your disposal. The less awareness people have, the fewer options they have to choose from.

If you are an expert in something, you have a vast amount of knowledge of the tools, methods and resources available. Let's take the example of a clothing stylist. A stylist not only carries a mental warehouse of clothing brands, materials, patterns and trends, but also knows what works best for specific body types, skin tones, events, budgets and so on. That experience and knowledge make the stylist an expert in tailoring a look specifically suited to each client.

In this same sense, members of the Global Tribe are experts too. They are able to pick and choose elements from different cultures that best suit their needs. I want to invest like an American, work like a German, travel like an Australian, make love like a Frenchman and relax like a Jamaican. The tribe is aware of these different ways of maximizing life's opportunities.

Freedom of awareness also makes the Global Tribe extremely good at adapting and being flexible. Like chameleons, they know how important it is to change oneself as the environment changes. This is a basic quality of survival, and in today's constantly changing world, it is a bankable quality to have.

IT'S ALL ABOUT MIND-SET

What I want to emphasize in this book is that it's not about money; it's about a mind-set. What makes the Global Tribe different from the rest of the population is that that they are using the global *mind* and not the global *brain*.

While the brain is about quantity and about a buffet lifestyle of constantly wanting more in order to feel like we are creating an identity, the mind is about quality. The global mind focuses on quality content. If we take the example of social media, we are bombarded with copious amounts of content. Twitter, for example, allows every individual with access to the Internet to spew out bite-sized information that often creates more noise than meaning. When filtering through dozens, even hundreds, of posts, we may find only one message that really states something relevant and important.

The global mind is also concerned about the structure and linkages between pieces of information. An idea is only an idea when our neurons are connected through pathways and build connections, but isolated information is devoid of meaning.

When a client asks me to help them define the code for a particular product or service, I always look at the underlying structure—how behaviors, individuals, objects and places relate to each other—rather than how these things operate individually.

When I did some work for the Ritz-Carlton a few years ago, I told them that we needed to understand the relationship between the service staff and the hotel's clients. It's not enough for the personnel to understand their jobs as waiters, bellboys or working at the front desk; they need to understand their relationship with the customers. We came up with a saying: "Ladies and gentlemen serving ladies and gentlemen." This put a demand on both ends of the relationship. Not only was the staff expected to behave as ladies and gentlemen—so were the clients. If a patron treated a member of the staff badly, the manager could ask them to kindly leave. This created a new philosophy and work culture where the staff could feel proud of their work, and the clients could also be happy with the results. This relationship is the "space in between." To borrow from anthropologist Claude Lévi-Strauss, we can say that a mother is not a woman, rather, that a mother is the space between a woman and a child. Without a child, there is no mother and vice versa.

As I mentioned above, the structures that connect us are what really matter to the global mind, because the mind understands that everything we do or want all goes back to our social networks. Why does anyone buy a new purse? They want to send a message to other people. Why does anyone buy a plane ticket? So they can visit other people. We are defined by our connections and the Global Tribe understands this.

Chinese culture eloquently uses the term *guanxi* to refer to the social networks we develop in the different realms of our lives—work, family, friends, and clubs or organizations. *Guanxi* recognizes how important it is to cultivate interpersonal relationships. Often, our greatest memories and joys come from our relationships with others, and so do our most intense pains and frustrations. We are in essence social animals, and it's through our social ties that we are able to define our identities.

ADAPTABILITY

We must constantly adapt and evolve in response to the pace of change. It's impossible to foresee changes, so we have no way of knowing what we will be doing in the next decade, or even the next year. Most of the jobs that exist today will become obsolete in ten years. The future is completely open, so we must be flexible in response to whatever comes our way.

Members of the Global Tribe are more successful at adapting to change because they don't put all their eggs in one basket. You may be a great lawyer, but if you want to survive and succeed you should probably consider buying real estate, investing in high-tech companies, writing a book or collecting art. The wise person will keep his or her eyes open for new opportunities of growth and income, even when that person is relatively comfortable and economically stable.

Being able to adapt with such ease is similar to the art of acting. The actor delves into the psyche of a character. The actor begins to think, feel and behave like the character. Empathy is the actor's greatest tool for truly capturing the essence of a character. Similarly, in order to adapt, we must have empathy.

Members of the Global Tribe are actors on the world stage. They must be able to arrive at a crowded market in New Delhi, observe and listen to the hustle and bustle of what's going on, and be able to adapt. If they don't want to get pick-pocketed or ripped off on their weekly grocery run, then they must quickly learn how to be aware of how a culture works and be able to effectively adapt and act. Tribe members put on the correct local attire, walk, talk and negotiate like a local. The same would apply if they were leading a business meeting in Shanghai, going to the opera in Vienna or touring the Amazon in Brazil. They are acting.

Now that we've discussed the hierarchy and rituals of the Global Tribe, let's explore where and how they live.

TWO

WHERE THEY LIVE

Now that we know who the members of the tribe are, let's explore where they live. We know that they move all the time, so they need a place conveniently located and well-connected to other places. If the purpose of this book is to explore and decipher how the Global Tribe is creating the Global Code, we can start by looking at how they've already defined the city of the future.

LOCATION. LOCATION. LOCATION.

Most tribe members have several spots that they consider home. These places are very specific locations, with very specific characteristics. I call them hubs or city-states, even if that's not their literal status (Istanbul or London, for example).

We know that today 53 percent of the world's population lives in cities and that number will be more like 60 percent by 2025. Understanding the evolution of cities is crucial to discovering the Global Code. But not just any city will do. Charleston, South Carolina, might be a beautiful city, but the Global Tribe needs multiple airports offering direct, nonstop flights to other hubs.

HUBS AND CITY-STATES

In 2008, I was commissioned to discover the code for city-states. We went to Hong Kong, Singapore, Dubai, Macau, Monaco and Luxembourg. Again, London, Istanbul and New York are hubs, not true city-states, but in reality they *should be* city-states. They are in many ways independent. Istanbul is not the same as Turkey, just as Hong Kong is not Chinese (as witnessed by the numerous student demonstrations claiming a Hong Kong national identity). Muslim Turkey will not be accepted in Europe, especially at a time when Europe is experiencing increasing anti-Islamic sentiment. Istanbul by itself, on the other hand, very well could be considered a European city.

Many folks have suggested that London would be better off if it had the status of a city-state, and also that New York City—specifically Manhattan—is not an American city per se but more of a world capital. It is the cosmopolitan hub favored by many global nomads, or *glomads*. Recently published statistics about how many Manhattan apartments are now owned by foreign nationals who live there only a couple of weeks a year reinforce this notion of NYC as a world city. New York City is where Russians, Chinese and Brazilians "park" their money by investing in multimillion-dollar apartments they almost never use. Of course it becomes very expensive for others to buy a home on the island, and many people who work in Manhattan have to commute. We heard in Manhattan that the people who live on the island refer to those who commute in as *BATs* (short for Bridge and Tunnel). Every day, BATs invade NYC.

It is clear that Manhattan's status as a world center is beyond question. Even after 9/11 and the destruction of the World Trade Center, it became clear to the terrorists that not only had they attacked New York, and America; they had also assaulted Western identity. Indeed, individuals from 27 different nationalities were working in the Twin Towers when they fell. Today, the Freedom Tower, the new building at the World Trade Center site, is the tallest building in the United States. It's a symbol of New Yorkers' power and their ability to come back from anything.

So what are the key characteristics of the city of the future? Why do such veritable city-states hold such power and attraction?

A City-State Is an Island

Being on an island, whether real or symbolic, gives a city a distinct advantage. It is usually an indicator that the city was a trading post, often associated with a strong navy, such as with Venice and London, as well as a strong shipping-based economy. Paris is known for its Ile de la Cité, one of the islands in the middle of the river Seine, which the Romans settled more than 2,000 years ago.

Place of Free Trade

The archetype of the free port, the trading post, the free harbor, *le port franc,* is still imprinted in the minds of those cities' inhabitants. Dubai was a trading post for the Arabs, Persians, Indians and Turks. Through commerce, they were places where not only products but also ideas and knowledge were exchanged. The merchants' boutiques were outposts of the cultures they represented. These cities were open, welcoming travelers and merchants from all over the world. They were dedicated to connecting disparate peoples and cultures.

Strategic Position

Such places are strategically positioned to channel goods, people and money from one continent to another. Istanbul and Singapore both have this strategic positioning. Istanbul is a bridge, a bridge between East and West, a bridge across the Bosphorus, and the gateway to the Russian territory and for the Russian navy. These places are bridges, passages, connectors; they are hubs. Modern technology has brought the Internet, and these cities are also the electronic relays, the multiple brain centers, used by the Global Tribe to communicate. Originally associated with water, the hub city today has the best electronic communication infrastructure and the best airports.

Airport Cities

The primary function of these cities is to link the world's places where people commute, change planes and connect. Airports are the centers of these cities, as are major airlines. Each of these cities has several airports and several major airlines. New York, for example, has JFK, La Guardia and Newark, plus many little airports for private jets. Hong Kong built an enormous new airport. London desperately needs a new one as Heathrow is running out of capacity. Dubai is now the number one airport in the world.

In fact, Dubai calls itself the world's center, as it is equidistant from East and West. Al Maktoum, the ruler and brand manager of Dubai, knows what he's after . . . he's after the best. The best airlines, the best airport, the best connection, the best shopping mall in the middle of the desert, the best tourist attractions (such as the ski slope located inside that same mall!). Old cities like London or New York now have to compete with new cities like Doha or Dubai. The Global Tribe is quick to spread the word if a city's airport has no jetways (Doha) or if it's famous for more delays than any other airport (La Guardia) or if, like Heathrow, it's a zoo best avoided.

Easy Access

A busy airport is not the only criterion, however. Connectedness to important places matters. So if it takes two hours to go from Charles de Gaulle to Paris, then Paris does not qualify.

Hong Kong used to have its airport right in the city, but the new airport is not too far away, so Hong Kong still qualifies. The beauty of the train between London and Paris is that you catch the train in the center of Paris and arrive in the center of London. This is a lot better and faster than taking a plane—unfortunately, there is no train to New York!

Business-Friendly

These successful cities harbor some of the world's most business-friendly environments. Hong Kong is still considered the world's number one most business-friendly city. Singapore follows closely behind, and other city hubs are constantly fighting for spots at the top of the list. Because topping that list has huge benefits, HSBC relocated its headquarters from London to Singapore, and now P&G headquarters for Asia are also located in Singapore. City-states are becoming the major service and financial hubs of the globally connected world.

ANCIENT VENICE AS A REFERENCE

The code for the Global City is *Venice*. This is the reference system. Of course I'm speaking about the old Venice, that independent city that ruled the sea and the world for centuries, until Napoleon came along.

Venice is the archetypal city-state. It is on an island; in fact, it comprises a group of islands. It had a technologically advanced navy; Venetian ships were well ahead of their time. It was very business-friendly, and found higher purpose in enabling international commerce. What Venetians will call a palace is in reality a warehouse on the canal, where a boat could dock and deliver merchandise. These locales had a first floor, *piano nobile* (noble level). Residents lived above their own shops and in turn became very rich.

One day, while enjoying a dry sherry in a place overlooking the Grand Canal in Venice, one of my friends, a Venetian count, told me that at some point a group of Venetian merchants had reflected on their successes. They said, "We are very rich, we have many beautiful properties adorned with the finest paintings and sculptures, we need to become nobles. We need titles!" The merchants quickly realized that acquiring noble titles would also be very beneficial for their businesses, as the added prestige meant they could charge higher premiums for their goods and services.

As a delegation, they went to see the Doge of Venice and shared their concern with him. The Doge, whose main interest was the prosperity of the city-state, immediately saw the financial advantages of improving the status of his Venetian friends. Thus all of the warehouses changed their names to *palazzo* and all of the merchants became counts. They did not have a hierarchy like traditional European nobility (with barons, marquis or dukes); they were all counts.

Today Venice does not exist as a city-state anymore and the "counts" are mostly all gone. The city has been taken over by Italian socialists and communists, who have transformed it into a garbage can for tourists. No counts live in the city anymore, and most of the native Venetians have left or are leaving. So if Venice has lost its status as archetypal model of the Global Code for a city-state, who has taken over?

I believe that Singapore is the new Venice.

SINGAPORE: THE NEW MODEL

"The gentleman has universal sympathies and is not partisan. The small man is partisan and does not have universal sympathies."

—Confucius

I would like to draw attention to Singapore for several reasons. First, as we discussed in the previous chapter, I believe that Singapore is the new model for aspiring global cities. Second, Singapore is unusual in that it's a young culture, created from scratch by a "Virtuous Leader," following Confucian principles.

If Venice is the past, Singapore is the future. It has most of the characteristics of a successful city-state, making it a good example of the hub needed by the glomads. Let's explore some of these characteristics. First off, it is an island, strategically situated to be able to connect different worlds. Second, it has one of the best airports in the world, as well as one of the best airlines (Singapore Airlines).

What's even more important is that Singapore is very stable, both politically and economically. The country experiences almost no corruption, as all the civil servants are well paid and very efficient. It has a large pool of highly educated citizens and boasts a booming high-tech industry and advanced higher education institutions. Many American and European universities have a sister campus in Singapore. Not only is Singapore extremely multicultural, home to Chinese, Malays, Indians and expats from all over the world; it is also very safe and extremely business-friendly. In our dealings there, most of the officials we spoke with mentioned that they just don't understand why people like President Hollande in France or President Obama take clearly anti-business positions. It is not just a question of taxes; it is a question of priorities and mind-set. Any successful city wants to attract the best entrepreneurs, educators and managers. If all the rich people leave, who will pay the taxes? Finally, Singapore (like London and Hong Kong) is very expat-friendly.

Size Matters

A large population of expats live in Singapore and feel very comfortable there. But they do not feel lost in a sea of locals. Singapore, like Switzerland or Sweden, belongs to the "minus ten" group of countries, which means that it has fewer than 10 million inhabitants. This group has quite the impressive track record, and includes cities and countries like Hong Kong, Macau, Switzerland, Monaco, Luxembourg, Sweden, Norway and Denmark. Such places stand in complete contrast with the "billionaire population club" of India and China.

Choosing Singapore

Why do many glomads choose Singapore as a home base?

We asked some members of the Global Tribe this question and received the following answers:

"I love Sing, it is very safe, the food is fantastic, my children get one of the best educations, it is clean."—a 38-year-old male Indian executive

"We have an apartment in London, visit very often our family in Mumbai, but this is one of the places in the world where I feel very comfortable."—a 29-year-old Indian woman

"Everybody speaks English, they love success and reward it, not like in my country of origin."—a 32-year-old French bank manager

Eduardo Saverin, the co-founder of Facebook, recently became a resident. With no oil, no gas, no land, and no natural resources, this tiny nation of 5 million people is a model of success. Let's explore this success story further.

Clean and *Kiasu*

Singapore is a perfect example of a place often chosen as a replenishment stop by members of the Global Tribe, independently of their culture of origin. It is already a multicultural place, with a large representation of

Chinese, Malay and Indians that keeps attracting the Global Tribe. This is a place where many members from China will come, invest, go shopping or send their children to university. A very large international expat population from all over the world feels very comfortable there.

Singapore is the archetype of the global city, the model that inspires many countries. I have been told that when Deng Xiaoping visited Singapore he asked, "Why isn't this us? We can do the same." He went back to China and started to move his country in the Singaporean direction. Recently a mission from Vietnam went to Singapore to see how they could apply this model to their own nation. Let's explore why and how Singapore became this global model:

"It does not matter if the cat is black or white, as long as he catches the mice."

—Deng Xiaoping

In Singapore, everybody catches the mice—independently of their race, color, or country of origin or culture.

Singapore Cleans Up

"Singapore is a country of only 5 million people, and it tops the world's best over and over again in terms of how to compete."

—Jon Huntsman, former U.S. ambassador to Singapore

As far as blows to a nation's self-image are concerned, few are more devastating than the one the Federation of Malaysia dealt Singapore in 1965. The city-state had been merged into the federation in 1963, but only two years later Malaysia expelled Singapore from its membership because it was poor, in economic decline, its streets were filthy, its people were desperate and frustrated, and its prospects were bleak.

For an entire nation to be "fired" is the sort of thing that can permanently ruin a population's psyche. Few countries could recover from this, much less a country with no land, no oil and no other substantial natural resources, one whose population is comprised of 48 different races speaking 54 languages. The future for such a nation might well include further degradation, a descent into violence, despair and surrender.

In 1965, Singapore's very survival was at stake.

Today, as I have learned from doing a considerable amount of work there, including several discoveries, Singapore and its citizens have accomplished one of the great national transformations of our time. Singapore is the envy of much of the world. It is ultramodern and sophisticated, one of the key players in the Asian economic resurgence, and a true global leader in finance and business.

How did this happen?

More to the point—how did the people of Singapore use their failed participation in the federation to catalyze their emergence as a model of the future-facing nation?

As it turns out, the first step was learning to be clean.

When basic survival itself is a challenge, true leaders know that reptilian priorities must guide decisions and initiatives. Basic survival is paramount. People must be fed; they must have clean air to breathe and clean water to drink. Only by ensuring the fundamentals can a nation pursue loftier goals.

The reptilian leader understands that to achieve these fundamentals, it is essential to show the people how to play their part—individually and as a society—in establishing, attending to and extending those basic reptilian priorities on which further priorities and accomplishments can be built. The leader who showed the way to Singapore's brighter future was Lee Kuan Yew, who became prime minister of the independent Republic of Singapore, established on August 9, 1965.

A longtime champion of Singapore's integration with Malaysia, Lee admitted, even as he pronounced Singapore's independence, that the failure of the federation "literally broke everything that we stood for." However, as a reptilian leader, he understood that nursing heartbreak and lingering over past failures does nothing to get the people fed, cared for and on their way to the future. Quickly, Lee Kuan Yew introduced a series of initiatives and basic principles aimed at defining and reinforcing Singapore's cultural identity. Central to this was cleanliness.

Clean: A Basic Reptilian Hot Button

Cleanliness has consequences, all of them positive. Cleanliness promotes civic and cultural pride; a clean populace stands taller, sees more clearly, works harder, raises stronger children. A 21-year-old Singaporean man told me this when I was holding a discovery session there in 2008:

> No matter where you go, you will find bins for people to throw their rubbish. Singaporeans are also considerate—they know how to dispose of their rubbish in a correct way. Furthermore, you can see cleaners doing their part in keeping the country clean by performing their duty every day without fail. All these help to keep Singapore clean and be termed as the cleanest and greenest country.

The qualities that the young man celebrated are also the qualities first noticed by those arriving in Singapore. Visitors, encountering a clean city, form immediate impressions that make them likelier to do business there, invest there and recommend the city to colleagues. Cleanliness, which serves as a self-reinforcing mirror of accomplishment for Singaporeans, also serves as a window on an appealing picture for outsiders. Reptilian principles have consequences beyond their immediate purposes.

More than just pride, cleanliness promotes hygiene, resulting in a populace that is healthier and better able to work harder, and in general be better prepared to create a prosperous future for themselves and their children. These were the goals and consequences, both overt and implied, that Singapore pursued as it began to clean itself up.

Understanding that only by cleaning the nation—and, crucially, keeping it clean—could Singapore move forward, Lee and his new government began a process of both education and regulation. Widely deploying slogans such as "Keep Singapore Litter-Free," and beginning a campaign to identify the new republic as a "clean and green city," Lee Kuan Yew sought to establish clean as a prime virtue and, more important, a prime responsibility for all Singaporeans. In doing so, he was making a reptilian point and delivering a reptilian message that mothers know instinctively: when your children are clean and practice clean behavior, every other virtue is given a far better chance at becoming established. Children wearing sloppy and dirty clothes often exhibit sloppy and dirty behavior.

Additionally, and equally important, Lee Kuan Yew understood that if Singapore presented a clean "face" to the world, the world would be far more favorably disposed to see its potential, attracting investors and employers, both of which were necessary in a nation possessing so little in the way of local resources. You can see the essence—and the impact—of the clean hot button in your own life and travels. Consider, for example, how you feel upon entering a dirty hotel room. Not only are you likely to check out of the hotel immediately; it's likely that you will take your business away from the entire hotel chain. This perception on a national level was one of Lee Kuan Yew's key insights, an example of brilliant reptilian leadership put into practice.

However, mothers also know instinctively what too many leaders fail to learn: success at putting reptilian priorities into practice is achieved only by reinforcement and incentives; education and slogans alone are not enough to transform a nation, or an individual.

Along with the educational campaign, and alongside the slogans, Lee's government instituted a strict system of fines and punishments aimed at eradicating bad behavior such as spitting or littering. The government introduced new laws widening the definitions of offenses, which by 1966 would include vandalism and graffiti. The fines applied to everyone, including visitors, and no infraction was too small to earn a fine. (Indeed, some joke to this day that Singapore is the world's "finest" city.) Clean, to Lee Kuan Yew's government, was an absolute: in Singapore there is no such thing as minor littering or vandalism.

Only by that level of insistence, reinforced by fines and punishments, could Singapore hope to transform its sordid streets into appealing avenues, boulevards of hope that bespoke gathering—and attentive—national and cultural pride. Singapore's clean initiative and its Pavlovian system of fines and punishments were not without controversy and objection, just as children sometimes object strenuously to being told to bathe. Some of that controversy continued long after the introduction of the cleanliness regulations.

In Singapore the basic form of punishment is caning, in which those convicted of an offense are struck with a rattan cane. The punishment is always administered in private, but it is *always* administered.

In 1994, an American teenager living in Singapore, Michael Fay, was convicted of vandalizing automobiles and given a fine and a punishment consisting of six strokes with a cane. The punishment was in line with that received by Singaporean males convicted of similar affronts (only males under 50 are subject to caning in Singapore). The case attracted large and sensational international press attention, leading Bill Clinton to attempt to bring the weight of the U.S. presidency to bear upon Singapore to win leniency for the 18-year-old Fay.

However, by 1994, less than 30 years—barely a single generation—after Singaporean independence, the nation had developed a large measure of justifiable national pride and openly resented and objected to attempts at outside interference with its national rules. The rules of Singapore, its people said through the press, extend to everyone who visits there. In the end, Michael Fay received four, not six strokes of the cane. Americans continue to visit Singapore—they spend the most money of any group of tourists—but they go there now a little wiser about the local regulations.

I am certainly not advocating caning as a way to correct the behavior problems of American teenagers, of course. But caning and fines work for Singapore (remember that you must consider all cultural practices within the context of a particular culture). Young Singaporeans understand the rules of their nation, know that the rules will be enforced, and feel that the rules *should* be enforced. A young male Singaporean pointed out to me that the enforcement of the laws is a reflection of the country's commitment to safety for its citizens:

> Singapore is a secure country. Crime rates are generally lower as compared to other countries. We have to give credit to our law enforcement for implementing strict laws and severe punishment to those who commit a crime. As I have just completed my National Service, I feel that I have done a part in protecting the country and the people. It makes me feel proud to be able to play a part in the security of the country.

We heard story after story during our discovery sessions from others who claimed to love Singapore because it is clean. Even those who have visited other great cities such as Paris or San Francisco would not wish to live anywhere but Singapore. Indeed, one 21-year-old woman told me that for her, as for most Singaporeans, her city and its character remained with her even when she was living abroad in Hong Kong:

> I feel more like a Singaporean there than I feel when I'm in Singapore itself. I realized and was reminded of the greatness of my own country. People asked where I am from. I said, "Singapore," and they go, "Oh! Wow, nice city!" I feel proud of my country, I feel proud of Singapore and being a Singaporean.

Such national pride cannot, of course, be beaten into citizens with a cane, nor did Lee Kuan Yew think that it would be. Rather, the Pavlovian incentives were and are aimed at establishing the discipline required to keep Singapore clean. Doing that teaches the people the value of discipline, of respect for rules and order, of personal as well as national pride.

Litter, graffiti and public filth are no longer problems in the nation. Singapore is not only one of the world's most prosperous cities; it is one of the cleanest. A reptilian leader would know, of course, that you are unlikely to have the one without applying yourself constantly to the other.

From Clean Comes All Else

Singapore's dramatic and rapid rise to its current global stature required more than cleanliness, of course. But the brilliance of Lee Kuan Yew's leadership lay in understanding the absolute centrality of clean to everything else he and his fellow Singaporeans wished to accomplish. Even as the nation set about scrubbing itself, collecting litter from the streets and refurbishing run-down and decrepit buildings, the idea of cleaning the nation extended to realms beyond the physical.

Widespread and endemic government corruption had been one of the large problems identified by the Federation of Malaysia when it expelled Singapore from its membership. Just as he guided the government to address littered streets, Lee Kuan Yew guided profound governmental and administrative reforms. Again, his abilities as a reptilian thinker served Lee and his nation well. There was corruption not simply because of lax policies and structure, but also because Singapore's civil service workforce was underpaid. When Lee's government swept out corrupt officials, it also instituted a more equitable salary structure for public employees, placing them on levels equal to their peers in business. Doing so raised both the government workers' incomes and their pride in their profession.

As with most Asian nations in the twentieth century, population was another problem that threatened Singapore's well-being and ability to generate prosperity and attract business. Once more, Lee Kuan Yew's leadership approached a fundamental problem with a combination of an educational campaign and Pavlovian incentives. "Stop at Two" became a national initiative, encouraging smaller families while making clear that fewer children could be better cared for and have more opportunities in adulthood. The government reinforced the campaign with tax and other incentives for smaller families. Those with two children, for instance, received extra educational attention, and their parents had access to better housing. The campaign proved effective, halting Singapore's population explosion before it became disastrous.

Of course, as we have discussed elsewhere, true leadership requires always being cognizant of the times. By the 1980s, Singapore was experiencing quite a different sort of population crisis. The nation's increasingly well-educated young female population was not marrying and becoming parents in numbers large enough to support Singapore's increasing success. Lee Kuan Yew's solution was to extol, publicly, the virtues of marrying educated women, and to offer a new set of incentives for "graduate mothers," including tax, housing, and educational benefits for mothers bearing three or more children. The "Stop at Two" campaign came to a complete halt in the 1990s as Lee's successor faced an ongoing population decline, a situation that, while serious, served as another differentiator for Singapore when compared to many other Asian nations.

Kiasu

By the 1970s, unemployment in Singapore had largely been eradicated; adequate, clean housing was being built; and the economy was beginning to grow and, shortly, to boom.

All because Lee Kuan Yew insisted that his nation become clean?

Of course—and of course not.

To assume that everything good will happen to a culture because it is clean is to miss the point. Children don't make straight A's simply because they are clean—they are better able to study and learn, to have sharper minds, to develop their curiosity and imagination, better prepared to discipline themselves in all areas of life because they are disciplined in this most fundamental aspect of life. A Singaporean taxi driver reminded me of this during a conversation. We'd been talking for a while about the quality of life in Singapore when he asked me a question

"How's my English?" he said.

"Great!" I said, honestly. "Why do you ask?"

"Singaporeans all have to learn how to speak good English, not 'Singlish,' so I go at night to take classes to improve my English. When I am working, I go in front of the big hotels to pick up foreigners, so I can practice my English. How am I doing so far?"

Like his country, the taxi driver was doing fantastically! Lee Kuan Yew's leadership, like that of Pericles (see Chapter 9), was aimed at showing Singaporeans they could excel in all areas of modern life, but that to do so required constant and unremitting discipline and effort. No scrap of trash would be overlooked, no blemish left uncleaned. Hard work during the day would be matched by serious study at night. From the moment the government implemented the first initiative to pick up the trash, Singaporeans were heading down a path to greatness. They have even adopted a Chinese word to describe how they will achieve and maintain greatness.

The word is an amalgam. *kia* means "afraid," while *su* means to "lose." *Kiasu* means Singaporeans are afraid to lose. At least it did when they first embraced the term. Now, though, the concept has evolved in the culture. Today *kiasu* means something related to its origins, but also far larger than them. Today, *kiasu* means "afraid of not being the best."

In today's Singapore, only the best is acceptable—the best economy and climate for business, the best-educated children, the best airlines and hotel, the best in every category Singapore chooses to compete in. Singapore is *kiasu,* and *kiasu* is Singapore.

A Global City-state with Its Own Culture

The results of Lee Kuan Yew's reptilian leadership principles have been nothing short of extraordinary. From the indignity of being jettisoned by Malaysia, Singapore has become, along with South Korea, Hong Kong and Taiwan, one of Asia's Four Tigers, the centerpieces and the engines of the region's economic surge. That Singapore has achieved such stature so quickly from such a challenging beginning is a tribute to the determination, discipline and concentration its leaders brought to its people.

Of particular interest is the fact that Singapore has created its own unique culture largely by welcoming other cultures. Singapore demands—and inspires—the best of immigrants from all over the world. Multiculturalism may be a difficult and dangerous issue in Europe and even in the melting pot of the United States. It is not an issue in Singapore. Wherever one comes from, one becomes part of Singapore—and devoted to it. I once asked Jacky, my Indian tailor, where he was from. "Singapore," he said without hesitation. "I am a pure Singaporean."

This pure Singaporean also has Ganesha, the elephant-headed Hindu god of success and prosperity, on his desk. Similar stories and examples, I am sure, could be found for every immigrant to Singapore. They know where their journey began, and respect it, but they know now that they are from Singapore, and of it. This transcends assimilation. It involves becoming a part of the national "family," as well as living under its flag, and can only be achieved by successful, clean, safe and appealing nations and organizations.

Respected and venerated, Lee Kuan Yew continues to offer the nation his counsel and wisdom. Part of that wisdom includes knowing when it is time to depart. For Lee, that time arrived early in 2011, when opposition party success in the elections led him to announce that he would step down from his role in Singapore's cabinet to provide the new administration the opportunity to put its own selections in place. Like George Washington, Lee knew that the time had come for others to continue the work he had begun, and to do so in their own way.

He also has long understood that one of the vital responsibilities of the modern leader is to prepare the way for other leaders. "My job really was to find my successors," he said in 2005. "I found them, they are there; their job is to find their successors. So there must be this continuous renewal of talented, dedicated, honest, able people who will do things not for themselves but for their people and for their country. If they can do that, they will carry on for another generation and so it goes on. The moment that breaks, it's gone."

Such an insight, and such an awareness of the stakes—if the chain of leadership breaks, all is ended—is another lesson in leadership from this great leader who understood that not only does everything begin with clean, but also that clean is the true beginning for anything one decides to seek.

WHAT "CLEAN" MEANS FOR THE NEW PILOTS

As this chapter illustrates, the leaders of many countries have much to learn from the best cultural practices of Singapore, from the inspiring message of assimilation to the rallying cry of *kiasu*. However, the reptilian practice that Singapore best demonstrates is "clean." Those leading the way into the emerging global culture need to make "clean" an essential part of their approach to connecting with the world.

One manifestation of this must be cleanliness of purpose. In a world filled with countless regional agendas, one cannot truly get one's message across to a meaningful number of people unless one has a clear and consistent purpose. This means that your message must be uncluttered and your communications as neat and as simple as possible. A grimy or inconsistent statement of purpose will not play effectively across the many channels it needs to cross to travel the globe. Local cultures can receive a clean statement and adapt it as necessary. A messy statement stands a much greater chance of misinterpretation and bastardization at the local level.

Another manifestation is cleanliness of presentation. Whether you are promoting an American soft drink throughout Eastern Europe or a new health initiative to developing nations, if the presentation is a mess, local cultures are less likely to embrace what you are promoting, regardless of its underlying quality. Just as the Singaporeans needed to offer clean streets to potential investors, the New Pilots coming from the Global Tribe need to present everything they seek to promote as cleanly as they can.

Yet another manifestation of cleanliness is the discipline underlying it. Cleanliness structures your mind, prepares you to be demanding, to respect the rules, to be proud of your accomplishments, to reject the sloppiness and the "casual" approach to life that is so prevalent in global pop culture. To be clean is to ready yourself for large things. Perhaps the most valuable by-product of Lee Kuan Yew's cleanliness campaign is enhanced levels of internal fortitude throughout Singapore. The Global Tribe has already adopted this as they lead the way into the global culture. Discipline leads to excellence—to *kiasu*—and excellence is a prerequisite for leading the world to a new future.

The lesson from Singapore is very powerful. You don't need oil to get rich. You need to be clean. Sounds surprising? To be clean you need discipline; discipline means education; education means evaluation, competition, and being the best. Step by step, with nothing at the beginning, Singapore became a model of success, and created from scratch a new culture. The reason I insist on describing Singapore's succession of events in such detail is because it is the global model for success: stop blaming other nations for your difficulties; just start at the reptilian level and build around it. We have seen in New York City how the broken window policy has reduced crime. Sloppiness does not pay.

Now we have seen how Singapore has become one of the busiest hubs of the world, with a fantastic airport and one of the greatest airlines. But we must return to what we learned in Chapter 1: that the Global Tribe wants no airport.

One of the key elements of the Global Tribe is movement. Through their travels, they discover, select and reinforce all of the "best practices" of the world, which is how they've elevated Singapore to such elite status in just a few decades. Let's see what else they find.

THREE

HOW THEY TRAVEL

We have seen that the Global Tribe lives in city-states or hubs like Singapore, and that they redefine luxury all of the time. If they are traveling all the time, this means they are in permanent orbit. So the question to ask them is not "Where are you?" but "Where are you going?" Not "What is your position?" but "What is your movement?"

Boeing, the aircraft manufacturer, commissioned me to discover the code for frequent travelers as well as the code for luxury travel. Recently Centurion (better known as the American Express "black card") asked me to do the same thing. What are the unaddressed expectations of the Global Tribe? How do they see luxury travel and the future of traveling? What unaddressed, unconscious, unspoken needs of theirs should we address? What is this tribe's code for travel?

David Livingstone was not merely traveling, nor was Ferdinand Magellan. They both had a higher purpose, a destiny to fulfill. Of course, other people, like tourists, travel as well. Some travel for business, to go to meetings, while others visit their family or take vacations. Thanksgiving, New Year's Eve and Christmas are all busy times for travel. But the Global Tribe doesn't follow this travel schedule. They are not sedentary people who once in a while have to go somewhere at a crucial time; the Global Tribe is continuously on the move.

To the Platinum Gypsies, this constant movement is not considered traveling. It has become second nature, like breathing. They are always on the go. We don't describe a satellite as traveling from point A to point B; a satellite travels in perpetual orbit.

For the average sedentary person, traveling is a special moment. But they always come back home. In contrast, the Global Tribe is always on the move, and because they have so many homes, for them the expression "to go back home" has a different meaning. It means "refueling," reconnecting with other members of the tribe. Enjoying a special moment, following the calendar. But this is just a stop before they're on to the next hub.

If they always keep moving, then their code is *satellite*.

THE SATELLITE TRIBE

From now on we will refer to the Global Tribe as the Satellite Tribe.

Fish do not occasionally swim. Likewise, members of the Satellite Tribe do not occasionally travel. They are migrating in flocks and following the *Agenda*. They do not travel solely for work or to visit family; rather, they follow the migration patterns of the tribe.

> "We are going to Davos and then to St. Moritz for the snow polo. Why? Because all of our friends are there."—a 65-year-old female socialite from New York

> "Did you go to the Red Cross Ball in Monaco this year? It is a must, you have to go next year."—a 70-year-old male Palm Beach resident

So let's explore *how* these people move from one place to the other. Remember, not everybody might have the financial means to do what they are doing, but we want to decode the standards that they are establishing. Not everybody was able to own a car in 1900. Today, in America, your driver's license is your identity, and cars are ubiquitous. So let's look at the way the Satellite Tribe travels to get a sense of the future of travel.

We already have seen that they don't want to go through the airport process. Understanding this, several airlines and American Express Centurion now offer a service that takes you through the airport at high speed. It's not quite the same as flying on a private jet, but it's certainly an improvement.

TRAVEL LIGHT: NO LUGGAGE

The evolution of the Satellite Tribe is movement. They do not fear change but rather they seek it out and embrace it. A duchess once inherited a one-thousand-year-old castle. When asked how she felt about acquiring this new home she responded, "It's not mine, I'm just a temporary caretaker." Just like the duchess, the Satellite Tribe is all about being transitional, not permanent. They are the first to understand that everything is temporary and that permanence is an illusion. Nothing lasts forever, and holding on to material goods is counterproductive to the Satellite Tribe lifestyle.

Their code for movement is *no luggage*. The Satellite Tribe has an assortment of carry-on luggage options, but they rarely pack large suitcases. To the saying "You are never too thin, and you are never too rich" I would add "You are never too light." They travel light, pack the essentials and leave behind the bulk. When life decides that our time is up, you won't find a luggage rack on the hearse. Material things in the end don't matter; it's our life experiences and memories that are buried with us when we die. This is because the Satellite Tribe is more concerned about quality than quantity.

While some may prefer to spend $100 on a fistful of cheap plastic jewelry, the Satellite Tribe would rather spend that $100 on a nice pair of classic earrings that can be worn for any occasion. The Satellite Tribe buys, packs and stores only the bare essentials and classic items. A garage filled with boxes of junk and broken home appliances that never got around to getting fixed is not on-code for the Satellite Tribe.

If you peek into the suitcase of an experienced traveler, you'll probably find only the essentials and versatile clothing. In a woman's suitcase, you'll find the little black dress that can be appropriate for any event, comfortable heels, a great pair of earrings, and a simple but elegant purse. For men, you'll find loafers, a versatile sports jacket, and two ties that go with anything. And, of course, it would be foolish to pack anything that requires heavy-duty ironing like fine linen. If traveling by plane, they'll do their best to leave the elaborate buckle at home, wear shoes easy to slip on and off, and bring a cozy sweater for the plane's cold temperature. It's all about being practical.

> *"All that we are is the result of what we have thought. The mind is every-thing. What we think we become."*
>
> —Buddha

When I want to understand the needs of a global traveler, the first place I look to is the hotel and airport shop. There I find the bare essentials: Advil, Pepto-Bismol, toothpaste, condoms, hand sanitizer, water and snacks. I can also find our entertainment needs like magazines, books, headphones and cell phone chargers. With a few variations, you will find these basics in any airport or hotel around the world. These shops hold the Satellite Tribe's universal survival kit. Anything more is just bulk.

Similarly, the Satellite Tribe makes sure to already have everything they need at their different destinations. In each home they already have new toothbrushes, floss and toothpaste. Some even buy three pairs of their favorite shoes to keep one in each home. When you've left all your ski equipment in Vail, you can easily have a service transport it to Whistler for you, or simply rent new equipment. It may be more expensive, but in the end it's the convenience of feeling light and baggage-free that makes it worth it.

They are not buying things. You will never see a member of the tribe bringing a sombrero from Mexico. These are for tourists. The Satellite Tribe does not buy souvenirs. A tablet and a smartphone can capture everything they might want to share with their network. They don't need to carry much more. They don't need anything, because they have everything waiting for them everywhere they go. Five-star hotels should learn these expectations and make arrangements accordingly. If they don't have the means to stay in five-star hotels, they stay with friends, as their network of tribe members is large and diverse.

No luggage means more freedom to move. If you've tied down your roots so tightly and have many bills to pay off, you probably have little opportunity to travel or move around if a better opportunity shows up. Being weighed down is what the Satellite Tribe avoids like the plague.

They take almost nothing with them. They may FedEx a package ahead of their travel plans, perhaps containing a tuxedo or five cocktail dresses, but when they travel, they travel very light. Some of them, of course, travel in private jets, where they can take all the luggage that they want. But the reality is that they can find anything they want wherever they go. They can shop in the Hamptons, Gstaad or Monaco. Why bother packing? Members of the tribe who are not rich also travel light—jeans and two T-shirts can last a long time, and as they visit friends, they can always borrow a sweater if the weather gets cold.

Of course if your network is wealthy, you get special treatment, your friends accommodating you as if you were in a five-star hotel: bathrobe, slippers, toothbrush, shaving cream—even your favorite perfume if they know you well. This is style. The agenda is actually the description of the journey, the orbit that the Satellite Tribe is going to follow, going from one refurbishing station to another. The mental structure that we discovered we call the "island mentality."

MULTIPLE HOMES, PASSPORTS AND LANGUAGES

One hubber who just bought a $15 million two-bedroom apartment in Singapore was asked by the real estate agent if she was going to move in soon. Her answer was stunning: "Look, lady, I have six homes. I move all of the time!"

To the global nomads, a $50 million penthouse in Manhattan is like a tent in the desert. It might be a good investment, but it is a temporary place to stay when you are in transit. Hubbers are not sedentary; they are free to move, not only physically, but also psychologically. As nomads, they are very flexible, with the mind-set that they are citizens of several city-states. The term *world citizen* is regaining its true etymological meaning in that these individuals connect their identities with cities (citizen) as opposed to, say, nations, cultures or states. They usually have more than one passport and speak several languages, including, of course, English.

COMMUTERS

Hubbers are global commuters; they commute all of the time. Where will they establish their business headquarters? Perhaps in Hong Kong or

Singapore. Where do they want their children to go to school? Perhaps in Switzerland. Where do they want to spend a romantic weekend? Perhaps at the Gritti Palace in Venice. Anything from a long menu of locations. But what is most interesting about their migrations is that they follow the flock, all of them going to the same places at the same times, following along with the rest of the Satellite Tribe. They decide what is in and what is out. Today, Berlin is more creative than Paris, and Gstaad is better than St. Moritz, which has been invaded by too many Russians!

NO TOURISM

The Court does not take pictures. Most of the time they do not even want their picture to be taken. They don't visit museums or ruins. Sometimes invited to private exhibitions, they may meet with other tribe members, but they never wait in line with strangers. If you have to wait in line with strangers, it means that you are not there yet—that you are "aspirational" and still on your way to the satellite status. Travelers not in the tribe may tell you they went to the Amalfi Coast, visited Capri, went to Naples, then to Florence. Unlike such tourists, Satellite Tribe members instead visit friends while following their tribe's agenda with a completely different perception of traveling. Our friend Jeffrey does not "visit" Mexico. He goes back to a place that he knows, one where he has many friends with whom he will stay. He knows other members of his tribe will be there.

The Satellite Tribe is a step in the evolution of mankind.

Obviously, such people spend a lot of time in the air. When someone asks me where I live, my usual answer is, "in airplanes." I recently spent more than 200 days in one year traveling. Icarus died trying to fly, but today we can do it continuously. For thousands of years flying was an impossible dream, but today, thanks to modern technology and companies like Boeing and Airbus, flying can be an everyday fact of life.

A few years ago, Boeing asked me to discover the Global Code for flying. They wanted to understand how frequent flyers like me felt about flying. Going around the world to understand how a frequent flyer felt, we came up with a lot of horror stories and frustration. What unconscious, unexpressed and unaddressed needs related to flying could we determine?

FLYING

The ideal, of course, is the private jet. But if you cannot go overseas with a private jet and must fly commercial, you never—absolutely never—want to have a layover. You know that layovers mean more airport time, delays, cancellations, rebookings and so on. So nonstop—which is better than direct; nowadays what airlines call "direct" sometimes includes a stop—is a must. When you fly commercial you want to be in the first row, preferably an aisle. Why? So nobody reclines his seat onto your lunch tray while you are eating, and so you will get the fish dish when people in row five will be left with the pasta. On long flights a flat bed is a must—and not "almost flat," which is so uncomfortable you cannot sleep. In fact, you might as well ask your travel agent to cancel any flight you have with Air France. Quality airlines provide their guests with pajamas, a large bathroom for changing clothes, and in some cases, such as Emirate Airlines, your own suite.

"The first time I flew Turkish Airlines from Istanbul to New York, I had my own closet to hang clothes, and the chef, dressed in all white (including a white hat), came to ask me how I wanted my steak to be prepared. That was great! But the last time I flew with them, a few months later, they no longer had a first class, and business class was a zoo. That was terrible. They lost me. I will never fly Turkish Airlines again."—a 45-year-old businessman from New York

"Why are airlines so dumb? They want you to stand in line, and then they make you wait and wait. I went to get a new Social Security card in New York the other day and they gave me a ticket with a number so that I could see when my number was being called. Given that I had about a half-hour to wait, I went shopping and came back five minutes before my call. This was great! Why can't airlines do the same? They just want to treat you like cattle!"—a 44-year-old female executive from Princeton, New Jersey

"Their boarding process is ridiculous. It does not make any sense. Why send people in wheelchairs first? They are sitting in the front row, are very slow to move, and are going to block the aisle. The same goes for people with children. The simplest and most logical way to accelerate boarding should be to board by row numbers and starting by the back of the plane. Business travelers just want to make sure that they will have room for their carry-on in the overhead compartments. So it should be forbidden for back of the plane passengers to use the business class overhead bins. Simple! Wheelchair passengers can come last. They are sitting in a chair already anyway, they can wait."—a 25-year-old male frequent flyer from Orlando, Florida

"Business only is a must. I need to work, and I can't when kids are crying for hours and bumping and hitting with their feet the back of my seat. Read *I Hate Other People's Kids*."—a 29-year-old male CEO of a start-up company, San Diego, California

It is clear that the Satellite Tribe wants to be separated from the masses; they require exclusivity. This is the contradiction that all airlines face today. Their real profit margins come from business class travelers and the Satellite Tribe, yet in order to survive they have to fill up the planes with as many people as possible, most of the time at very cheap prices. Like oil and water, the two do not mix very well.

While discovering the code for frequent flyers for Boeing, we discovered a very disturbing trend. The code for frequent flyers is *dead*. Here are some excerpts from the imprinting sessions.

"The only way to survive the horrific treatment of the so called 'security process' and the endless lines you have to wait through is to disconnect completely. To become a zombie, and to not pay attention to anything."—a 55-year-old male from Dallas, Texas

"I stop fighting and arguing. It is not worthwhile. So I try to be, in my mind, like somewhere else. It's like being dead in order not to feel anything."—a 42-year-old male from New York

For the airline, it's even more dramatic:

"We need to *process* the passengers as fast as possible, the less luggage the better; they should not be allowed to have carry-ons."—a 55-year-old female flight attendant

The ideal passenger is mute, docile and never asks for anything—the code is *suitcase*. You should be like a suitcase: never speak, never complain, never ask questions, and be able to stay several hours stuck on the tarmac without needing the bathroom. Recently the suitcase code was confirmed rather dramatically: airlines regularly lose luggage, but now they also seem to lose passengers—not long ago an airline was supposed to take a passenger in a wheelchair to a corresponding flight and managed to lose him.

HOTELS

For the Satellite Tribe, which is always on the move, the hotel experience should be a perfectly orchestrated one. No check-in line, no questions asked and everything ready the way you like it. The same coffee machine, so you don't have to spend an hour figuring out how to turn it on; the same shower mechanism so you don't ruin your hair when you just want to freshen up. Turning the light on should not be a test of your patience; you should not have to wait ten minutes for the hot water to arrive. Everything you need should *always* be at the same place. The Satellite Tribe doesn't like surprises; they love simple routines, consistency and rituals. When a hotel can provide that, it receives their undying loyalty.

When I worked with Horst Schulze, former president of the Ritz-Carlton Hotels, we used current technology to give the best service to our customers. *Anticipation* is the code for the best service; you should never have to ask for something. If a customer asked once for five pillows, this information should be sent to all the Ritz-Carltons in the world. When he arrives for the first time at the Ritz in Santiago de Chile, he should hear, "Welcome back, Mr. Brown. Your five pillows are already in your room."

This being said, we know that those who belong to the Court never go to hotels; rather, they visit friends. The aspiring Courtesans, the new middle class, go to hotels. But their aspirations are programmed by the Court. The code is *being invited*.

BEING INVITED

Your friends are happy to see you; they take care of you. Their butler knows how you drink your coffee and what you like to have for breakfast.

At the St. Regis in New York, you have a butler who comes with the room. He or she is supposed to be your personal butler. But the experience is different. You do not have your own personal butler but rather several butlers in a row as they change according to their shift. So you never know who is going to come next when you call. When a new one arrives, you have to repeat the instructions—quite different from what you get when staying with a friend.

When you pay $1,000 a night at the Carlyle in New York, or $1,200 at the Little Neil in Aspen, you should receive the Invited Guest treatment. There is no such thing as "bad" service, just dumb service that misunderstands customer expectations. There are no "bad" employees, just bad training and bad management. When Horst Schulze used to say, "Ladies and gentlemen serving ladies and gentlemen" he was not just referring to providing quality service; rather, he meant it as a larger philosophy. A butler is a gentleman's gentleman, so he can anticipate, and you never have to ask.

This is the model created by the Satellite Tribe. It indicates the direction that all the travel industry should take, along with the principles it should follow. Hotel chains are challenged today by bed-and-breakfasts, where owners treat you like family, and Airbnb, where your experience is closer to the Invited Guest standard. People prefer these rather than the depressing "Next in Line" treatment most hotels provide.

When you board a plane and the underpaid and overworked flight attendants are in the middle of a discussion and don't even look at you, you don't feel welcome. It is time they realize they are not merely carrying "suitcase" passengers from one gate to another, but that they are in the hospitality business. The broken window theory should also be applied to the travel industry. New York airports are like war zones where you want to go through as fast as possible and can only hope that you survive. When they process you like cattle, you feel subhuman.

The lesson from the Satellite Tribe is clear. The new middle class knows what good service really is; the global network of information has raised their awareness and changed their expectations. They might not be able to afford a private jet, or be able to stay with friends, but they dream about the "One Step" experience. Consequently, all travel professionals should concentrate their efforts on reducing the number of steps rather than making things more complicated. *Simplify* should be their motto.

The consequences are very clear. Reduce completely the airport experience. Make it simple and fast. Transform your hotels not to feel like home but like the guests are invited into somebody else's home—the home of another member of their tribe. It's why boutique hotels are so appealing to the Satellite Tribe. You don't want to wait in line in a hotel lobby that looks like a train station or have coffee in a place that looks like a university cafeteria. You want to be invited into a private home. Many boutique hotels in London give you this feeling. Rooms should not have numbers, but names. The Andy Warhol Room, the Rossini Room. You should never wait in line—they should know your name and anticipate your needs.

In the following section, I'd like to explore how members of the Satellite Tribe set the standards for beauty, luxury and pleasure.

PART TWO

HOW THEY SET THE STANDARDS

If the Satellite Tribe benchmarks everything and sets the standards, we can expect them to look at the best of the best everywhere.

They have a bird's eye view and are not stuck in the mundane aspects of daily life. But the question remains: Did they create a common universal standard of what is best?

What is perceived as "universal" might vary according to history, culture or geography. If we have a chance to discover a universal Global Code, from where will it come? Is the Satellite Tribe creating it, or just discovering it because of their bird's eye view?

When several of our clients asked us to discover the Global Code for beauty, we went around the world applying our methodology desperately looking for common elements or structures beyond cultural differences.

Our mission was not to discover an abstract concept of beauty, but what it really means to women in their everyday lives. We already know that men don't want to be rejected, but we also know that the fundamental universal logic of emotion for women is to be chosen.

For a woman to feel beautiful, she must be chosen. It became clear that the Global Code for beauty had to be understood though the reptilian brain, whose main purpose is survival and reproduction.

Let's try to understand what helps women be successfully chosen.

FOUR

THE GLOBAL CODE FOR BEAUTY

What we are going to present here is not guessing. It is not an opinion but the result of scientific research into beauty conducted worldwide during several decades and for several of the Fortune 100 companies. Of course you might be attracted by somebody's sense of humor, poetic writing, or talent with the cello. As a woman, you might enjoy a sweet, caring gentleman; as a man you might like a "mother" figure who is a great cook. Of course what is considered beautiful might vary from one culture to another, between rich and poor, or even between generations. But here we are looking not for the differences but for the common instinctive impulse, the irresistible attraction that makes men want one woman more than another. What is the trigger, what is the code?

Readers of *The Culture Code* already know that women's beauty is man's salvation, but do we have a universal code, a Global Code, for beauty? And is it the same for men and women?

Going around the world to understand beauty for L'Oréal, Richemont, LG and others, I was puzzled by the strong differences between how beauty is perceived in different cultures—and not just women's beauty, but how all people perceive one another, and what they prioritize. If we believe that stereotypes have any value and that clichés are sometimes illuminating, we can appreciate some differences between the Japanese and the Brazilians.

In general, Japanese men, for example, like shy, naïve women, stylized like schoolgirls, whereas many American men are attracted to the Dolly Parton type, with her "special advantages." Brazilian men will tend to value the "*bunda*," and the French value legs and the way a woman walks (after all, they invented the catwalk!). Many Japanese men find the woman's neck very sexy, and the Chinese prefer a skirt with an opening on the side that reveals the legs.

At first it seemed impossible to find a common thread. But after many investigations, looking at patterns and repetition, I was able to discover common elements, always looking for the space in between.

As noted earlier, Claude Lévi-Strauss famously said that a mother is not a woman; a mother is the space between a woman and her child. To understand beauty, it is the *space in between* that we must understand—the space between men and women. So what did we discover by looking at structures, patterns and repetitions rather than the content?

Women want to be chosen. If all the men want you, you have a choice, but if no one invites you to the prom, you are in trouble. Men don't want to be rejected. Studying deodorant for young men for Colgate, we came across this reaction.

> "I had a terrible time with my son for years. He never wanted to take a shower or change clothes. Then one day, he was 14 and half, a girl told him that he stank, that she will never go out with him, that his smell was disgusting, like he had a dead rat in his pocket. He came home in tears, spent an hour under the shower and went to the supermarket to buy five deodorants. Since then, he has been so clean. She succeeded in two minutes where I had failed for years."—a 39–year-old man, Cincinnati, Ohio

The perception of beauty is also clearly influenced by cultures, taboos and mating rituals. We all know that devout Muslims have a very strong and rigid practice of prohibiting their women from advertising their beauty in public, whereas in France, women see no problem with topless beaches. Could there really be any common element between these cultures? Do they have a common code for feminine beauty?

As it turns out, yes, they do. Even if in most Muslim countries women are supposed to be strictly covered, they still love belly dancers, who shake their hips in a provocative way. When I looked at women's saris in India, I suddenly discovered a common element. Both Indian and Muslim women were showing their belly buttons.

I always believe that when I see something once, it is a reference point. If I see it twice, I can draw a line between the two points, thus making a connection. When I see things three times, however, it becomes a structure. The Tao Te Ching states:

The Tao gives birth to One.
One gives birth to Two.
Two gives birth to Three.
Three gives birth to all things.

THE BELLY BUTTON

I went looking for that third belly button, and that is when I realized that American young women were wearing very low-waist jeans and high-riding T-shirts to show their belly buttons. Of course, they were not necessarily doing it on purpose. Often they were just following a trend. But it was no accident that Arabic, Indian and American women were doing the same thing.

So I did some research to try and understand what was so magical about the belly button. When men think about sex, it's not necessarily the first part that comes to mind. So what does it mean?

The belly button has many symbolic dimensions. Most advertisements for losing weight focus on the waist and the belly button. The ideal is not to shrink your hips, but rather to shrink your waist. In France, advertising for yogurts shows women's waists, and of course, their belly buttons. It is the center of the body, the point of attachment to the umbilical cord, the last connection that we have to cut with our mother in order to be brought up into the world. It activates—worldwide—a strong emotion reminding us that this is where life begins.

Doing some research in India, we could not miss that the religious statues adorning the front doors of many temples featured belly buttons as well. We started doing research, and this is how we discovered, through the work of Dr. Devendra Singh, the Global Code for women's beauty. The code is *0.7*.

What is 0.7?

It is the ideal ratio between the waist and the hips of a woman.

Devendra Singh and his wife studied waist-to-hip ratios around the world and found a constant throughout many cultures and over time. Not only did they study how people reacted to different ratios, but they also analyzed ancient Greek statues, medieval paintings and Indian temples. In the Western world, we might speak of the "hourglass" figure, but what we really mean is this 0.7 code—the unconscious indicator that a woman is ready for reproduction.

Now we understand why corsets were invented 5,000 years ago by the Egyptians and could be found 2,000 years ago in Greece. The French invented the *robe a panier* and the *faux cul*. The same goal was always in mind: to reinforce the 0.7 ratio. Dita Von Teese has made a profession of her waistline, advertising her very small waist. She also gives references on tight-lacing.

Ethel Granger holds the record for the smallest waist, at 13 inches. Empress Elizabeth of Austria's waist measured 16 inches. Polaire, a French actress, had a waist that measured 16.5 inches. Cathie Jung, 15 inches; Dita Von Teese, 16.5 inches, and so on.

The magic number for waist circumference is 18. "Any number below eighteen becomes extremely potent—yes I would say magical," says a Mr. Pearl in Von Teese's book *Burlesque and the Art of the Teese*. In the same book, Von Teese looks to ancient Greece, citing a "Cretan statue of a snake goddess dating from 2,000 BC who dons something that cinches her waist and pushes up her breasts. For me, there is something subtly erotic about wearing a piece that has been with humanity for so long, that women have historically endured for beauty."

During our sessions for discovering the codes of health, beauty and seduction in Europe, Asia and the Middle East, we did find that a smaller waist attracted men more. But the reality is that it is the ratio that truly matters. Men will be very clear: large hips signify that a woman can give birth to a healthy child, large breasts signify that she will be able to feed the child. A small waist is a way to show, by form of contrast, the generous bust and the large hips.

In their study, the Singhs discovered that the ratio was significant worldwide, and they also found that women who had a 0.7 waist-to-hips ratio lived longer, suffered fewer cancers and had more children. The message to men is a reptilian one: with these women, there is a future for your genes, perhaps a long one.

From Greek goddesses to Victorian silhouettes, from corsets to *robe a panier,* 0.7 transcends time. Even today, take a look at perfume bottles: You'll notice that most of them have the 0.7 ratio. Hervé Leger, *J'adore* (Dior) and so on. Unconsciously, designers are following the code.

In the Western world, we pay a lot of attention to fat, and according to statistics, 50 percent of Americans are obese. So not getting fat became an obsession. However, the reality of the Global Code for beauty is the following: it is not fat that really matters; rather, it is fat distribution.

New Zealand anthropologist Barnaby Dixson said, "It is likely that perfect 0.7 ratio sends a biological signal to men that that woman is most fertile and most likely to produce a healthy offspring, no matter what size that woman is."

Anecdotally, we find some women concurring.

> "I had a small waist before becoming pregnant . . . after my pregnancy
> I asked my doctor for a tummy tuck. I wanted to recover my small
> waistline."—a 35-year-old shopkeeper, San Diego, California

Why do women want to have a smaller waistline? To attract men and to get pregnant. Pregnancy erases the waistline and produces the opposite: a big round belly. Once the baby is delivered, women want to go back to the size they were before bearing a child (i.e., a small waist, with a ratio of 0.7 when compared with hips). What for? To get pregnant again. It may seem crazy, but of course this is all unconscious—part of our species' reptilian program. Seeing as we have 7 billion and counting on this planet, I think it's fair to say that this program works.

And sometimes women stop sending that signal.

> "I have four children. I'm done. After my last child I didn't lose weight
> as I did before. I was a size two and I became a size twelve. I cannot fit
> into my jeans anymore, but that's OK. I have to take care of my children
> and feed them. I'm done."—a 52-year-old mother of four, Newark, New
> Jersey

The message is clear. No more waistlines means, "I checked out, I have done my biological reptilian work, I can concentrate on being a mother."

When we did some work in Russia, on fat and food for Barilla and LG, we discovered a clear transition. Young Russian women, even in freezing weather, would wear high heels, mini-skirts and tight clothes to show their waistlines. They advertise. Yet, when they are grandmothers (*babushkas*), they relax and enjoy a round shape. They are no longer into sex, but they are into food.

This ratio has a powerful unconscious effect on men. Working for Gallo, a Californian winery, I was asked to design a bottle for a white wine associated with seduction and romance. Regular bottles have no "waistline"; they are simply cylindrical. Our idea was to create a bottle that respected the 0.7 ratio. When we tested it, we saw men caressing the bottle and saying "Wow, nice bottle!" We sold 20 percent more of this wine because of that bottle.

Our discovery has a lot of consequences for product design around the world. A successful 911 Porsche has large hips; the Corvette has a large, elevated bottom; jeans with a low waistline that shows the belly button are very successful. The classic iconic Coke bottle has a very nice waist-to-hip ratio, and most of the water bottles carried by models have a waistline evoking the 0.7 ratio. The intellectual alibi behind this design might be that the bottle is easier to carry, but we know the Global Code and how it programs our unconscious.

A good friend of mine in her mid-fifties recently went to Bangladesh. She caught a terrible disease, was not able to eat for three weeks, and was vomiting continuously. A few weeks after she got back to New York, I invited her for lunch. She had more or less recovered by this point, and so I asked her how she felt. "I'm so happy," she said. "I can fit into my old jeans, I can wear a mini-skirt again. I feel like I am 18 years old again." What she was telling me is that she was back in the game.

Dixson confirmed these findings. She was looking for what makes women attractive to men. She asked a simple question: What do Kate Moss, Marilyn Monroe, Jessica Alba and Victoria's Secret model Alessandra Ambrosio have in common? The perfect figure, 0.7. Studies show that men in the UK, Cameroon, Germany and China agree with those polled in New Zealand.

A study conducted by the University of Regensburg in Germany confirmed the finding, reporting that the hourglass figure was considered more consistently attractive than even athletic types or long-legged, big-chested "Barbies."

So if the Global Code for women's beauty is 0.7, what is it for men? What makes men attractive to women?

Women are in charge of propagating the species. That statement might not be politically correct, but they are the door of life; we all come from a woman. To create life is a long, complicated biological process. Sex is just a small, short element. For women, it is much more complex. Much research has proven that, most of the time, because of their biology, women are more selective than men about when and with whom to have sex. They need a reason, a good reason—whether it's to please their husband because they feel guilty, or to have something to tell to their girlfriends, and so on. Men need only one reason: *opportunity.*

So what is it that attracts women? What is the Global Code for the beauty women see in men?

Dixson maintains that men were wasting their time pumping iron in a gym, as women invariably preferred a leaner, less muscle-bound physique. "On a biological level," Dixson writes, "women are more likely to pick a leaner, even slightly more effeminate man, as they equate those physical traits with being more caring and gentle and therefore a better prospect as a partner." However, depending on whether a woman was looking for a casual fling or to create a family, her priorities change. It's a tough world out there, and you want to make sure that the man you choose is going to protect you.

Working for Match.com in Japan, we discovered that cuteness was not a priority, nor was being lean. A good job on the other hand, certainly was.

"Does he have a job, a good salary? Is he stable?" a 19-year-old Tokyo woman asked. Rich and cute is the ideal, but very rich can compensate for not too cute.

Why?

Once again, it's our reptilian brains in action. Women are wired toward survival and reproduction, just like men. What about Einstein? How many women would choose him?

STRENGTH IN MEN IS BEAUTIFUL

Worldwide, women want a "strong" man. A man who can protect them and their children. Strength might lie in the form of muscles, money or intelligence. Cute is fine, but it's just the icing on the cake. If he is strong, rich and cute, he probably won't be available very long.

So if strength is the code, let's explore what it means. First comes physical appearance: tall and broad-shouldered. Big is also good. A skinny Buddha is very rare. American football players are not fat, they are big, which means strong. The best visual aid for this is to think of an upside-down triangle—the reason for shoulder padding in men's suits. Tall is also very important. This is why President François Hollande, who is smaller than German Chancellor Angela Merkel and definitely dwarfed by U.S. President Barack Obama, wears platform shoes.

In political races, the tallest man wins 80 percent of the time. Bill Clinton, Obama and current New York Mayor Bill de Blasio are all very tall.

Second comes the realistic expectation: power and money are sexy. There is an axis between cute on the left and rich on the right. The richer you are, the less cute you need to be. Billionaires need trophy wives. And if she manages not to have to sign a prenuptial agreement and is 30 years younger, the chances that she will become a billionaire herself are very high.

Studying the Satellite Tribe, we met several of these multiply-widowed billionaires. In their late seventies, sometimes early eighties, most are still very active and engaged in promoting charities. One very famous billionaire widow in Palm Beach is 95 and still going strong. She goes to charity balls almost every night, and each time with a different dress.

But the reptilian brain for reproduction is programmed to select the male who will give your children more chances to grow and thrive. The female reptilian brain knows that sex takes just a few minutes and often does not last very long after marriage.

The qualities that might make a man most attractive for sex might not have anything to do with feeding, protecting and raising a family. For women, looking at men, "beauty" means *strength*. But it also means commitment. It takes nine months for a woman to create a child, and many years to raise a human being. For the man, the act of procreation might take just a few minutes. So the woman wants to make sure that the man will stay around to fight the lions when she delivers the baby, and to bring food for the child for many years to come. Consequently, the Global Code for men's beauty is *committed strength.*

We found a common structure worldwide, a common "space in between" all around the world. As our mission is awareness, I believe that it is important to emphasize this common aspect of the expectations between men and women.

Women are like nature, and nature is unpredictable and beautiful. Paradisical sandy beaches can be transformed in moments by a tsunami, just as beautifully quiet mountains can unpredictably spew flows of volcanic lava. Female biology, especially, is a succession of transformations.

THE GLOBAL CODE FOR WOMEN: TRANSFORMATION

The key word to understand women's biology is *transformation.* Hormones, menstruation, pregnancy, breast-feeding and menopause are all transformations. But this code also applies to their psychology, personalities, search for identities, mood swings and multitasking abilities. When you have three kids, a job, a husband and your old mother to take care of, you definitely need all these talents. Men don't go through these same biological transformations. They are programmed for production, quantity and speed; they continuously want more, and they want it faster. When a couple cannot have children, the first thing we do is a sperm count. Men produce billions of sperm in their lifetimes (while women are born with a limited amount of eggs) but to be successful, the sperm has to move, and move fast. The right time for men is *now.* Remember, they only need an opportunity.

The notion of time is also different for women. The definition is *timing.* Women cannot get pregnant all of the time, they are not always biologically available. Men are—and since the advent of Viagra, even beyond the natural limits that age once imposed.

You know the saying, "Women marry a man thinking that they are going to change him, and he never changes." Well, men have the opposite scenario. They marry a woman thinking she will never change, and she always changes.

As one 65-year-old San Francisco man told me, "I have been married three times, and each time, one day, I wake up and cannot recognize the woman in my bed. Where is the sweet, loving lady that I met? Who is this woman? It looks like I will never learn."

Worldwide, we see the same structure. Of course, some cultures accept this reality better than others, creating rules, institutions and taboos to address these differences—polygamy, polyandry, short-term marriage (Islam), no marriage (Hollande has several children from several women and never has been married). The nineteenth-century Chinese Empress Dowager Cixi was known to have a harem of young men, and the famous Amazons, after becoming pregnant, were believed to have killed the men with whom they had copulated.

Of course in some countries, some women do not really need men's protection. These women are financially independent and do not need a strong, muscular man to fight the lions. But the reptilian brain is very slow to change. When Maria Shriver fell in love with Arnold Schwarzenegger, one has to imagine that even though she was a wealthy, intelligent, independent woman, her reptilian brain fell for the muscles. (I certainly never heard that he was writing poetry.) Billions of women in the world today are fighting hard just trying to survive and feed their children. They have a better chance when they meet *committed strength*.

Strength means success, and around the world success means access to the best of everything. The best is sometimes called *luxury*. Women's beauty is perceived in many cultures as a way to access luxury. But luxury is not always associated with money. For the Satellite Tribe, as we will see next, luxury is more an attitude and a lifestyle.

FIVE

THE GLOBAL CODE FOR LUXURY

"It is not expensive, it is expensive to make."
—Hermès

"Art is not luxury. Art is a necessity."
—Yukoz

THE TALENT OF AN ARTISAN

A few years ago, my wife and I wanted to buy a new sofa for our apartment in Paris. We went into different shops for days, but finally we found the perfect sofa at Hermès. We absolutely fell in love with the sofa. When I told the shopkeeper, "We'll take it!" he responded with, "Great! Your sofa will be ready in six months." Six months? "Sir, this sofa isn't for sale, it is a model. You must be involved in the process and choose all the finishing," he told us. We were taken to a separate room to look and feel all the different types of leathers they offered. We could choose the wood, the varnish, and all the details we wanted. What's more, we had a professional give us his expert opinion the entire time. The process was so personalized that we knew that this sofa was made just for us: there would be no other like it in anyone else's home.

These experiences, along with many others and the work I have done with clients, have helped me discover the Global Code for luxury. Luxury is about having something handmade, unique and made just for you.

Because I always go back to the reptilian for insight and my mantra is "the reptilian always wins," I wanted to know what the reptilian has to do with luxury. If we go back to the time when we were infants, our bond with our mother was the most pure and unique experience we could ever have. The milk our mothers produced in their breasts was made just for us. It creates a profound biological connection on a person-to-person basis. The global unconscious is forever preoccupied with re-creating this reptilian moment of when we felt very happy, safe and special. The comfort we felt in our mother's womb for nine months is universal. So luxury has everything to do with trying to re-create this moment where we felt special, unique and comfortable.

MADE JUST FOR ME

Think about the opposite of luxury. Plastic and virtual stuff. Something made in a factory in China is not luxury. It's the difference between plastic and brick and mortar. A house made of stone and wood, built 100 years ago by someone who put a lot of planning into the details, the layout and the architecture is very different from a planned neighborhood in Houston, Texas, with 30 homes each looking just like the other, all of them made with plaster and plywood.

When it comes to credit card services, American Express's brand is built upon the notion of by *hand*. Someone who spends nearly $10,000 to receive the American Express Centurion Card expects very high-quality service and special treatment: an array of luxury services like a dedicated concierge and travel agent, access to airport clubs and lounges, personal shoppers at select shops, among others. When I call up my credit card company, it's not a luxury to be attended by a recording that makes me jump through a series of hoops and asks a list full of questions before I may speak to a human being and express my concern. It's luxury to be able to call your credit card company and immediately be received by a person on the other end of the line—one who immediately attends just to me.

THE GLOBAL CODE FOR LUXURY

Machines don't have talent. But artists, designers, architects, writers and decorators do. So what is the Global Code for luxury? How could we capture it in one word? What is it that characterizes what all these people do?

Our discovery here was commissioned by the Richemont Group (Cartier, Van Cleef, Mont Blanc, etc.), L'Oréal Luxe and Boeing. It turned out that the Global Code for luxury is *hand*. More particularly, *made by hand,* as opposed to *made in France* or *made in England*. Once we discovered the code, it was obvious that it expressed humans' strong reaction against the machine, mass production and a culture of disposable goods. The unique value of luxury resides in the talent of an *artisan* working with patience, passion and commitment, to create a unique piece—something you'll want to transmit to the next generation. For the Satellite Tribe, "legacy" is a keyword; for the masses it is not. Luxury brand advertisers tap into this desire. For example, *"You never actually own a Patek Philippe, you merely look after it for the next generation."*

"Bespoke," *"sur mesure,"* "tailor-made" . . . these are the keywords associated with *made by hand.* Hermès is a perfect example of this Global Code; they do not like to say that they are in the business of luxury. In fact, they rarely mention the term *luxury,* because they do not believe it represents what they do. They believe that they are in the business of *art, talent* and *passion.* They are proud of their artisans, who create a unique and beautiful object that you are going to want to keep forever.

We return to our earlier example. A handmade Hermès sofa in Paris costs $50,000 and takes six months to produce, meaning that you have to wait. You select the leather, the color and the size according to where you plan to place it and what kind of atmosphere you want to create. It is tailor-made to you, to your apartment or house, to the room where it is going to go. You have to pay up front, and no negotiation is possible. Hermès organizes a tour to show you all of the ateliers and studios where their artisans are working, or rather *creating.*

MANIPULATION IS GOOD

The hand is reptilian, and we know that the reptilian always wins. To touch is a reptilian verb, powerful and dangerous. How many times do children hear "Don't touch that!" But in order to learn, they have to touch.

In the United States, we've discovered that doctors who have less physical contact with their patients are statistically more likely to incur lawsuits. Such is the remarkable power of the hand. Interestingly, *manipulation* (bearing the suffix *mano,* for hand) has become a bad word. Nobody wants to be manipulated by politicians, the media or lobbyists. Even if he is being fed by a machine, a baby cannot survive without physical contact with its mother; this is fundamentally reptilian. The hand is the reptilian imperative, a symbol of love and survival. The verb "to touch" has two different meanings, one reptilian and the other limbic. AT&T used to say, "Reach out and touch someone," by which they meant to touch someone emotionally rather than physically. But both are crucial to our thriving as a species.

Luxury is not independent of the reptilian. In fact, luxury is meant to enhance our reptilian needs. Concierge medicine is a luxury because it personalizes our reptilian need for good health. For an annual fee, a patient doesn't need to wait months for an appointment with a doctor; they are guaranteed attention on demand when needed. The 24/7 availability is a luxury—what the Satellite Tribe wants. Whereas "open Monday through Friday, 9:00 a.m. to 5:00 p.m." is not luxury.

> *"Luxury is in each detail."*
>
> —Hubert de Givenchy

I want to emphasize a crucial point: luxury is not about money, nor is it entirely reserved for one percent of the population. Rather, luxury is a mind-set; it's an art. The problem we have today is that we associate luxury with money. But money doesn't guarantee good taste, which is inherent in the concept of luxury.

When I went to Algeria to give a workshop in the 1970s, I decided to take a stroll through the desert a day before. I brought my Walkman, put on some Pink Floyd tunes and took a long walk through the desert to watch the sunset. I was awed by the colors and beauty of the desert. As nightfall arrived, I thought to myself, "I could go back to the hotel, or I could just stay here and take advantage of this perfect view of the stars." I opted for the latter. I made a bed in the sand, looked at the stars and listened to the music: this was luxury.

THE SELFISH BAG: WANTING WHAT YOU CAN'T HAVE

Two women walk the streets of New York City, strutting and walking with purpose. Their gaze is fixed straight ahead; they do not dare glimpse into the eyes of passersby because they wouldn't want to insinuate that any plainness has caught their attention. They both work in the fashion industry and run within the same circles of friends, but they've never met before. Both have a sort of timeless and elegant beauty, both of them dressed head to toe in next season's trends. Except there's one problem. They have the exact same bag: the new Prada bag that their mutual friend in Milan promised them was not even on the market yet.

"No one can know you have this," Marcello had said to each of them separately. "We are only giving five of our closest friends in the industry this bag before we launch it in a year."

"Perfect," each woman thought. "I'll probably never see another woman with this bag. I'll be the envy of all my friends!"

As they both turned the corner, they caught each other's eyes. They skimmed one another up and down, each thinking to herself, "Nice hair, pretty perfume, cute dress, Marc Jacobs spring/summer collection 2014, my best friend has those shoes, and her bag . . . *what!?*" Neither of them could avoid stopping dead in the middle of the sidewalk, their jaws agape. Maybe in an ideal world both would smile at each other, make a compliment, giggle and walk away. But what happened in fact was that the women scoffed at each other and stormed off furiously. Each one had her day ruined.

Why does this happen? Because when it comes to luxury goods, we simply cannot share.

Contrary to luxury, brands like Levi's and the Gap succeed because they are the American uniform. Everyone is encouraged to wear jeans, a white T-shirt, hoodie or flannel shirt. While this uniform model works well for brands that want to appeal to the masses, the market for luxury goods is the opposite.

"Ubiquity tends to be the antithesis of luxury."

—Milton Pedraza

Luxury is not for the masses because it's an aspiration. Mass production is associated with cheap, superficial and poor-quality products. They are temporary and won't last long. You simply don't buy a hoodie from Old Navy and expect your children to inherit it; but you do buy a Cartier watch hoping to hand it down to your daughter.

Louis Vuitton has always had a strong image as a luxury brand. The code for luxury, *hand,* certainly holds true for Louis Vuitton and their famous suitcases and trunks made of wood and aged leather. But when the global economy was in full upswing in the 1990s, Louis Vuitton did the unspeakable in luxury: they marketed to the masses. As populations became more affluent and had more disposable income, luxury goods attracted them. Louis Vuitton made their products more available, their image more pronounced, their prices more competitive, and improved their accessibility. Soon enough nearly everyone had a Louis Vuitton bag (some real, some fake), and the image became easier to copy, boosting the market for counterfeits. Louis Vuitton's reputation has weakened because the whole backbone of luxury is creating an aspiration.

The easy conclusion to this dilemma is to raise prices and reduce production, right? Wrong. Again, there's much more to luxury than money. The origin of luxury goods should be linked back to an artist, the creator who put in effort and is showing the direction of the trends. Some brands have been highly successful at attaching a face behind the brand, as is the case with Coco Chanel and Karl Lagerfeld for Chanel, and John Galliano for Christian Dior. It's important to have a signature, a name that personifies the brand. It goes back to the *hand* code. It's about having something exclusively made just for you by a professional, an artist.

"When things become too popular they are always fading away for something else."

—Karl Lagerfeld

The charm behind haute couture clothing stems exactly from this imperative. A couture piece is created by an artist who makes only one, rather than thousands in a factory. Handmade, with each detail—the fabric, stitching, adornments like beads and jewels—all carefully picked out and put together by skilled craftspeople. Rather than just a simple garment, haute couture is a collectible form of art.

As in the art world, those who purchase haute couture belong to a very small, private and elite club of buyers who are highly knowledgeable about what they are investing in. Haute couture is not for just anyone—but not because the price is so high, rather because only a real connoisseur can appreciate the work put into the craft. Every piece such experts acquire is tailored to fit them like a glove, safely kept and maintained, and stays with them for a lifetime. In haute couture, as in luxury, the relationship is between the artist and the connoisseur.

Luxury needs a sense of refinement, patience and intention. It means taking a brute stone from the land, one that is not beautiful yet, but with the right expertise can be cut and polished into something beautiful. The whole purpose of such refinement is to reach a higher level of pleasure.

Eroticism is in essence refinement. By nature we are sexual beings, but each culture has a way of refining our animal instincts. The kimono in Japanese culture is linked to luxury because it has this element of refinement. The way a woman moves subtly in her kimono, revealing her nape and elongating her neck, is a subtle message, a code, for men to know that the woman is trying to seduce him . . . she has an intention but it's subtle. Seduction can be either vulgar or discreet, and the latter is much more pleasurable and luxurious because it has a hidden message that triggers your reptilian reaction.

Refinement evokes that sense of subtlety and discretion. Luxury is about the attention to small details, like keeping the champagne glasses in the freezer to keep the champagne cold and more pleasurable to drink—a small detail that makes all the difference. Coco Chanel understood the value of simplicity and the subtleness in the details. Her attention to detail and the little things was impeccable, like with the carefully designed buttons on a coat or dress.

"Luxury lies not in the richness of things, but in the absence of vulgarity."

—Coco Chanel

This idea ties back to the Satellite Tribe, the select few individuals who can appreciate the true luxury of things. It's true that many tailor-made luxuries like haute couture have a high cost because of the artistry, craftsmanship, time and effort invested in creating each piece, and naturally only a small percentage of the population can afford this. However, what I want to emphasize here is that it doesn't matter how wealthy you are: luxury is perception and tradition. Even if you can afford all the yachts, homes, clothing and diamonds your heart desires, the Satellite Tribe mentality knows how to appreciate the intention behind luxury, the tradition attached to it, and the most discreet and subtle way to celebrate it to reach the highest level of pleasure.

TIMELESS: THE CONSTANT SEARCH FOR THE REFERENCE

The most successful luxuries are timeless: the little black dress, great riding boots, a diamond ring, good whiskey, and finely made cigars. Timeless in the sense of never going out of fashion, lasting forever, and based on a tradition refined to perfection.

Many alcoholic beverages stem from a long line of tradition and perfecting of the craft. The history of champagne, for instance, stems back to when the Romans grew vineyards in the Champagne region of France. But it wasn't until the medieval period that Benedictine monks began to produce sparkling wine by bottling it before fermentation ended. Though historians now refute the popular claim that Dom Pérignon invented champagne, his contributions helped perfect the art. For example, in the seventeenth century, his ideas solved the problem of exploding champagne bottles whose fermentation process was incomplete. Shortly after his death, Canon Godinot published a set of wine-making rules influenced by Pérignon's contributions. These moments were one step in the long perfection of this luxurious tradition. In French we use the term *la reference* (the reference) when talking about when perfection was almost accomplished, about the reference point for everything else we want to build on.

To take another beverage example, German beer took hundreds of years to perfect, centuries of effort invested in ensuring that newer generations will acknowledge and respect the perfection of the tradition.

"In the luxury business, you have to build on heritage."

—Bernard Arnault

Traditions need people to maintain and preserve them, and today these people are the Satellite Tribe. Throughout history, kings and courts would be the protectors and purveyors of culture, investing in art as patrons. Painters and artists could survive only if sponsored by the royal court. Leonardo da Vinci died in the arms of King Francis I of France, and despite being Italian, his most famous piece, the *Mona Lisa*, remained in France and still does to this day. In our time the Satellite Tribe resembles those courts: they have the knowledge, culture, time and resources to make sure that refinement is preserved and traditions behind luxuries carry on.

But this doesn't mean that the Satellite Tribe are closed off to change, nor that just because something is tradition we should keep it and practice it exactly as is. The refinement of goods and rituals takes place over a long period of time until we reach *la reference*. Nevertheless, we don't want to be Luddites, foolishly enamored of the past and averse to the natural order of change, evolution and improvement. The best luxuries strike this perfect balance between preserving tradition and innovating.

Let's move to an automotive example. At the beginning of the twentieth century, the first automobiles were coming out of the United States, England, Germany and Japan, a huge demonstration of their economic might to the rest of the world. The United States was famous for pioneering industrial manufacturing processes with the standardized black Ford Model T, a vehicle designed to be accessible and affordable to all. Karl Benz pioneered the automobile in Germany and though they were perhaps less accessible to the public compared to the Ford Model T, their distinguishing features were high performance and advanced technology. Cars manufactured in England were quintessentially English in that they were inextricably tied to "the gentleman." Every true gentleman possessed two cars: a Rolls-Royce, which was driven by a chauffeur, and a Bentley that he drove himself. According to tradition, Rolls-Royces are inherently more complex—gentlemen sent their chauffeurs to certified courses to learn how to properly drive them. Simpler Bentleys were considered sportier and easier for the busy English gentleman to master.

When Volkswagen bought Bentley in 1998, the risk of the iconic brand's prestige dying out was very high. But the outcome has been better than anticipated: Bentley sales have gone up. Why did this happen? Because Volkswagen was wise enough both to respect the tradition behind the Bentley brand and to innovate to make it even better. Still a prestigious vehicle with handmade elements and true to its traditional production process, the Bentley now had a great German engine, too.

Mini Cooper has done likewise. It's still a very English car, but now with a BMW engine. The best luxury brands both preserve the story behind the brand and also capitalize on innovation. When Volkswagen came out with the Maybach model, a car that was valued at half a million dollars, it was a huge failure. Nobody wanted to buy it because nobody knew it. There was no point of reference. It had no past that people could refer to in their minds. Nobody sees a Bentley and thinks of it as a VW car, but people saw the Maybach as just an expensive Volkswagen. Luxury is built upon a history, and it must have a reference of prestige.

A LUXURY BRAND IS A REFERENCE

The English gentleman is the point of reference of luxury for the rest of the world. Everything he owns is bespoke and handmade just for him: his suits, shoes, furniture, jewelry, and so on. He prefers the handmade item created just for him by a specialist in the craft. The English gentleman is the epitome of luxury also because he builds upon heritage.

Imagine this scene: A group of English gentlemen plan a weekend in the country. They stay in their friend's home, one that has been in his family for centuries. They decide to invite their American friend, Jack, who just moved to London to work for a major bank, and show him a little about English culture. Upon arrival, each gentleman unloads his luggage—beautiful leather travel bags perfect just for a night or two, with their initials engraved and the leather rather worn-out. Jack rolls in with a black Samsonite with wheels.

The activities planned for the day include a stroll of the grounds on horseback and then a few hours of clay pigeon shooting. They settle in their rooms and meet out front by the stables. Each of the gentlemen is wearing old leather boots, family heirlooms once belonging to their fathers and even grandfathers. Jack wears Nike tennis shoes. After a long day outside, they relax a moment in their rooms and freshen up for a brandy before dinner. When they all come down to the sitting room by the majestic fireplace, they are each sporting a velvet smoking jacket in different shades of burgundy, pine green and black. Jack has on his college hoodie.

What do we learn from this? Few, if any, luxury brands are 100 percent American. This is because one key element of luxury is the heritage attached to it. English gentlemen are living vestiges of their ancestors, history and traditions. This carries with it an element of luxury that the whole world wants to copy.

The Satellite Tribe is intimately familiar with luxury. Some years ago we discovered the code for luxury in America, a culture where titles and clear symbols of nobility do not exist. In the United States, the code for luxury is *civilian stripes*. Men will wear their Rolex as a general wears his first star. It is not just status but a stripe announcing your position in a subtle hierarchy. As the saying goes, don't dress for the job you have, dress for the job you want to have. Luxury in America is an expression of the desire to go up in this hierarchy.

A WORLDWIDE REFERENCE POINT

How is the Satellite Tribe creating and developing the Global Code for luxury—an ethic that could transcend cultures and become a worldwide reference point?

The three-brain theory is useful here. The cortex is rational intelligence, the limbic is emotions, and the reptilian is survival and reproduction. The laws are cortex, love and seduction are limbic, sex and violence reptilian. Necessity is not luxury. Air, water, food, and shelter are not luxury. They are basic survival (or reptilian) needs. At the limbic level, love, caring, and friendship are not luxuries either. They are essential to human thriving. Finally, at the cortex level, rational thinking and long-term planning capacities would still not be considered luxuries. They will be necessary at some point for humans to survive long enough to pass their genes along.

So why do people buy Rolls-Royces? It's not to go from point A to point B. Why do people buy Rolexes? Obviously not because it's the only way to keep time. Why do people build 40,000-square-foot "start-up castles" in Florida? Not just to be protected from the rain! The same is happening in China, India, Russia, Brazil, Turkey and the Middle East. More and more people in the world can now afford luxury—and they crave it. It's simply human.

So we decided to study these newly emerging populations to go deeper into the Global Code for luxury. We went to Korea, China, India, Brazil, Singapore, Hong Kong, Dubai, Istanbul, Paris, London, Berlin. Our clients also asked us to add Africa to the list. The Richemont Group, which witnessed a 25 percent growth in China over the last decade, is more and more interested in studying what they call the "New China": Africa.

This is the future of the luxury market.

NO MACHINES

"I hate machines," recounted a 45-year-old Indian man. "I never speak to a robot or an answering machine. When I get a call and a robot asks me questions, I hang up immediately."

"Press one if you speak English, two if you speak Spanish, three if you are under 25 . . . they should have added a press four if you hate this process!" said a 50-year-old woman in Dallas.

"We are invaded by machines, technology everywhere!" said a 22-year-old Brazilian woman. "What happened to humans, human contacts?"

Hatred for machines—this was the first big insight into the Global Code for luxury. Whereas the ubiquity of robots and technology might seem like progress, they don't connote luxury. Technology, unlike true luxury, quickly becomes available and accessible to everybody, rather than the select few.

When I had my first telephone installed in my car in the 1970s, it was a big box in the trunk, with a long antenna on the roof and a big handset hanging from the dashboard. At that time, this was luxury. Today everybody has a smartphone. Technology grows exponentially more powerful and affordable (Moore's law) and as a result loses its elite status very quickly. We discovered that, everywhere, people feel addicted to machines of all sorts yet profess that they would love to free themselves. Luxury is a counterforce to the machine.

TIME IS LUXURY

The second insight came when people start speaking about time—how much time they need to do something or go someplace. When we ask Boeing frequent flyers what they thought of flying first class, we immediately got tons of horror stories.

"Trying to go to Charles de Gaulle at 5:00 p.m. to catch a plane is a nightmare," said a 52-year-old French businessman. "Two hours in traffic, the highway is too small . . . it takes more time to go to the airport than to fly to London."

"When you arrive in Atlanta, this is when the real journey begins," a 68-year-old woman from New York told us. "You have to wait in line at the airline counter, then you have to wait in line for somebody to check your identity, then you have to take off your shoes and belt and wait to go through a machine manipulated by ex-convicts who look at you naked, but then it is not finished. You have to wait in line to take a train, to go to the gate, and guess what? Once at the gate, you have to wait in line again. And you have to try to be in front of the line if you want to find room in the overhead bin for your carry-on. And of course the rule of the airline is that the flight attendant cannot help you to put your carry-on in the overhead bin."

"In some countries," said a 35-year-old male consultant from Rio de Janeiro, "they keep adding steps: identity check, visa check, police check, luggage scanning, customs . . . sometimes there is another line to pay some airport taxes. They are very creative at making our lives miserable. I wish I could find a way to avoid all these steps."

ONE STEP

We have seen that people hate airports. It takes so many steps to get to your seat. Airlines make a big mistake seeing their job as taking people from departing gates to arrival gates. For passengers, the trip is from their home and back to their home. But nobody in the business looks at it this way. So engineers and security guards keep making traveling more and more complicated every day. They keep adding *steps,* and the more they add, the farther they get from luxury.

So, to survive, they have to squeeze more people in the plane and give them less and less service (never give you a *hand*). To compensate, they try to seduce you with cheap tickets.

> "This is hell. Cheap as hell is still hell!"—a 50-year-old American manager in San Francisco

So what is the opposite of hell? What is luxury? Who can answer the phone for you, eliminate all the machines, give you a hand when you need it, carry your luggage and drive you to the private jet, where in one step, you will be in your seat? Your *butler*.

THE BUTLER

Of course very few people can afford an actual butler, but we are speaking here about the Global Code, created by the Satellite Tribe who can afford almost anything they want. So let's look at something in the butler concept that everyone should consider. A butler is the opposite of a machine. You are known; your voice is recognized; you don't need to spell your name; he knows exactly what you want. Luxury starts when you don't have to ask. So you don't need a real butler to be on-code. Consider the following stories.

> "When I go for dinner in my favorite restaurant, by the time I sit down, my drink is already there. They know me, they know what I drink, I never have to ask, I love it."—a 50-year-old male Palm Beach resident

> "When I arrive at the Fasano hotel in Sao Paulo, Marie Anne takes me directly to my suite, where a caipirinha, my favorite Brazilian drink, is waiting for me. She has already filled out the form as she has all the information; the coffee machine is ready, as I drink a lot of coffee; and the TV is already on CNN."—a 48-year-old male manager of a cosmetic company, Atlanta

This is luxury. Everything is one step, and done by hand—a hand that knows you. Centurion (American Express's black card) is one of my clients.

They recently introduced an international arrival service, with a guide who leads you through the airport and arrival process, like a private butler waiting for you at Shanghai, Mumbai or Seoul. His mission is to make your arrival as close to the *one-step* principle as possible. And he *will* give you a hand. As the new Business Centurion brochure promises, "Be unencumbered by both luggage and logistics. No need to lift a finger—your guide will assist with carry-on luggage, as well as coordinate with your local driver."

HAND

"Handmade," "made by hand," "bespoke," "tailor-made," "just for you"— these are the keywords for global luxury. You are unique and want a unique treatment, a unique product. Technology and the increasing automation of everyday life have created a nostalgia for the "real thing." From the spa, where we pay dearly for an hour of being touched by hand, to the handmade leather of the Rolls interior, *hand,* the Global Code for luxury, signifies a return to the basic reptilian life, when we are touched and manipulated by our mother, when food is homemade and handmade by her.

Of course, luxury products are generally expensive. But as I have been told by a famous luxury brand, "This is not *expensive,* this is expensive *to make.*" The time, talent, passion, and commitment of an artist or artisan along with high-quality materials and precisely selected components result in luxury being "expensive to make."

THE COURT BUTLER

The Court has a butler, and the Courtesans copy it. If you're lucky, you don't even answer the phone: your butler does it for you to protect you from the outside world. General de Gaulle preferred to be telephoned rather than calling somebody. He would thus make it be known, by means of his staff, when he was available to be reached by someone. In the same vein, members of the Court never answer the doorbell and go to open the door.

In America this might sound pompous and out of touch with simple American life. Not every member of the Satellite Tribe has somebody to open the door for them and receive their guests. Yet a large majority of the emerging middle class worldwide aspires to this luxury. It's one of the reasons why they all love *Downton Abbey*: seeing how the Court lives and imagining they might be able to one day as well. The challenge is more psychological than material.

I met a top executive of a luxury car brand to speak about the future of the brand. "Our dilemma," he said, "is how to appeal to the new money, or nouveau riche, without losing the loyalty of old money, our traditional clients. Buying a luxury product has to be acquiring a new stripe, without devaluating this stripe. When the French government gives the Legion d'Honneur to everybody it loses its value and generates a lot of resentment among the ones who do bear the medal and feel that they actually deserve it. How do we attract a new generation without alienating our loyal customers?" A top executive at Richemont phrased the same dilemma differently: Can you increase your volume and market share without diluting your brand?

PERMISSION TO BUY

We soon realized that some people need a "permission to buy" and a permission to identify themselves with the new aspirational level they want to join. Most of the time, people with new money are not sure they belong. They are not sure they know the rules and are afraid of the faux pas that might disqualify them. We saw it very clearly when we studied the code for Cartier in New York.

> "When I went to the store, the way people were looking at me made me feel that I was at the wrong place, I was feeling that I didn't deserve it, that I didn't have the style."—a 25-year-old male start-up billionaire, Dallas, Texas

Despite these challenges, Ralph Lauren is a company that has been successful at creating a series of luxury brands (Polo Ralph Lauren, RRL, Purple Label) that achieved universal appeal, becoming unconsciously synonymous with affordable luxury. Not just affordable from a price perspective (roughly $80 for a polo shirt), but affordable in the sense of giving a wider range of people "permission to buy."

The executive at Rolls-Royce concurred: "With the Ghost, a much smaller Rolls-Royce model, we are giving clients 'permission to buy.' Some clients, though they may have the money for it, cannot psychologically 'afford' to buy a model like the Phantom. Too big, too ostentatious and too in your face." One way to get these new customers familiar with the Global Code for luxury is to have different levels of products, and to tell the right story with each one. Although it might be expensive, there is a reason for that: its true value is in that it is made by *hand*.

BMW, which owns the Rolls-Royce brand, decided to opt for the "rich but shy" angle. Even the Flying Lady hood ornament on the new Phantom Drophead Coupe is smaller and retractable. Yet loyal clients don't want a shy Rolls-Royce; if they buy a Rolls-Royce, it's because they've been successful and they want to show it off. So when the Mandarin Hotel in Hong Kong bought a fleet of 12 Rolls-Royces to pick up their loyal customers from the airport, they bought the long-bodied Phantom model. Very impressive indeed. A good marketing tool for Rolls-Royce: potential clients will associate themselves with the luxury of the car as someone who needs to be picked up at the airport in a Rolls. The hotel's brochure explains how these cars—made "by hand" in England—represent more than just money. They represent a commitment to the very best.

The main competitor to Rolls-Royce is Bentley. Many years ago, both of these brands essentially produced identical cars, differentiated only by their hood ornaments—the Flying Lady for Rolls-Royce and the Winged B for Bentley. Being so similar was, of course, a mistake—one which almost cost Bentley its existence at one point. The two car brands should manufacture differentiable models given that they already have different symbolic associations: the Rolls-Royce, a butler and chauffeur, the Bentley for hunting, with you at the wheel and your dogs in the back. One formal, one sporty. The two cars cannot be the same.

CIVILIAN STRIPES

Very few American nouveaux riches can afford both from a psychological and sociological perspective to buy a Phantom, so they opt for the Ghost or Wraith models instead, as they are more discreet. The Rolls-Royce executive: "We are very happy with our new products. They sell well, since

60 percent of our customers are new customers." Given that the code for luxury in America is *civilian stripes,* if the Drophead Coupe Phantom is a four-star general, the regular Phantom is a three-star general, the Wraith a two-star general and the Ghost a one-star. Much like actual military stripes, you have to prove that you deserve them, usually by showing your courage in combat. You have to earn your stripes. Which starts with "permission to buy."

MONEY IS NOT THE GOAL

Civilian stripes signify that you are a good fighter. You took risks, failed, tried again, never gave up, and one day you made it. So you know that you are good. The goal was never to make money; money is only the *proof.* The proof that you worked hard, succeeded, and now you deserve the symbols of your status. Now that you are a general, how many stars are you going to wear on your shoulder?

Civilian stripes also mean that you know where you are in the Satellite Tribe's hierarchy. Court symbols are different from those used by Courtesans. A Courtesan will never dare to wear a crown, which is reserved for the queen. The Global Tribe's hierarchy of symbols has to be equally clear and precise. To have money is not enough; you need to feel confident in how to use it. Any luxury brand should have a clear positioning, and be a clear indicator of position. In *Downton Abbey,* the white tie is for the lord, the black tie for the butler; there is no room for confusion.

MOVING UP

However, the code of *civilian stripes* is uniquely American and does not govern some other cultures, whose relationship with luxury can be vastly different. When we explored the notion of premium cars for Fiat in Brazil, we discovered that many Brazilians thought Fiat was in fact a Brazilian brand. For many people, Fiat had been the first car they could afford. Yet just like their American counterparts, Brazilian consumers want to *move up* and succeed. But the desired pace is different. Whereas Americans like breakthrough scenarios, Brazilians take a slower approach—*melhorzinho,* or what we would call "baby steps."

We decided to create products that followed them as they moved upward, giving them a new clear symbol of achievement at every step. Brazilians keep fighting to succeed; even in very difficult times, they never surrender or give up. But they do take things slowly. So when they succeed, they deserve it—but it's not part of the culture to suddenly become a billionaire at 15. Fiat recognized that they needed a line of products that would match their customers' evolving life stages. Each new car was designed to correspond to a stage in a customer's road to success and serve as a clear indicator of a new position. That also shows their customers the path to the next level, creating new aspirations.

Showroom floors are designed to show the potential buyer of a $5,000 car what they could have for the next level up—say, $7,000. Buyers see the social progression, a new identity, a new status. The carmaker will create loyalty and guide customers toward the company's premium products.

However, when Rolls-Royce in the United States made their product more "shy" to appeal to new customers needing permission to buy, they offered them what I call an intellectual alibi. Intellectual alibi means a good reason for me to do what I want to do anyway. We know that the reptilian always wins, that the emotional level is always full of tensions and contradictions, but the cortex or logical brain just needs to provide the reptilian with a good excuse, like a rebate or a competitive price.

DON'T BE SHY

Modesty about luxury consumption is not for everyone, though. A large part of the global luxury market in China, India, Southeast Asia, Africa and the Middle East is not populated by shy customers. When these customers are rich, they want the real thing. They *want* to show it off. The new Bugatti is priced at around $2.5 million, yet one Asian customer bought 12 of them to give as presents to his family members.

Today, China is the number one market for luxury and luxury cars. A *People* magazine review of Kevin Kwan's 2014 book *Crazy Rich Asians* noted, "There is rich, filthy rich and then crazy rich." If Europe is still fighting its long recession, and rich Americans are becoming shy, the future of luxury is sure to be found in other places, such as India, Asia and soon Africa. So the newly arrived might show their art collection, their wine cellar, their car collection. They always are attracted by what they cannot buy: style and sophistication, art and talent.

LUXURY IS NOT WORK

After all, the French don't like to work. As one French business publication *Enjeux* clearly spells out on its cover page: "Travailler nuit gravement a la santé" (Working is very detrimental to your health). Another bestselling book in France, written by Corinne Maier, is titled *Bonjour Paresse* (Hello Laziness), and explains how to pretend to work without really doing anything. In the French culture, working to make money is considered vulgar and *petit bourgeois*. However, to be either an artisan or an artist is noble. You do not *work;* you create beauty, style, sophistication and elegance. This is your divine mission, your contribution to the evolution of the human species.

EACH CULTURE HAS A CONTRIBUTION TO MAKE

Each culture or continent is going to contribute to the Global Code of luxury. We have brands selling handmade whiskey in Brooklyn. Rolls-Royce and Bentley claim that they are still handmade in England. Dom Pérignon champagne from the French. Hermès has created a Chinese brand, Shang Xia, with stores in Paris and around the world, but Shang Xia's jade comes from China. All of these brands have one creator at their origin.

If the code for luxury is *made by hand,* instinctively our reptilian brain needs to know whose hand it is. Who is the creator?

A BRAND IS A SIGNATURE

A brand should be a name—a signature. Even better, the logo should look like a handmade signature: St. Laurent, Dior, Ralph Lauren, Rolls-Royce and Coco Chanel are all brands associated with individual creators, passionate artists with a higher purpose whose artistry went beyond just making money. The hand has a name, a human dimension to counterbalance the mass-produced disposable goods that dominate the marketplace. The aspiration of the masses is always going to tend first toward freedom, but from there toward style, status and luxury.

We now understand that the Global Code created by the Platinum Gypsies has several elements that we can start putting together. What words and phrases describe what the Satellite Tribe wants? No airport, one step, no luggage, made by hand, by invitation only, unique and legacy. A brand is a signature made by a hand belonging to an artist. The brand is his or her name, face, style, and story (again, think Coco Chanel).

The Satellite Tribe is familiar with the best of each culture. They test, benchmark, select and promote by word of mouth. When they find it, they expect continuity and consistency. A Rolls should always be a Rolls; a Chanel dress, a Chanel dress.

LOYALTY, PURPOSE AND PASSION

If brands want their customers to be loyal to them, they need to be loyal to their customers. Don't change the structure, because the structure is the identity, the essence of the brand. You might be able to change the content occasionally, but be sure to preserve the DNA of the brand. The Mini Cooper is a real Mini Cooper: same structure. At the same time, it is a newly imagined car (new content). *West Side Story* has the same structure as *Romeo and Juliet,* but the content is different. We know that people don't drink the wine, they drink the story. So to be loyal to your customer, you have to respect the story—your story. From Dom Pérignon to Coco Chanel, Château Beychevelle to Rolls-Royce, they all have a story to tell.

Luxury has a higher purpose: the achievement of real global value. The elevation of the mundane into a higher and more educated level of beauty, sophistication and talent. This is *higher culture,* a level of sophistication that the Chinese reached thousands of years before the Europeans.

High-density cultures are those cultures that, at a certain period in time, created the global reference system imitated by everyone else. Japan, for example, was once the reference for quality control. France was and largely still is style and elegance; Germany is high-performance systems.

Finally, what the Satellite Tribe most admires is passion. For them, luxury is not a treat, but a necessity. "We are all going to age and die, luxury is the best revenge," is how an 85-year-old female expat in Singapore put it to me.

It is worth noting that luxury has different meanings depending on your level in the Tribe.

The Court sets the highest standards. The Courtesans use luxury to signify that they are ready to join the Court. The Aspirants will try their best to avoid a faux pas that will disqualify them; the Suppliers will provide the appropriate products to the different stratification; but the biggest market is, of course, all the people who will buy a brand that will give them a little bit of the dream, the little polo player on their chest. The brand and its creator must inspire passion. The artist and the designer are modern poets who defy mortality. Along with *hand,* the Global Code for luxury is *passion.*

Rolls and Royce wanted to build the best car in the world, Coco Chanel to liberate women from the corset, and Patek Philippe to help you begin your own tradition. Each set a higher standard, the reference system, the pillar of society, a mission for the Satellite Tribe to follow.

As we saw earlier, Patek Philippe says, "you never actually own a Patek Philippe, you merely look after it for the next generation." This is what global luxury is all about. This is the mission of the Court, to create with passion a reference system of refinement and sophistication for the next generation. To defy death by creating rituals of higher pleasure.

The reptilian instinctive brain learns and progresses through pain and pleasure. To survive, we try to avoid pain and to satisfy our basic needs to look for pleasure. The search for pleasure is a universal quest. Around the world, class is very often associated with a higher level of appreciation of pleasure. In many ways, the Satellite Tribe has managed to master the quest for higher pleasure.

SIX

THE GLOBAL CODE
FOR PLEASURE

THE THREE LEVELS OF PLEASURE

Lust, Love and Limits

When we usually talk about pleasure, we tend to think about pleasure in a sexual sense. In common speech, pleasure is most often attached to sexuality, and maybe sometimes to food, like the pleasure we feel from eating a bar of chocolate or a savory meal. But I want to show you how pleasure comes in all different shapes and sizes.

Pleasure is one of our most basic sensory experiences, and not just as humans but also as animals. It infiltrates all aspects of our lives. Pleasure is an important element in all our lives and should therefore be explored in terms of the Global Codes. The way we perceive and act upon pleasure varies greatly from culture to culture, person to person, but I believe that the Satellite Tribe is setting certain trends regarding pleasure that are worth observing and even following. But before I can talk about the Satellite Tribe's codes for pleasure, I need to outline the different types of pleasure and how they relate to our three brains. This is a critical step when it comes to my analysis and how I've reached these Global Codes, so I must guide you through it.

THE THREE BRAINS OF PLEASURE

Let's consider the three-brain theory and see how it can help us decode the Global Code for pleasure. At a reptilian level, just fulfilling your basic needs while avoiding pain is already a sort of pleasure. Feeling full after being hungry is a basic form of pleasure, as is reaching an orgasm after sex, or falling asleep when you are tired. We call these *animalistic pleasures,* and we have them in common with many other species. But if we move up in the brain hierarchy, we discover a culture of higher pleasure unique to humans.

Our most primordial pleasure is physical. We experience physical pleasure from being sexually aroused or taking a hot bath, from eating a delicious meal or receiving a back massage. It's the satisfaction you get when drinking a glass of water when you're thirsty, eating food when you're hungry, or having sex when you're turned on. When the alcoholic, smoker or drug addict ingests their poison of choice, they are experiencing a physical and chemical reaction inside their bodies and minds; it's a completely physical sensation of pleasure.

Then we have emotional pleasure, the warm, fuzzy feeling when someone gives you a hug or a baby smiles at you. It's that feeling you get when you haven't seen a loved one in a long time and meet them at the airport with a hug.

Physical pleasure can be experienced alone, while emotional pleasure tends to come from our relationships with others. It has to do with family, friends and connecting with people on a social level. You can't feel emotional pleasure from receiving a present without someone else giving it to you. You need someone else to say "I love you" in order to feel this type of pleasure.

Emotional pleasures like these are associated with the limbic brain and follow what we call the "logic of emotion." If you are in a restaurant where everybody is rude and you get the feeling that the staff hates you, you might not really enjoy the food. But if you go to a place where everybody knows you and loves you, the same food might taste better and your pleasure might be enhanced. If reptilian pleasure is associated directly with sex and food, limbic pleasure has more to do with attention, seduction, caring and love. Identical physical events happening in different environments change your experience of them.

Finally we have cortex pleasure—what the French call a brilliant idea—like the pleasure of discovering a mathematical formula or a new law of physics. This is intellectual pleasure, and it definitely includes the search for the perfect rituals. Words like *sophistication* and *refinement* take their full meanings here.

Like physical pleasure, cortex pleasure is primarily experienced alone. Can you recall a time when you worked really hard on a project and succeeded? You were experiencing intellectual pleasure. It's that feeling of self-satisfaction when you have a goal and achieve it, like graduating from college at the top of your class, reaching your goal weight after months of exercising and dieting, or finally being able to ride your bike smoothly without the training wheels.

We already know that the reptilian always wins; I always use the example that you cannot go to the opera if you cannot breathe. However, when your basic needs are met, you might want to enjoy those necessities in a more refined manner; this is when a culture of pleasure begins to develop. Food and sex, for example, become art: we now enter the world of culinary *art* (as opposed to "cooking") and eroticism (as opposed to sex).

Furthermore, it's interesting to notice that in many cultures these two often go together, from the Roman orgies, through medieval *ripailles* to contemporary orgy parties. We can explain this by visualizing the reptilian space as a circle containing two arrows, one directed toward the inside of the circle and one directed toward the outside. Everything that goes in and out of your body is reptilian and directly associated with pain and/or pleasure—everything that goes inside (air, liquid, food, sex), and everything that goes out (bodily functions, sperm, babies, blood).

The art of pleasure consists in transforming those basic needs into higher satisfaction. You need to drink liquids every day, but savoring a Château Haut-Brion 1985 is very different from merely topping up on fluids. "You don't drink the wine, you drink the story. Look at the Château Beychevelle, what a name and what a story. I love this wine!" said a 60-year-old American wine connoisseur from Napa Valley, California. You need to eat something, preferably every day, but to enjoy beluga caviar or foie gras au torchon is entirely on another level.

The Satellite Tribe is setting the standards for higher pleasure. Just as we have haute couture, we now have *haut plaisir,* or a higher level of sophistication. Such experiences require refinement. When you find a diamond, in the ground, it does not look like a Cartier or Harry Winston diamond until after the process of cutting the original stone into the final jewel. In some cases refining takes a long time and implies a complex process that requires talent, patience, hard work and pain to attain higher pleasure. Think of the time, energy, knowledge and talent needed to go from pen and paper to an opera being performed and executed by hundreds of musicians, singers, set decorators and administrators. From Wagner's original compositions to the Bayreuth Festival commemorating his oeuvre for thousands of visitors each year . . . what a journey!

Culture is important, because you cannot appreciate a Wagner opera or a Japanese Noh performance if you have never been educated and prepared to experience that kind of pleasure. Like coffee, these are acquired tastes. You need somebody to initiate you. In the movie *Pretty Woman,* when Julia Roberts's character attends the opera for the first time she is greatly moved by the experience. (Asked for her reaction to Verdi's *La Traviata,* she exclaims, "Oh, it was so good, I almost peed my pants!")

Despite these varying types of pleasure, no one form is superior to the other; all are very important to our survival, each with its particular function. If we didn't take pleasure from sex, we wouldn't want to have intercourse and reproduce the species; if we didn't get pleasure from connecting emotionally with other people, we'd have fewer chances of surviving on our own than working together as a team; if we didn't feel pleasure from achieving our goals, we would be content with a sedentary and uncompetitive lifestyle. All of these pleasures are crucial to survival as a species and as individuals in this world.

> *"Nature has placed mankind under the government of two sovereign masters, pain and pleasure—they govern all we do, in all we say, in all we think: Every effort we make to throw off our subjection, will serve but to demonstrate and confirm."*
>
> —Jeremy Bentham

Naturally, our three brains perceive pleasure in very different ways. For the reptilian, pleasure and pain relate to our nervous system, the physical sense of pleasure. What's more, our imprints—our first life experiences that are ingrained in our unconscious—relating to reptilian pleasure and pain are signals that serve our survival. Unconsciously, our mind recollects the way we were first nourished—did mother give me plenty of milk? Was I fed whenever I wanted or only on her schedule? Did I breast-feed for a long time or was I given formula as an infant? All of these imprints and unconscious memories impact how each individual personally feels about different behaviors, in this case, eating. Depending on our first imprints of eating, we will attach eating to either pleasure or pain for the rest of our lives.

This phenomenon explains why, in most cases, individuals who were sexually abused or molested in childhood tend to display promiscuous and reckless sexual behavior from a young age and well into adulthood (though of course this varies from person to person). Their first imprints of sexual pleasure were connected with a sense of loss of control, bringing up emotional pain. Hence, deciding to actively engage in promiscuous behavior gives these individuals a sense of regaining control over their sexuality and decision making. Our first imprints are crucial signals that always relate to pain and pleasure, and they directly impact our behavior in the future.

Our limbic pleasure involves feelings of security. It's about feeling free to express your feelings because you are in a safe space. As infants, our mother provided us with security through patterns and repetition. We need order and structure in our lives because this creates predictability and reliability, and when this happens we feel comfortable to move around as we please and express ourselves and our emotions in their truest form.

Public speaking, for instance, can be a limbic pleasure or limbic pain. Some people are great at speaking in front of their class or giving a toast at a wedding because they probably have positive imprints from childhood that gave them a feeling of security and confidence to express themselves openly to strangers. Ironically, though a great comedian on screen, Rowan Atkinson (known best for his role as Mr. Bean), has shared in interviews his fear of public speaking, mostly due to a stutter and speech impediment he developed as a child. In the limbic world, pleasure has to do with emotional comfort.

Finally, the cortex. Here we see a completely new definition of gratification and pleasure. Ruling the realm of logic and reasoning, our cortex isn't seeking short-term pleasure. It involves seeking a heightened sense of pleasure rather than an immediate one. While driving on the highway, our reptilian brain is tempted to stop along the way and pig out at the closest gas station with sweets and potato chips, while our cortex encourages us to be patient, keep going, and think long-term, where a great meal awaits us at our destination.

The cortex is all about the sophistication of pleasure. It's about taming the reptilian within, not to silence it, but to train it to be patient for greater pleasures in the future. The Satellite Tribe is great at this. By observing their behavior, how they seek out pleasure, I've discovered the Global Code for pleasure.

DELAY

There is no pain without pleasure, and no pleasure without pain. They are two sides of the same coin. Our nervous system uses both pain and pleasure as signals of what we ought and oughtn't do to ensure our survival.

You might remember the first time you burned your hand on the kitchen stove, fell while climbing a tree, or got a deep scratch on your arm from teasing the cat. These imprints of pain serve as mental notes that our actions can have damaging consequences. Similarly, sometimes escaping pain gives us pleasure—another survival technique our biology has bestowed upon us. After a long afternoon of shoveling snow, a warm shower is very pleasurable because exposing our bodies to low temperatures for too long can be detrimental to our health, so the relief from pain is meant to feel good.

"It is always by way of pain one arrives at pleasure."

—Marquis de Sade

The Global Code for pleasure has everything to do with this inextricable relationship. Postponing pleasure now and enduring temporary pain leads to greater pleasure later. Athletes know this very well. They train entire days under strict regimens that are both physically and mentally challenging, following less-than-pleasant diets for months and sometimes years until that brief moment where they compete to win. All their hard work and suffering comes down to a few minutes. But all that effort and pain they went through is worth it for a potential victory, a much greater pleasure than if they had decided to relax on the sofa instead. The same goes for music virtuosos who perfect their instrument for years before they perform in ways that make their every move appear so natural and even intuitive to the audience.

Hence, the Global Code for pleasure is *delay*. To experience more elevated pleasures, we must first be patient, work hard, endure temporary pain, give up short-term satisfaction, and reach goals with higher payoffs.

When I did work for Vichy, part of L'Oréal, we worked on developing the code for makeup and skin care. We found an interesting revelation about Frenchwomen: They spend a lot of time and money on makeup, but only to look like they aren't wearing any. For Frenchwomen, it's vulgar to look like you put too much effort into your makeup. Avoiding a theatrical look, they opt for a more natural look, secretly putting in a lot of work to look effortlessly and naturally beautiful.

Japan's geisha tradition also follows this sophistication of pleasure through delay. Geishas were created not as mere sexual objects but rather to train these women to be the best lady they can possibly be. They were taught how to look, behave and dress appropriately, how to eat politely and how to initiate pleasant conversation. Hard work and effort led them to become the ultimate lady. They were seeking a higher level of pleasure beyond immediate satisfaction.

"A woman does not exist before the age of 30."
—Honoré de Balzac

Pleasure has a lot to do with releasing tension, a very biological concept connected with our circle-and-arrows diagram described above, in which our body works in terms of opposites: in-out, up-down, pain-pleasure. When we ingest food, it must come out through digestion. When we lie down at night we must get up in the morning. We work hard but play hard too. Childbirth is extremely painful, but the pleasure a woman experiences once the baby is born is not just from seeing her child for the first time but also from the release of tension, the relief from pain. Nightmares bring pain and suffering, but once you wake up you feel relieved because you escaped pain. In the wild, predators must be patient and build up tension when hunting their prey because they know a bigger reward awaits them if they succeed.

"Pain is temporary, quitting is forever."

—Lance Armstrong

The Satellite Tribe follows the Global Code for pleasure because they know that delay means higher returns on investment. While studying in medical or law school, students will turn down invitations to parties, spend sleepless nights at the library, and take out numerous college loans to pay for their education. The only reason a future neurosurgeon would put herself through such strain is because she knows that if she succeeds and graduates, the rewards are very high—she will be making a valuable contribution to society, receive a very attractive salary and possibly retire at a very young age to enjoy the perks of living well.

Delay is what differentiates the equestrian from the buffet-eater. Equestrians are disciplined and focused; they must endure the pain of training before they experience the pleasure of winning. Buffet-eaters do the reverse. They would rather gorge on piles of high-calorie food at a cheap price today and risk the pain of high cholesterol, heart disease, increased body fat, and expensive doctor visits. They prefer experiencing the short-term gains right now at the cost of pain later.

Likewise, someone who has a lot of unprotected sex today might risk the pain of getting a sexually transmitted infection in the future. This is the reptilian at work, thinking about short-term satisfaction and immediate gains over long-term consequences. Obeying the rule of delay means prioritizing the thinking done by the cortex, which involves reason, foresight and thinking long-term; however, delaying does not therefore necessarily deny us our reptilian needs. In fact, we should view such behavior as the cortex *celebrating* the reptilian and actualizing it in the best manner possible.

The art of seduction is limbic, but when done right it's the cortex manipulating the reptilian to our advantage. Seduction and delay is a woman's game. If she likes the guy, she might feel she can't simply give in and have sex with him on the first date. She has to entice him and tease him by dressing sexy and making the rules of when and where she is available to see him. In other words, women are masters at playing hard to get.

I had discovered the code for seduction for L'Oréal in seven different countries, and I was so fascinated by the results that I wanted to create a course on seduction at the University of California, Los Angeles, where I was already teaching. When I proposed my idea it was immediately rejected. "No way! Feminists will immediately jump down our throats and we'll get lawyers knocking at the door in a heartbeat!" Americans perceived seduction as a man sneakily taking advantage of a woman to get her in bed. As a Frenchman I see seduction completely differently. I see it as being a game where delay is your best strategy. It's a dance between two people—if you will, an art.

Since I always look back to the reptilian for insight, I discovered that women invented seduction and the art of "delay." Why? Because women live in cycles—first as an infant, then as a young woman going through puberty, then as a mother, then as a woman in menopause. Every month she returns to the cycle of her hormones. Men don't go through the same cycles as women do, so "time" for men is all about now—wanting sex now. For women, time is all about tim*ing*. It is way easier for a woman to go out to a bar with girlfriends and not sleep with the first man that shows interest. Men, on the other hand, find it difficult to say "no" when even a not-so-attractive woman propositions sex. Women are great at delay because they know that it's better to wait for better gains in the future.

If there is no tension, then there's no desire, and if there's no desire then there's no satisfaction. We need to feel like we fought hard for what we want in order to feel accomplished and satisfied. Desire by definition is to want something you don't have. When you can't have something right away, then you experience greater pleasure when you actually do get what you want. The buildup of tension is what leads to a higher level of satisfaction and pleasure.

"Nothing in the world is worth having or worth doing unless it means effort, pain, difficulty . . . I have never in my life envied a human being who led an easy life. I have envied a great many people who led difficult lives and led them well."

—Theodore Roosevelt

The reptilian demands pleasure now, but the cortex tells the reptilian to wait, be patient, and work hard for greater rewards in the future. Yale Law School professor and author Amy Chua was scrutinized for the harsh parenting techniques she endorsed in her book *Battle Hymn of the Tiger Mother*. In it, she described how the strict parenting style of Chinese mothers was preferable to the lax model common in Western homes.

Though many of her stories appeared shocking and even cruel to many readers, what Chua was really professing was delay. In one telling anecdote, Chua describes forcing her daughter to sit at the piano with no dinner or bathroom breaks until she mastered "The Little White Donkey" by Jacques Ibert. But Chua defended her actions by saying that her intent was not merely to teach the mastering of self-discipline but rather to enable her daughter to feel an immense sense of elation and self-confidence once she perfected the piece. Chua's parenting method was all about the principle of delay—enduring pain and abstaining from temporary short-term pleasures in lieu of far greater future rewards and basking in the fruits of her efforts.

You will probably never catch Amy Chua at a restaurant buffet. The Satellite Tribe steers clear of the buffet lifestyle. They know very well that anything worth having is worth fighting for. They seek out activities that give them a higher level of pleasure.

"How do you get to Carnegie Hall?" an old joke runs: "Practice" is the answer. A symphony orchestra demands the hard work, practice and dedication of every performer involved. Each instrument, each note, in isolation is mere noise, but together they create beautiful music. An elevated sense of pleasure depends on learning how to postpone and delay temporary follies for greater things to come.

BEAUTY IN SIMPLICITY

The Sophistication of the Chimp

There is an inevitable sense of nostalgia when it comes to pleasure. Our first imprint of pleasure was our feeling warmth, protection and love in our mother's arms. This is the home base for pleasure, our bunker of comfort in simplicity. But it never lasts for long. Eventually we stop breastfeeding, gain independence and leave the nest to venture on our own. Forever longing for the simple comfort mother offered us, we seek it out through other forms of satisfaction.

"We are all in a post-hypnotic trance induced in early infancy."
—Ronald David Laing

More and more we are seeing the Satellite Tribe opting for retreats to isolated destinations rather than crowded resorts. We gain a certain sense of satisfaction when we find a deserted beach where we can frolic with the ones we care for, unplug and disconnect from the noise and chaos of the rest of the world. The Satellite Tribe is drawn to places like spas and yoga retreats or boutique hotels embedded in the natural landscape. They remind us of a simpler life when we were infants cared for by our mothers.

Thus I've found a second Global Code for pleasure: *beauty in simplicity*. The more we feel like we are returning to the nostalgic simplicity of childhood when everything was easier, when we felt immense joy from climbing a tree, playing on the beach or laughing with friends on the playground, the closer we are to the Global Code for pleasure.

The Banyan Tree luxury resorts take simple pleasure very seriously, re-creating a time and place that is untouched and pure where we can unwind, heal, reflect and relax. Each Banyan Tree hotel scattered throughout the world is located in a secluded and hidden natural place and constructed so as to blend in with nature. A place where time stands still, a refuge away from the madness of the city, these hotels create a paradise for visitors, a "sanctuary of the senses" as they call it. The Banyan Tree's success and attraction stem from our craving to return to our simplest pleasure: comfort, safety and peace.

The beauty of simplicity can also come from eliminating artifice. Just walking through your local supermarket aisles, you'll see how product labels are now covered with the word *no*: *no* additives, *no* artificial coloring, and *no* saturated fat. We are seeing a rise in organic produce where we want the real thing, the natural thing. The finest restaurants are cooking with all natural ingredients, organic vegetables and cage-free organic chicken. The way of the future is less is more, and purity is better— beauty in simplicity.

We are regressing to a simpler way of life because of this nostalgia we carry of wanting to feel those purest forms of pleasure—our mother's comfort, care and love. We crave this feeling and retire to small villages with no pollution, trash on the streets, or electric cables hanging everywhere. We want to go back to the very beginning.

But simplicity isn't the same as *being* simple. Being simple means that you don't know any better. Simplicity comes from a long line of efforts. The French are great at dressing down and still looking fabulous only because they know what it's like to dress *up*. Simplicity is about making something look so effortless. As with learning how to master an instrument, you must put in hours of practice to make playing look so easy. Ballerinas who move so gracefully that their gestures look simple enough for anyone to do are masking the physical pain and strain it takes to pull off these moves. If you ever have the chance to see a ballerina come offstage after a performance, you'll see her immediately collapse to the floor, heart racing and chest pulsing up and down as a layer of sweat begins to cover her body. Her beauty looked simple, but it took a lot of work.

> *"Simplicity is the ultimate sophistication."*
>
> —Leonardo da Vinci

The greatest pleasures come from the simple things in life: a smile, dinner with friends, receiving flowers, strolling through the forest or watching the stars. While the reptilian seeks immediate gratification, the cortex seeks out greater pleasures. So you don't drink wine because you're thirsty or to get drunk, you choose good wine for the art of tasting it with all your senses: smelling it, admiring its colors, observing its texture as it slides off the glass, and of course, the nuances of its taste.

The Satellite Tribe is expert at finding refined pleasure in different cultures around the world. In France, the expressions "*l'art de vivre*" (the art of living) or "*la joie de vivre*" (the joy of living) embrace taking pleasure in even the most mundane aspects of life. It's not just about survival, getting by through mere eating, drinking, sleeping and having sex. It's about learning how to take pleasure in the beauty of life, appreciating the simple pleasures. It is a philosophy of life that doesn't require money or other resources.

When it comes to fashion, Frenchwomen take beauty in simplicity very seriously. A Frenchwoman will combine pieces from her closet that she has collected over the years that are both classic and eccentric. When she steps out of her home she looks fabulous, effortlessly chic, but in reality she put a lot of thought into her outfit. Before she walks out the door, she takes one last glance in the mirror, and by rule, she must take off one accessory piece. Too many accessories imply that she is trying too hard. She is accomplishing simplicity after hard work and years of learning how to combine clothing pieces.

Japanese culture has always embraced the concept of refinement, heightening pleasure by seeking greater quality over quantity and fostering a culture of patience. Japan's Muromachi Period between 1337 and 1573 marked a new cultural and artistic era whereby new forms of literature, art, architecture and rituals arose, including *chadō,* the Japanese tea ceremony. In Western culture, tea is just another beverage. We buy it in boxes from the supermarket or order it at Starbucks, sweetened with sugar substitutes. But for Japanese culture, tea was considered a luxury. Originally tea was used for religious purposes in Buddhist temples; Japanese culture began to embrace the ritualistic pleasure acquired from the tea ritual during the Muromachi Period. The art of preparing and drinking tea became a status symbol and an indicator of refinement. The royal court would organize tea-tasting parties and set up special sites for conducting the tea ceremony. Tea was much more than a simple drink; it was an art and a lesson in the values of patience, harmony and peace. The sophistication of pleasure elevates the ordinary to the extraordinary.

"Tea with us became more than an idealization of the form of drinking; it is a religion of the art of life . . . Teaism was Taoism in disguise."

—Okakura Kakuzo

The same framework applies to human sexuality. For example, many people still assume that the *Kama Sutra* is merely a sex book detailing exotic sex positions. But in reality, the *Kama Sutra's* objective was much more sophisticated. Intended to be a guide on how we can live more fulfilled and virtuous lives when it comes to family, love, work and sex, it's about seeking the highest levels of gratification in a virtuous and honorable manner. It's about the art of sensuality, desire and pleasure.

Different cultures deal with reptilian needs like sex, eating and sleeping in different ways. But the ones that are more on-code are the ones that are concerned with seeking a more refined quality in simple pleasure rather than opting for immediate gratification that leaves little room for experiencing true and more meaningful pleasure.

TWO TYPES OF SIMPLICITY

There are two types of simplicity: Simple Dumb and Simple Einstein. Simple Dumb is being plain and uncreative, not making an effort to actualize yourself and open your mind to new possibilities. It's the fear of branching out and trying new things. Simple Dumb is a world void of imagination that stays within the confines of the comfort zone: people remaining simple because they just don't know any better and really don't *want* to know any better.

Simple Einstein is about working so hard, learning so much, and reaching such a level of complexity that you eventually make it effortless. Albert Einstein, a math genius, had a mind able to conceive of complexities the average person could not even begin to comprehend. But even in his world of intricacies and elaborate constructions, he narrowed his preeminent discovery down to a simple equation: $E = mc^2$. From someone as smart as Einstein, most would have expected a book-long equation, but he surprised the world with his principle of simplicity: "Everything should be made as simple as possible. But not simpler," he said.

Zen Buddhism is another form of Simple Einstein. Before you can reach a state of peace, you need to expend effort on reflection and meditation. You cannot simply jump all the work and reach serenity. It takes time, self-reflection, patience and practice to train the mind to reach an elevated state of consciousness. Once you reach nirvana in Zen Buddhism, you are able to experience the divine stillness of the mind that is, in essence, the mind in its purest and simplest state.

"See simplicity in the complicated, seek greatness in small things. In the Universe, the difficult things are done as if they were easy."

—Lao Tzu

Pleasure is about reaching a higher level of sophistication. It's about moving past the basic demands of the reptilian and using the cortex to celebrate the simple pleasures of life. If you are starving, you are likely to eat anything in order to satisfy your hunger. But if you plan ahead, think with your cortex, and delay your desire for immediate satisfaction, then you can move past the reptilian talking inside your head and choose to eat something you will truly enjoy.

The Satellite Tribe has an abundance of choices because they expose themselves to a variety of lifestyles, so they are much more apt to choose elevating their pleasure over accepting the first option available. They can analyze their options, weigh them, and choose what gives them the greatest amount of pleasure. If we want to move forward as an interconnected global community and make the best decisions for our future, we must learn from the Satellite Tribe about how they view concepts like pleasure and how much they value delay and simplicity.

A MEANS TO AN END?

The various cultures we have studied all have their unique relationship with pleasure. Of course, they all share the same basic reptilian, animalistic, and instinctive forces. But they manifest in different ways. In America, for instance, people are prone to eating large quantities of food as fast as possible when it is available, as if somebody else were about to come along to steal it from them (see fast food and buffet dining)—the main purpose being to fill up the tank, and to feel sated.

On the contrary, the Japanese have very subtle rituals, such as when preparing sushi. For them, the aesthetics of food is definitely part of the pleasure. The French have "le trou Normand," a shot of Calvados to clear your palate to better enjoy the next dish.

Each culture has a goal, an unconscious goal, which reveals that culture's priorities. For Americans the goal is money; for the British it is social stature; for the Germans it is order. But for the French it is pleasure. So the French have discovered many ways to enhance their pleasure and created many rituals to this effect. For this reason, French gastronomy has been designated by UNESCO as part of the Intangible Cultural Heritage of Humanity, which is to be preserved and protected. From fine wines to gourmet cheese, if you wish to attain the highest pleasure, you have to follow the rituals.

RITUALS OF PLEASURE

Another piece of the Global Code for pleasure is *ritual*. At the reptilian, animalistic level, you just eat. For the sophisticated Satellite Tribe, however, "eat" is a vulgar word. Animals eat; we have lunch, dinner or supper; we savor and appreciate the subtlety and gradual intensity of taste. The purpose is not to fill up the tank but to experience the highest pleasure.

Take wine, for example. If you are thirsty, drink water. Before drinking a fine wine, you have to prepare your palate, so you must eat something . . . but not just anything. For certain wine you might want to have a specific cheese, or a certain type of bread. In some cases, the wine has to be brought to life, especially if it is a 10- or 20-year-old bottle. In this case you should use a decanter to oxygenate the wine (it has to breathe), as well as a candle to check for any residue.

Certain wines have to be drunk at room temperature, others might need to be chilled, but you never put ice in your wine (only Americans do that!). The first instance of pleasure comes by looking at the wine. Look at the robe, the legs (*la jambe*), the thighs of the wine, the color. Of course, the French use similar language to appreciate the beauty of a woman as they do to describe a fine wine. And the metaphor does not stop there, as the smell of the wine is also to be enjoyed; the word *bouquet,* used to describe a flower arrangement, is also used to describe the characteristics of a wine.

Part of the ritual might include cupping your hands around the glass, which was specifically chosen to hold the wine you are about *savor* ("drinking" is what animals do). The purpose of this gesture is not just to show your affection for the beautiful wine but also to check the temperature and perhaps to slightly warm the wine up, as usually the cellar temperature is a little cold. This also has the function of bringing out the flavor, opening it up and releasing the subtlety of the wine. "This 15-year-old bottle," said a 66-year-old Parisian wine aficionado, "is like Sleeping Beauty. You have to slowly bring her back to life, warm her up. This is like foreplay."

The next step of the ritual is to slowly swirl the wine in the glass using a very gentle motion, in order to stir it and further oxygenate it. Then you smell the wine, putting most of your nose in the glass. Only once these steps have been completed might you consider taking a small sip and swishing it in your mouth, in order to stimulate all your sensitive papillae. Remember you're not *drinking* the wine, you're *savoring* it, so much so that it might even look as though you are savoring a steak (your mouth moves as if you were chewing the wine). Only after this might you consider swallowing it, which is optional.

Enjoying cheese is another pleasure that is enhanced by ritual. *"Du pain, du vin, et du boursin"* (bread, wine and boursin) was a famous slogan for a popular French brand of cheese. It suggests that you cannot appreciate and enjoy the pleasure provided by the cheese you are going to eat without having the appropriate bread and wine. Goat cheese does not go with the same wine as Camembert. But when you have a cheese board/platter, the order of consumption is crucial. You have to start with the mildest cheese and move up in terms of intensity of taste. You might start with a Brie and end up with the Bleu d'Auvergne. If you do the opposite you might not appreciate the mildest one at the end. Once again, the ritual is there to enhance your pleasure.

In the same vein, in France you are not supposed to start with a salad as is customary in the United States. Why? Because the salad dressing usually has vinegar (from the Latin *vyn egre,* meaning sour wine), which kills the taste of wine. So if you start with a salad, you cannot enjoy wine with the rest of your meal. Of course, Americans might have Coke or coffee with their dinner. So they might not care. But for the pleasure-minded French, that departure from pleasurable ritual is not just a mistake; it is a tragedy.

PLEASURE IQ

We all know about measuring intelligence; we call it IQ. We even have associations or clubs where only those with the highest IQs can join, like

Mensa. In the 1990s, psychologist Daniel Goleman described another form of intelligence called emotional intelligence. Very intelligent people are sometimes emotionally incompetent and disturbed. It is clear that knowing too much might be a source of anxiety and instability, making your relationship with others very difficult. Likewise, most paranoiacs are usually highly intelligent. But very few people have developed their *pleasure intelligence*—the art of mastering pleasure rituals to attain higher levels of enjoyment and appreciation.

FREE FROM CULTURAL DOS AND DON'TS

Every day, the Satellite Tribe experiences the *relativity* of norms, mores, and taboos, which they do not necessarily follow based on culture or religion. Constantly benchmarking the world, the tribe members follow their own judgment and pleasure principles. They can choose where to be and constantly move from one pleasure to another. They have an unconscious mental scale of what brings them the greatest pleasure; they know the *rituals* that deliver what they want.

> "I like my champagne very cold, and always in a chilled glass. I only want half of a glass, so that it does not have time to get warm. I drink it and then get another half glass, still cold."—a 65-year-old man, Los Angeles

> "I want the best in a spa. When they give me a massage in Shanghai, at the Peninsula, they put a bowl of hot steaming water below the table, close to my face, so I can breathe the lavender that they put in it. It opens my nostrils and I can breathe better, it is very relaxing. Once you have experienced it you want it all the time. The other day, in Beijing, they did not even know about this. I was disappointed."—a 28-year-old woman, Hong Kong

THE SPA OF PLEASURE

A massage is a massage. Right? No, it can be an incredible pleasure or a bad experience. Everything will depend on your expectations. The Global

Tribe keep raising the bar, and its members know what is the best. They expect it and want it. The lighting, the music, the perfumed steam, the special body oil, the green tea, the special room to relax after, the service—every element of this experience is there to enhance your pleasure.

Being touched is very reptilian. Being cared for with special attention is very limbic (emotional), the purpose being to relax your body and your mind. Finally, at the cortex level, you have the best intellectual alibi that you could imagine to justify getting a massage, which is that a massage is the best way to deal with stress and jet lag. If you are relaxed and in good shape you will be more efficient.

Detox is a magic word. You need to detox your body and your mind. Once you have a clear reptilian pleasure, in a perfect emotional experience, it is easy to find the right intellectual alibi. The purpose of the intellectual alibi is to give you a good reason to do what you are going to do anyway, and a good alibi will liberate you and increase your perception of pleasure. Just as with luxuries where we sometimes need "permission to buy" certain things, we also need to give ourselves "permission to enjoy" things.

LESS SEX, MORE FOOD

Sex is a delicate subject, associated with so many taboos. But it is also one of the most fascinating subjects, the foundation of life and the survival of our species. Many cultures control, regulate and repress this fundamental reptilian imperative. Some even feel it should be reserved solely for reproductive purposes. Some cultures practice female castration, whereas others believe that female pleasure is good because it increases fertility. On one hand we have the *Kama Sutra*, which praises sexuality, and on the other, we have puritans preaching abstinence. Cultural restrictions about sex are a clear indicator that some cultures are still afraid of their basic reptilian instincts, even if today the biological consequences of sex (and therefore reproduction) can be controlled. Sex is still perceived in many cultures as "dangerous" even if the actual dangers are not fully articulated. So we formulate cortex-driven excuses to avoid sex. "I need to know you better" is a typical argument provided by the inhibiting and controlling cortex brain. It resembles the "Just Say No" advertising campaign promoted by Nancy

Reagan to attempt to reduce drug use and the abstinence campaign to reduce teenage pregnancy—needless to say, one whose efficacy was highly debatable.

"If sex was available like McDonald's, everywhere and at the same price, we would have less violence and less obesity."—a 22-year-old male, East Los Angeles

"Food is safe sex, so why bother with sex?" writes a 19-year-old female from East Los Angeles. The result of this relationship between food, sex and pleasure in America results in incredibly high obesity rates in adults. Instead of "make love, not war," I think America needs the slogan, "more sex, less food." But the biological difference is too obvious to neglect. Many women told us in America that "food is safe sex," and many men claim that they never get enough sex.

TALENT

If the purpose of the Satellite Tribe is to follow the *pleasure principle* and to bring instinctive reptilian needs to a higher level of sophistication, what is the result? What is the Global Code for pleasure that fits all cultures?

The French code for pleasure is the *talent* to create rituals.

Sex and food, for instance, are animal urges that can also be elevated to the level of art. But art is not just technique, recipes, and knowledge; art requires talent, and that is where the difference lies. The Satellite Tribe is always looking for talent. "It is not what you have, it is what you do with what you have," wrote a 65-year-old female participant in Paris.

Talent implies intention, focus, refinement, sophistication and ritual in the pursuit of higher pleasure; and it is hard work to get there. Before you can play the violin like Yehudi Menuhin, you need to practice and practice and practice. But even if you acquire all the technique possible, only talent can help you reach a higher level of pleasure.

Pleasure is associated with beauty, and talent is the pleasure of creating beauty. Creating each moment of your life as if it were an *oeuvre d'art*. What the Satellite Tribe taught me is that *intention* is the key. Pleasure is not simple or casual. It requires attention to detail, the wherewithal to combine everything that you have to attain a higher pleasure.

For the Satellite Tribe, pleasure is derived from the combination of multiple talents. Music, culinary artistry, decorative flair, artfulness and sex. It is about creating everlasting *moments of eternity* that transcend time and space.

"We are so mobilized by everyday chores and routines, that we do not take time for pleasure, *real* pleasure," explained a 44-year-old woman in Rio de Janeiro. "But when we do, when we forget about the cell phone and the tablet, and can combine the perfect environment with the perfect partner, we experience what I call a 'moment of eternity.' It is like entering another dimension." I think the whole world can agree with that.

In the past three chapters I have insisted on the Global Codes for beauty, luxury and pleasure, as they in many ways define the basic standard of success. But of course there are plenty of possible, individual variations. Beauty is in the eye of the beholder, as the old adage goes. My pleasure might not be your pleasure, and luxury for me is a cup of coffee on the beach.

The reptilian brain teaches us that pleasure won't protect you from pain. You might be on the beach drinking a margarita and enjoying a beautiful sunset when a suicide bomber attacks your hotel and brings a lot of pain.

The Satellite Tribe knows that to enjoy the best you must always be prepared for the worst. One common element that unifies all of the inhabitants of this planet in their thirst for pleasure and survival is the increased awareness of common enemies who might not just destroy their pleasure but end their lives.

It is time now to explore the more collective dimension of the Global Code. Common enemies are becoming more and more powerful, forcing us to adapt and change to survive. Meanwhile, new technology has created a new generation of Millennials who almost seem to be another species altogether. How will the Global Code dictate the future of our planet?

PART THREE

GLOBAL CODES

SEVEN

THE GLOBAL CODE FOR SURVIVAL

The Satellite Tribe has a better chance of survival than the sedentary masses when common enemies strike. Because they are in constant movement, hyper-connected and permanently informed, they might choose to avoid certain parts of Africa because of Ebola, and certain parts of the Middle East because of Islamic terrorist threats.

The reptilian brain's program is about survival and reproduction, which is the survival of the species. So far we have 7 billion people on this planet, and it looks like the program works. But other species have flourished and then disappeared. Are we like the dinosaurs, destined one day to vanish and be replaced by aliens or robots?

For the first time in the history of this planet as we have known it, we have a species—humans—that possesses the power to change, transform and destroy this world. This is the age of the Anthropocene. Everybody has heard of weapons of mass destruction, terrorists, atomic bombs, biological warfare, global warming, pollution, desertification, overpopulation, etc. Many have predicted the end of the human species. Science fiction has enjoyed many a blockbuster success with its perpetual warnings of doomsday just ahead.

But so far, humans have managed to survive. The Satellite Tribe, thanks to its perpetual circling of the globe, has become well aware of common enemies and the danger they represent. Satellite Tribe nomads benefit from an aerial view of where our planet is headed.

Some years ago, I had the opportunity to implement some of my research methodology for a very exciting client. NASA contacted me because they wanted to know why the American people were no longer passionate about the space program, a disinterest that was having a direct impact on their funding, which depended on the public's support. I conducted imprinting sessions all over America and invited an astronaut to attend one of the sessions. And this is what he told us:

> I was over there in space, on my way to the moon. Then I looked backward and suddenly saw planet Earth. It looked so small, isolated, almost lost in the universe. I had a big moment of illumination—this is *home,* this is the only home we have, this is my home. It is precious, has an incredible value, [and] we should all pull together, forget about our differences—race, religion gender, politics—and fight to preserve it. This little ball in space needs our protection.

We know that too many generals are still fighting the last war. For example, one terrorist had a bomb in his shoe, and for years to come we must take off our shoes when we check in to a flight even though the next terrorist is going to take us by surprise again. The 9/11 attack did not result from lack of intelligence or military power but rather a lack of imagination. Nobody in Hollywood would have been able to come up with this scenario. Such a small investment: 12 airline tickets, and such incredible destruction. Think about the incredible return on investment. We spend billions of dollars to create the most sophisticated weapons, they spend a few thousand just to buy tickets and use our own airplanes as weapons, and they beat us. Is our problem lack of intelligence, of determination, of imagination, of anticipation?

We know the problem once we see it. But it is usually too late. So how can the Satellite Tribe change that?

If we take that astronaut's view of our planet, we realize that if we have the power to destroy it, we might also have the power to protect it, enhance it, and transform it for the better. If our main simple goal is to create a better world for our children, what is the model?

The first thing we have to do is identify our enemies, to name them. Then develop a strategy, a plan and tactic. Finally, we have to take action.

THREATS TO SURVIVAL

The Global Code for survival is *common enemies*. And the key elements to survival are awareness, anticipation and preparation. The Swiss are always prepared, so let's look to them first in identifying our common enemies. Here are a few of the larger common enemies to global survival.

Natural Disasters

Natural disasters kill people without distinguishing between races, religions, ages or political affiliations. Solidarity, of the kind we witnessed after the 2004 Indian Ocean tsunami killed hundreds of thousands of people, is not enough. We need to anticipate and be prepared for such events. Thinking about San Francisco, the question is not "Are we going to have another earthquake?" but rather, "When is the next earthquake going to strike?" The key to survival here is to educate and train people to manage under these terrible circumstances.

Pandemics

Ebola began in Africa but also managed to affect the rest of the planet. The real problem is going to be how to deal with the next global pandemic, the one we are not prepared for, the one we are not even aware of yet. Nowadays, some of the old, supposedly "eradicated" diseases are making a comeback (e.g., tuberculosis). We now live in a different world, where people travel more freely around the globe. This mobility poses a new kind of threat, especially when you consider diseases with long incubation times such as Ebola. To compound this complication, there are many ethics issues that come into play when considering such protocols as quarantining and passenger screening.

Viruses fly first class, and we need to be prepared. The danger does not come from what we know—like Ebola—but from what we don't know.

Terrorism

Terrorism is unacceptable and cannot be excused. Mothers who send their own children to kill innocent victims with bombs strapped around their chests should be ashamed, as should the teachers, imams, extremists, apologetics and preachers who try to justify the killing.

A 19-year-old female student from Istanbul told me, "It is not the religion, it is the preachers who indoctrinate poor lost souls to become martyrs. This is just a license to kill; it is a 'victim's' alibi and a false promise of a better after-life."

"Twenty-six virgins waiting for you in heaven? Come on!" said a 20-year-old male student from Istanbul.

Bureaucracy

Although less headline-grabbing, bureaucracy is a serious common enemy; in fact, it can best be described as "total power given to total idiots." When given any kind of power, individuals who perceive themselves as mid- or lower level sometimes behave in a very authoritarian way, seeming to enjoy using their power to abuse others, especially those whom they perceive as superiors.

Bureaucrats use regulations as a way to cover their backsides, to get power, and to immobilize everything. By adding steps, bureaucrats become a common enemy; they delay solutions and encourage procrastination. Think about politicians in Washington, who have managed to produce a tax code so complicated not even the IRS can explain it to you. Or an even better example, the bureaucrats in Midway, Georgia, who shut down some little girls' lemonade stand because they did not have a permit.

France has more bureaucrats than wealth producers. One French author, Corinne Maier, even wrote a bestseller on this topic called *Bonjour Paresse* (Hello Laziness), or "how to pretend you are working and not doing anything." A humorous critique of French culture, it expounds on the theme of getting away with not actually doing any work. The author lived as a full-time bureaucrat employed by the French government in her early years. She obviously was an expert and had all of the credentials.

Weapons of Mass Destruction

Many—too many—nuclear devices are sleeping in too many places where they are not being watched by responsible people. Terrifying scenarios of nuclear holocaust have long permeated Hollywood movies. When former president of Iran Mahmoud Ahmadinejad says he wants to destroy Israel and is simultaneously building an atomic bomb, we have reason to be concerned. Can you imagine what Kim Jong-un might do when he has one? So we have more and more crazy people with the tools to destroy the planet and we appear to be getting weaker and weaker. This dangerous situation should be enough to motivate people to overcome their differences and to copy the Swiss model of preparation and collaboration, which we will explore presently.

Genocide

After the Holocaust the world said "never again." But tribal warfare in Africa has killed millions. The future of Africa depends on the model they try to emulate. North Korea or Switzerland? Mexico or Singapore? The Chinese are all over Africa already, but not to promote their culture—just to get the natural resources that they desperately need. We have interviewed several members of the Satellite Tribe in Africa. Slowly, a large middle class is emerging, but the road ahead is full of minefields. One interviewee, a 17-year-old male student, from Johannesburg, said, "South Africa is different. We were pariahs because of apartheid, but look at what is happening in Zimbabwe, or Congo. Nobody says anything, nobody does anything. I wish I could go to America."

Illiteracy

Illiteracy may not be as spectacular an enemy as most of the other common enemies described here, but it is one nonetheless. I'm referring to those people who are being kept from learning how to read and write. Being educated is perceived as a danger by many Islamist tribes; the Taliban, for instance, have killed children attending schools in Pakistan and girls who want to learn how to read. This is a real outrage, and without a doubt a common enemy. Burning books has never been a good sign of progress, and neither has keeping girls away from knowledge and schools.

RETURN TO THE DARK AGES

The work we have done around the world made us aware of strong opposing forces that are shaping our planet today. On one side we have modernity, and the fairly recent rise of hundreds of millions of people out of poverty. But paradoxically, the incredible speed and acceleration of technological change has also created a very strong resistance to modernity in some quarters. When people are lost, they want to go back home. Virtually everyone might have a cell phone today, but that doesn't mean they all embrace what it represents.

Many political and religious groups are afraid of modernity and technology; some preach a return to Sharia law, to isolation, and to a rejection of Western values. Some have started to kill those who disagree. Such people are also a common enemy. Beyond the direct threat they pose, they encourage a dangerous cleaving of the world.

Meanwhile, members of the Satellite Tribe are, on the contrary, *early* adopters—people who are ahead of their time and have access to the most advanced technology. Because of the exponentially growing rate of change, the distance between the Satellite Tribe and the sedentary "little people," as Confucius says, is widening. Despots who resist modernity are taking advantage of this chasm to keep their people in the dark.

The dark ages, or Middle Ages, were a time when wealthy people lived inside fortresses with drawbridges and private armies to protect them. It might surprise you that around the world some countries or cities are replicating this model.

One country, which has roots in several cultures, was born of the fundamental desire to survive. The Satellite Tribe knows that these people may represent the best tribal model for survival. Of course, I am speaking about Switzerland, also known as the Helvetic Confederation. We found that the Swiss model is always present in the Global Mind. Why?

Because the key verb to decode the Swiss mind is: *to worry.*

In 1291, three cantons got together—Schwyz, Uri and Nidwalden—in what came to be known as the Rütli Meadow Oath. They were all tired of being regularly invaded by their neighbors, the Austrian Counts of Hapsburg. They decided, on this occasion, that despite their differences they would help defend each other against violence and injustice.

We know that the Satellite Tribe loves Switzerland. Not only because it is a place to put their money, but also because Switzerland is the best personification of the Global Code for survival. Their natural disposition is to worry so much that they are always over-anticipating potential dangers. The Swiss increase their chances of survival with a simple-to-understand strategy: be prepared.

BE PREPARED

The Swiss have developed a keen ability to detect danger before anybody else; they believe that only the paranoid survive. For that reason they require by law that every new house must have an atomic bomb shelter with three weeks' supply of food and water. They want to be prepared, in order to survive.

It's why nearly every able-bodied man and woman of a certain age is trained and enlisted in the military. They all keep guns and ammunition at home. They are ready to fight—prepared—just in case the Austrians want to come back. Of course, today there is very little chance that Austria would invade Switzerland, and the country itself pointedly remains neutral in any conflict that threatens to draw it in. But when Vladimir Putin invaded Crimea, the Swiss said: "You see, always be prepared. You never know. You have to make it too costly to invade, too risky." The Swiss, like the Israelis, have a citizen army. In five minutes they can have half a million soldiers ready to fight. The roughly 1.5 million military-grade weapons in Swiss households are at hand for defending some 8 million citizens. The Swiss Army knife is the perfect symbol of this mind-set.

I remember one day, I was driving on the highway in Switzerland, when out of nowhere, the Swiss police appeared and stopped the traffic. As you know, you are not supposed to argue with the police in Switzerland. Even the Germans are afraid of the Swiss police. So I obeyed. All of a sudden, the "mountain" by the side of the road opened up to reveal a huge hangar, out of which a brand-new military jet fighter emerged and taxied to the highway. It took off using the highway as a runway. Then the hangar disappeared, the police signaled, and I resumed my journey. The Swiss are ready for anything.

The Satellite Tribe feels safe in Switzerland. They love to send their children to schools and universities in Switzerland and to have one of their multiple homes in Gstaad, Verbier or St. Moritz. They all like to go to the World Economic Forum in Davos to be together, with the alibi of trying to make the planet safer.

For them, Switzerland is the ultimate replenishing hub. The Swiss have managed not to be invaded for centuries. It's country as fortress—hence, one of the Satellite Tribe's favorite Plan B's.

If we want to go further in understanding how the Satellite Tribe, following the Swiss model, has a chance to help this planet to survive, we might want to listen to them.

> "We cannot trust the politicians. They only think short-term—as far as the next elections. They have to please the masses to be reelected, and the masses are like children, they believe in Santa Claus and don't want to make any efforts."—a 65-year-old male banker, Davos

> "This planet is getting less and less secure. Think about earthquakes, volcanoes, terrorist madness, Islamist invasion, nuclear weapons proliferation, and tsunamis, to name a few. Are we prepared?—a 42-year-old female marketing executive, Verbier

> "We are all in the same boat; It does not matter where you are, how rich you are, how educated you are. You and your children are still in danger."—A 35-year-old mother of three, Geneva

We know what the Global Code for mother is. It is a very reptilian code common to all mothers, whatever their culture. The code is *total paranoia.*

Mothers know that one second of inattention can be fatal. The maternal reptilian brain does not need any training. It's characterized by immediate, instinctive reflex. In this sense, the Swiss disposition is very maternal: always worrying, over-prepared.

This model appeals to the Satellite Tribe. Because of their permanent movement and position above the clouds, they can predict and anticipate better than most. They are not afraid of profiling; they know how the Israelis managed to survive for more than 60 years, how they've endured several wars and the constant threat from neighbors who want their destruction. They anticipate. Americans are, by contrast, not good at anticipation. We are the sleeping giant. We need Pearl Harbor to wake up the dormant Superman in us. Then we fight and go back to sleep. But the common enemies never sleep.

Humans are born unfinished. A little foal can survive by itself very quickly, but we humans need years of attention from the previous generation to survive. Without a mother, or a mother substitute, we have very little chance.

Terrorists know that we are weak. Free speech laws in England allow extremists to recruit and convert young people and to send them to the Middle East to kill innocent people as suicide bombers. Imams preaching the end of England, the end of free speech and the triumph of Sharia law (which calls for stoning adulterous women and other such incomprehensible punishments) are allowed to express their views because England respects their freedoms. Such is the price we pay for upholding Enlightenment values.

The Satellite Tribe is aware of these global dangers. They are telling us to be prepared, to collaborate, to pull our resources together, and to forget about our differences. The Swiss model—with its four official languages, many different cultures and a tough, mountainous environment—is a good example of what can be accomplished when people pull together and set their differences aside. If the Swiss have survived 800 years in the middle of European wars, perhaps the bunker mentality sometimes is the best. But their way has also hindered them in promoting change and adaptability. Switzerland is a refuge. It is not the cutting edge. So who in the world could give us some clues of what should be the Global Code for adaptability?

One special country has had to go through many difficult times, but because they have never given up, they are stronger today. Let's look at how the Koreans are a model of adaptability.

EIGHT

THE GLOBAL CODE FOR ADAPTABILITY AND CHANGE

When I first visited Korea 20 years ago I immediately became aware of an odd but omnipresent phenomenon.

Whenever I visited a temple, information placards read "built in 1752, destroyed in 1785, rebuilt in 1820, destroyed in 1852, rebuilt in 1890" and so on. Everything had apparently been built and destroyed time and time again. But they always came back. I resolved to learn more about this fascinating aspect of the Korean culture. Because of its geographic location, Korea is a connector, a passage between India, China and Japan. Buddhism had to go through Korea in order to pass from India to Japan.

The Global Code for adaptability is *Weeble*. Advertising for the Weeble, a children's toy that became popular in the 1970s, used the slogan, "Weebles wobble, but they don't fall down," referring to the primary quality of the egg-shaped toy, which automatically corrects itself to a standing position, regardless of how it is handled. The best example of this incredible resilience is South Korea.

Rigidity is often a defense mechanism. The symbol of a wall is often very significant: It stops movement. Some cultures or nations choose to isolate themselves, like Japan in the eighteenth and nineteenth centuries (up until the Meiji era). The Berlin Wall had a purpose, which was to stop people from leaving. The wall between Mexico and the United States is to stop people from illegally entering the United States. Today, many cultures are still closed and difficult to penetrate, like Saudi Arabia; others have shown incredible adaptability.

America has the Comeback Kid archetype. This includes everyone from Nixon to Clinton in politics to Trump and Chrysler in business. In the American culture, you are supposed to always have a second chance, and a third. Celebrities are all famous for going down and coming back again. The American code for celebrities is *rehab*.

These terms have also become part of the Global Code for adaptability.

The Satellite Tribe is extremely adaptable. They just go to another place when they don't like where they are. But they can also change *themselves* very quickly, because they belong to several cultures, speak several languages, and have experienced several emotional systems. They have this Weeble capability. They are not stuck in one ideology or religion or one culture. They combine the two basic principles of adaptability: the ability to transform or change your environment, and the ability to change or transform yourself.

First, they never stay down. American culture has many aspects of this Weeble capability. Never take no for an answer, learn from your mistakes, always try again, never give up, be optimistic. The American culture always gives you a second chance and sometimes a *second* second chance. However, you should always forget the past. No blame game. Concentrate your next move on going up again.

For the past 50 years, I have heard the Europeans, and especially the French, constantly predict the end of America, especially after events such as the Vietnam War, the Kennedy assassination, the Nixon resignation, the Japanese buying Rockefeller Center, 9/11, China becoming the number one economy and all of the most recent economic crises. "Now they are done, decadent, finished" read the headlines, and every time, they are surprised to see Americans coming back again. Like the Weeble, America's natural tendency gravitates upward.

"I am 70 years old and made my first fortune in real estate," said a man from Houston, Texas. "Then I lost everything. I made my second fortune in oil, made the wrong move and lost everything again. OK, this is great; I am bankrupt so I have no choice. I am going to make it again."

Adaptability, recalculating, flexibility—a quality required for surviving in difficult situations.

The South Koreans have proven that they have most of these qualities in spades—and the right attitude.

Having been occupied by the Japanese for 35 years (1910–1945), they had to adapt to survive. They were forced to take Japanese names, to speak Japanese, and to adopt the Japanese culture. They had no choice other than to adapt, yet they never gave up their own culture. As soon as the Japanese were defeated and left, the Weeble just stood back up. They learned from the Japanese. Copied their quality control approach. Today Korean cars compete and sometimes beat the Japanese products. Being down was a temporary situation, one in which they learned as much as possible from their invaders. As soon as the Weeble could stand back up, they were successful again. The South Korean economy is an incredible example of adaptability considering that the country is still at war with North Korea and permanently competing with two great powers—China and Japan.

The Korean culture has something in common with the Satellite Tribe. They share a multicultural mind. Like the Third Culture Kids, they are a 3K culture. Because of their location, they have been subject to many cultural influences coming from India, China and Japan. They also have been invaded many times, and each time learned something new. Korea is a hybrid culture. At an unconscious level, they have both German and Italian elements.

German because they like systems, processes and quality control. In this aspect, the Germans, Japanese and Koreans are very similar. Koreans also like Verdi and Puccini, Italian opera and design, and the Italian expression of emotion. Unlike the Germans or the Japanese, they are very emotional, and, like the Italians, the Korean mama is the center of the universe.

Student demonstrations in Korea are extremely noisy, violent, and intense. Politicians who disagree sometimes punch each other in the face in front of television cameras.

Korean expats will burst into tears when one of them sings "Arirang" (this is the equivalent of "La Vie en Rose" for the French). Mama, kimchi, "Arirang," and then they cry. Many members of the Satellite Tribe that we have met were originally Korean. Very few were Japanese. It is very difficult for Japanese people who have lived overseas to go back to Japan and re-adapt. The rigidity of the Japanese culture is such that the former expats have a very hard time reintegrating into the Japanese culture, and it is almost impossible for Japanese women to do so.

The lesson from Korea is clear. In many ways their culture has some American traits: never give up, try again and again, learn from your weaknesses and keep going. They are eager to learn, to understand world customers, to beat the Japanese at their own game. LG, a Korean company, asked us to discover the codes for home cleaning to help them sell their vacuum cleaners, washing machines and refrigerators in China, Russia, Spain and the Middle East. Many times what we discovered forced them to reconsider their whole positioning, their product design and their communication. They were open to change and not trying to justify what they had done in the past; they were ready to move on. Their adaptability had a fundamental rule, which is a key element of the Global Code: they prioritized the future, not the past. In many ways they were applying the GPS philosophy of re-calculating. Let's see how this technology permanently used by the Satellite Tribe is becoming the Global Code for adaptability and change.

CHANGE IS THE ONLY CONSTANT

Through our special quest to find the first experiences that were imprinted in people around the world, we explored imprinting regarding adaptability. We discovered two basic attitudes, summarized as the following: change the system or change yourself.

Change the system:
For the Germans, it is a question of engineering. They want to create the best system, as exemplified by the BMW slogan, "The ultimate driving machine." For the French, it is political. The prevailing attitude is one of: "Nothing can be done until we change everything."

Change yourself:
Americans largely believe that instead of changing the system, you have to change your attitude. Believe in yourself, and everything is possible. "Yes we can!!!"

For the Singaporean, this means hard work and high standards. But in both cases, adaptability means that you never stay down.

"I can't take it anymore! This so depressing. It does not look like the French are going to change their system; the bureaucrats are too powerful. I am leaving for London."—a 22-year-old male French business school student

"Practice, practice, practice. My mother wanted me to practice every day, but when I was 10, I was already very good, then I wanted to become the best."—a 24-year-old female Chinese violinist

"I've read all the books from Andrew Carnegie's rags-to-riches biography written by David Nasaw, to *Seven Habits of Highly Effective People* by Steven Covey, and *Unlimited Power* by Anthony Robbins. Self-confidence is key. You have to trust yourself, get the right attitude, and everything is possible."—a 24-year-old male American student, University of Texas, Austin

Edison failed a thousand times but never gave up. In the American culture, you learn from your mistakes, and improve all the time. This quote from Churchill illustrates how the rest of the world might perceive this relentless transformation: "You can always count on Americans to do the right thing—after they have tried everything else." When the Japanese make a mistake, on the other hand, they might kill themselves. The Japanese culture might be good at copying, improving, but not so good at "wobbling."

The Satellite Tribe is extremely good at wobbling; they are the archetype of adaptation, moving so quickly that they always go where the conditions are the best. It's their way of changing the system: move to a better system. But they are also good at transforming themselves all of the time. The Third Culture Kids are also sometimes called Chameleon Kids. They change color with the environment. "In Rome, do as the Romans do" is their motto. Because they have multicultural literacy and experience, they are the opposite of rigid. They can adapt to any environment.

After all, they feel, it takes too much time to change a culture. It is faster to change cultures—to move. We believe that technology *is* the new philosophy. It structures the way we think and function. A new supersonic business jet, the Aerion AS2, will soon allow us to go from Paris to New York for lunch and back the same day, just like when the Concorde was still running. This will truly change our whole perception of time and space. But how is the new technology preparing us to *change* in a personal sense? Changing our aspirations, our objectives, directions, dreams, values and priorities? Do we have a Global Code for *change*?

Following the Satellite Tribe around the world, we found it very clear that they had developed an incredible capacity for change.

RECALCULATING

The Global Code for change is *recalculating*. The GPS has changed how we go from one point to another: we don't use a map anymore; we just follow instructions. But how is this new technology shaping our minds and our attitudes toward *change*? What are the morals and values of the new Global Code? Let's explore.

Know Where You Are

"Know where you are" is rule number one. You need to know your exact location. Think of the wisdom behind this simple statement. You may want to move, to go somewhere else, to change your life, but before taking action you need an assessment. It could be a damage assessment, or an evaluation of your resources, or your emotional, intellectual and physical state. You need to know where and who you are.

You want to get an MBA, but where are you in your life journey? How much do you know, what is your experience in business, what are your expectations, how many resources do you have right *now*? This is the function of your personal GPS.

Know Where You Want to Go

Rule number two is: know where you want to go. You cannot just say "I want to go to New York"—you need to know exactly where; which city, which state, what zip code. Make up your mind before you start moving, and always know your destination.

In the American mind, action is salvation and procrastination a sin. But don't let that goad you into taking off before you're ready.

How many times have you heard people say that the journey *is* the destination? When I was teaching at Thomas Jefferson College in Michigan, one of my students gave me as a present a little jean vest with an embossed inscription that read "Keep on Trucking!" We know that at the reptilian level, life is movement, so we always want to keep moving. Sometimes, though, the GPS is slow, telling me that in 20 feet I should turn left when actually we are already at the street, so I keep going and miss it. I made a mistake. I should have turned left . . . maybe I was going too fast. Oops! This is where my GPS, despite her tone of voice, does not react as my mother. I don't have to say I am sorry. She does not blame me.

She does not even try to educate me; she simply suggests another way. The magic word is *recalculating*. In the globally connected present, your mistake is your new starting point.

No Blame Game

It is useless to say that you should have done this or that. What's done is done, and the past no longer exists, so whatever you did is irrelevant. You now have a new starting point, which is the present, your new reality. The blame game is over; let's keep moving. Of course most of us never really learn from experience and keep repeating the same mistakes, but it is a waste of time to blame yourself or others. You want to buy a house, but when you are finally ready, the house is gone, sold to somebody else. Of course you could wallow in regret: "I should have made my decision faster, I will never find another house like that, I'm cursed now!" However, the new GPS philosophy encourages us not to look backward. Life is in front of you; keep moving. Recalculating is such a fantastic word. Just make the next move.

Here is a classic conversation:

"The car's not starting!"
  "So?"
"Well, I need to go to the airport."

"So?"

"Maybe you did not close the door properly last night, and the battery went out."

"So?"

"OK, I will call a taxi."

This is recalculating. To know why the car does not start is not going to take you to the airport, but calling the taxi will.

Permanent Feedback

You always know where you are, and the GPS tells you in advance what is going to be your next move so that you are prepared. Two hundred yards, a hundred yards, ten yards, now turn. Can you think about managing your money this way? What about your life, or your children's education? It is like having a dashboard that gives you feedback in real time. Yet the most controversial and challenging element of this new philosophy is how it ends.

You Have Arrived

You have arrived at your destination . . . so the journey is over? I am not sure I like that; I am not sure I want to stop. I like to be on the road; I like to keep on moving. Now I realize that my first choice when I punched in my destination was in a way a sort of prediction of my future life. But the Satellite Tribe is always on the move, they never really "arrive." Water never really stops flowing, and the moon is never really still. Americans are permanent adolescents, always in search of their identity: "I am 70, and I still don't know what I am going to do when I grow up, because I never want to grow up."

To have arrived is akin to being done, having finished, being dead. However you choose to look at it, it marks the end of the journey. For the Satellite Tribe, on the other hand, the journey never ends. So we might need a new GPS for these Platinum Gypsies—one that would allow you to program several journeys in a row, with some tentative trips. It would include a program which would tell you where your friends were and what possibilities you have to plan visits. Instead of being told "you have arrived," the GPS voice should tell you "your new destination is . . ."

As we will see later, the GPS philosophy is also a useful one for higher education. In truth, your learning experience should never stop; you should always be on the move, learning and growing. If this new philosophy is our new global philosophy, we need global leaders on-code. So let's see what is the new Global Code for leadership.

NINE

THE GLOBAL CODE FOR LEADERSHIP

THE NEED FOR NEW LEADERSHIP MODELS

The emerging global culture requires new leaders and especially new *models* for global leadership. The old, hierarchical, traditional leadership models and roles do not work, as a glance at any news service—or city street—shows. Our current leaders are like generals always fighting last year's battles.

Yet a new model for global leadership is already taking shape, with different elements and best practices appearing in different cultures, different contexts. I have seen these, having worked with new leaders in governments and corporations, and I have helped develop some of the new leadership methods.

In the course of my research around the world, I have detected patterns, codes and best practices that can be applied to global leadership challenges, creating a template for the new global leader. The template is flexible, strong and able to face the myriad challenges and obstacles that global evolution must confront.

First we'll examine the elements that leaders must master to thrive in the global culture, and then we will identify the best practices and their culture of origin, practices that are central to effective leadership in the modern world.

THE AGENT OF CHANGE

What have we learned? "Keep moving, recalculating, do not look at the past. No blame game. It is not the group or class responsibility." But can you imagine applying those principles to a culture, a country or a nation?

Moses didn't look backward. He moved forward. "I have seen the promised land, follow me."

The pilot should know the destination. You need a flight plan before you are allowed to take off. But we have very few leaders like this.

Where is Moses when we need him?

When leaders are change agents, they should follow the GPS philosophy. When Vladimir Putin wants to return Russia to the ways of the Soviet Empire and blames the West for his problems, he is not a GPS leader. When Obama wants to blame the rich, fault the business world and increase redistribution, he is a leader looking backward. He does not lead change. Some leaders have changed the world. Moses, Lincoln, Churchill. The archetypal leaders are GPS leaders. They have seen the future. Some other leaders have even worked hard to change their own culture (Mustafa Kemal Atatürk and Sheik El Maktoum). Some have even created a new culture, like Lee Kuan Yew.

If planet Earth needs a new pilot, do we have a Global Code, a global archetypal model for moving this planet ahead and creating a better world for our children?

ON-CODE AND OFF-CODE LEADERS

First let's explore three modern leaders who are not on-code with the leadership that the planet needs: Presidents Obama, Putin and Hollande. Three failures in leadership.

First, Obama: a lot of words but no content. In this sense, he is a leader of the iPhone, new Millennial generation. When the planet needs a strong leader, Obama goes to play golf. He is the golfer-in-chief.

Putin presents the opposite picture. He shoots first and takes action. He invaded Ukraine, and since nobody moves, he keeps invading. When Obama objects, Putin's response is, "So, what are you going to do? Nothing? I will keep invading."

The worst of the modern leaders is definitely Monsieur Hollande. The Santa Claus leader. "Vote for me and you will get everything for free. Work less and you will get more. The rich, the bad, evil people will pay." Of course when people get killed, the masses rally behind their leader, whoever he or she is. Soon they go back to the reality of empty promises.

Obama famously said, "Yes, we can." We can what? If this is about improving conditions for African Americans, it looks like African Americans are worse off under Obama than under previous presidents.

Putin: "We will be an empire again." Yet, so many Russians want to leave the country. The economy is a disaster, and the sanctions against the "bully-in-chief" have had a devastating effect on the Russian people. Now Czar Putin has a very practical solution: cheap vodka.

Hollande: "Vote for me, I am Monsieur Normal. I have six known children, maybe more, from different women, but I have never been married. I put my favorite mistress at the Elysée Palace but leave at night on a scooter to visit my other younger mistress." Of course, all of this is considered normal. Although Hollande promised to reverse unemployment rates, Santa Claus did not deliver and more and more people are unemployed. The young, intelligent, French entrepreneurs are leaving for London and the United States. Monsieur Hollande refuses to look at where France is today. He refuses to have a clear indication of where he wants to go. He just does not apply the GPS philosophy, instead blaming Germany for all of the failures and problems that France is encountering.

Let's briefly review what makes these three non-GPS leaders so off-code when it comes to leadership.

Barack Obama

The code for U.S. president Barack Obama is *dreamer*. In his historic speech, Martin Luther King proclaimed, "I have a dream," and indeed this still holds true today . . . what he sought is still a dream. African Americans today are worse off under President Obama (an African American president) than they were under George W. Bush. The issue of illegal immigration still has no clear solution, and those who do immigrate to the United States call themselves the dreamers. Of course, if Obama is to be a dreamer, perhaps it is easy to get his attention, and maybe he will just close his eyes to what we call illegal immigration. So the dreamers are dreamers but they are still illegal.

Obama knows how to use the words that resonate with the American code. "Yes we can" and "Hope!" are two excellent examples. Nevertheless, he remains a dreamer who got a Nobel Peace Prize for doing nothing to promote peace. He even managed later on to get Osama bin Laden killed and send more troops to the Middle East. It is a cliché in the United States that liberal presidents who are supposedly against war always seem to be the ones starting them. Enemies of the United States seize their opportunities and attack when America is weak.

We know that when Obama states that he has drawn a line in the sand when speaking about the crisis in Syria, his convictions should be questioned. Indeed, when President Bashar al-Assad did cross that line, Obama simply shrugged it off and went to play golf in Florida instead.

Vladimir Putin

Let's explore another leader with another code, Vladimir Putin. The Global Code for Putin is *warrior*. In almost diametric opposition to the dreamer, who does nothing but dream, we have Putin, the warrior. When Obama spoke in Europe, people loved his speech. But they said, "This is a great speech, but I don't know what he spoke about." Obama is a great orator, but he has nothing to say besides clichés and stereotypes like the Nike slogan "Just do it" and "Hope!"

On the other hand, Putin is quite sparse with his words, but he acts. He is a warrior with a mission to re-establish Russia's greatness, to correct the big disaster that happened to Russia, which according to Putin was the dissolution of the Soviet Union. Putin sees this loss of territory as disastrous, and his mission is to reconquer the lost territory and re-create the Russian Empire. So, let's take Crimea—done! Let's take Ukraine! Kiev was once the capital of Russia, and so Putin used that as his divine right to attack Ukraine. What about Belarus, the Baltic states and Poland? Obama the dreamer is content with saying a few words after Russia's invasion of Crimea, and Putin the warrior invader couldn't have cared in the least.

François Hollande

The third leader I want to explore is even more abhorrent than the previous two; I'm of course speaking about Mr. François Hollande, France's current president. The Global Code for Hollande is the *séducteur* (seducer). Paris used to be the number one city for tourism, yet now this position has been taken over by London. France, at one point, was supposed to be the number one place for international companies whose executives wanted to enjoy the French *art de vivre,* but this recently has been lost to Holland, Ireland and Singapore.

There is one dimension where France is still number one. It is that of ridicule. France has a president who is the champion of ridiculousness. On the one hand, you have Obama who takes Air Force One to go play golf in Florida, and on the other, you have Putin who gets photographed barechested on a horse in order to build a personality cult.

Hollande fits the Don Juan archetype, the seducer. The definition of a Don Juan by Littré dictionary is the following: "A seducer, a man without morals and without conscience. He is pleasant in his manner but makes a game out of destroying women's reputations." Case in point: Hollande managed to destroy Valerie Trierweiler's reputation with all of his sneaking around, after he had promoted her to First Mistress (they were not married, so she could not be First Lady) and installed her at the Elysée Palace.

Here we have three leaders, three different styles and three different archetypes: the dreamer, the warrior and the seducer. The approval rating of the dreamer is one of the lowest of a second-term president in United States history, and his party lost many seats in the 2014 election. Thanks to his dreaming, the Republican Party got the biggest majority in both houses of Congress that they've had since 1928.

Hollande is a total disaster for France. He is again Mr. Three Percent (i.e., only three percent of the members of his own party are in favor of him). The warrior, on the other hand, receives incredible support from the Russian people and has never been so popular. With his media and public relations propaganda going full speed ahead, the frustrated Russians are all behind their leader; according to a Levada poll, his approval rating is around 86 percent.

Three leaders, three images: Obama playing golf, Putin shirtless on a horse and Hollande with his nocturnal scooter visits to see his mistress. None of these leaders are global leaders. What is the Global Code for leader? Winston Churchill, Angela Merkel, or Xi Jinping? England, Germany or China? What does it take to be a game-changing leader?

THE GLOBAL CODE FOR LEADERSHIP

According to Buckminster Fuller, planet Earth is the only spaceship without a pilot. Some leaders have changed the world, Moses, Churchill, Lincoln . . . they are archetypal leaders. Others have changed their cultures: Mustafa Kemal Atatürk, Lee Kuan Yew, Sheik Al Maktoum. The Anthropocene needs new leadership. Let's review three modern leaders and their legacies to see if their substance and style can teach us anything for the future.

Mustafa Kemal Atatürk

The first one I would like to mention is Mustafa Kemal Atatürk, or the "Father of the Turks." After rescuing his nation after the First World War, his vision was to create a modern Turkey, a more European one. He was a military man, but there are more pictures of him dressed in a tuxedo, an elegant symbol of European fashion, than of him in uniform. He tried to change the way that his people dressed, to change their mind-set to be more European than Muslim, more secular than religious. He may have succeeded in doing so in Istanbul, but he had a much harder time of it in Anatolia.

Turkey was supposed to become the global leader among the countries of the Middle East and the broader Islamic world, to serve as an incredible model combining democracy and Islam. But are Islam and democracy compatible? At its peak, the Ottoman Empire ruled a large part of the world, from Vienna to Africa. Today, however, while appealing mainly to the vote of the poor, less educated and religious majority in Turkey, President Recep Erdoğan and his party have proceeded to arrest and imprison

Kemalist generals and political opponents in attempts to reinstate the veil. The veil as a symbol for Islam has become incredibly politically charged in Turkey, a message that Mr. Erdoğan and his wife, Emine, openly reinforce.

Mustafa Kemal Atatürk may have saved Turkey from oblivion, but he failed to steer Turkey away from religious extremism and toward the modern world. As we learned, some Muslims are not just in support of the veil they stand against modernity and modernism.

Mohammed bin Rashid Al Maktoum

Another great creator of culture, this one slightly more successful than Atatürk, is Mohammed bin Rashid Al Maktoum of Dubai. The Global Code for Al Maktoum is *brand manager*. He presides like a CEO, and at the same time, a brand manager. He doesn't need to be elected; he doesn't need to have a group of politicians deciding the budget. He simply states things and they come into being. "I want the tallest building in the world, just do it, here is the money." And they do it! He doesn't have to manipulate voters. The results are stunning. Dubai is becoming the "World's Center," the number one hub not just of the Middle East but also in the rest of the world. Emirates is one of the best airlines in the world, and so many people are traveling through Dubai that London's Heathrow is going to give way to Dubai International as the world's busiest airport.

Dubai will be the global hub—the connector between East and West, passing through China, India, Africa and Europe. *La plaque tournante* of the global world is not New York, London or Paris; it is Dubai. All thanks to a new global leader who thinks less like a politician and more like a brand manager. Of course it helps that he does not have to worry about money right now, but at the same time, he needs to think long-term (i.e., past the time when oil runs out). Already Doha in Qatar, and Abu Dhabi and Dubai in the United Arab Emirates have a plan. Knowing that oil and gas will not last forever, they are banking on everything else: education, health, tourism, finance and so on. They want to attract all of the hubbers, members of the Satellite Tribe, and they are succeeding.

We saw that Atatürk's influence is waning with the direction that Turkey's democracy has taken. Turkey is a good example of the saying "one man, one vote, one time." That is, if radical Islamists who oppose democracy get democratically elected, then they can use their democratically elected authority to destroy the democratic process itself. On the other hand, we can see how an authoritarian leader who works as a manager and CEO, but whose priority is not to enforce an ideological or religious agenda, can succeed in creating the miracle that is Dubai in the middle of the desert.

Next I want to return to a leader who triumphed against all odds to create a successful nation in a completely different manner and under extremely different circumstances. This leader is of course Lee Kuan Yew, the first prime minister of Singapore.

Lee Kuan Yew

The Global Code for Lee Kuan Yew is *Mr. Clean*. In many ways his accomplishment, the Singaporean city-state, reflects a unique mix of Confucian philosophy and English predictability. Let's see what works; let's integrate our different heritages; let's combine the English common law system, Chinese Confucian philosophy (respect for hierarchy), Indian and Malaysian cultural strongpoints and expats from all around the world.

Today Singapore represents the world. The Chinese, the Indians, Malaysians, Europeans, Americans, Brazilians and Russians . . . they are all in Singapore. Why? As we saw in Chapter 2, starting out with nothing—no land, no oil, no gas, no natural resources and no money—Lee Kuan Yew has proven that you can create a culture of success that today is the envy of the world. Today Singapore has an unemployment rate of less than 2 percent. Perhaps Mr. Hollande should go for an internship in Singapore in order to learn a few lessons from their economic model. The country has one of the world's lowest corruption rates, so Mr. Narendra Modi, the prime minister of India, should also join Mr. Hollande in looking for an internship in Singapore. With one of the lowest tax rates and most business-friendly environments in the world, Singapore attracts investment from all over the world. (Mr. Obama, who has so often expressed his disapproval and contempt for the business world, should also join these two internship seekers.)

Some people who look at the accomplishment that is Singapore might try to argue that it is not a real democracy. But who is to say this system is any worse than an American-style democracy? We could also argue that even though American-style democracy might be good only for America (that is also debatable in and of itself!), it is not necessarily a good model for everyone. In fact, many nations reject it, as it goes against their own national beliefs and group identities.

So maybe in Singapore you're not allowed to chew gum (a rule which in reality is not at all strictly enforced), but you can go back home late at night without feeling at risk of being assaulted or mugged. A 19-year-old Singaporean woman who had visited Paris and spent time in San Francisco told us that she prefers to be in Singapore because "the trade-off is an obvious one." She said, "Would you rather not be able to chew gum, or risk being attacked at night when you go home?"

So we have three codes for leaders who tried to change the world. Atatürk, the game changer. Al Maktoum, the brand manager. And Lee Kuan Yew, the culture creator.

THE PERICLES PRESCRIPTION

"The age of Pericles resembled our own in the variety and disorder of its thought, and in the challenge that it offered to every standard and belief."

—Will Durant, *The Life of Greece*

Our ever-evolving moment requires new visionaries, people capable of embracing, understanding, and interpreting the enormity of information and change hoisted upon us daily. We need a new kind of leader.

Or maybe we need an *old* kind.

Considering Pericles

Twenty-five hundred years ago, Pericles changed Athens. In doing so, he also changed the world forever. What is most fascinating and most relevant to those of us considering the future two-and-a-half millennia hence is that Pericles did this not by forcing his will upon his city-state. Instead, he did it by inspiring the people of Athens to change by challenging their minds with new ideas and new models of thinking. He showed a new way, plotted a new course, and in doing so lifted Athens to heights that we still revere today. Though he died in 429 BC, Pericles is very much a flight instructor for our New Pilots.

Pericles navigated his city-state toward a specific destination—heightened greatness and the respect of the world—while attending to factors in constant flux. While the rate of change in ancient Athens would seem glacial compared to our times, new ideas were presenting themselves at a then unprecedented rate. Meanwhile, two key reptilian challenges left many Athenians dubious about survival: the constant threat of war and an extremely high level of poverty.

The essence of Pericles' greatness and the greatness of his vision was rooted in both his scrupulous honesty and his understanding that people need not only a strong, trustworthy leader but also a leader who can show how a different, better future can be created with their help, even in difficult times.

And indeed he was facing difficult times. There was the constant risk of invasion from Sparta, at the time Greece's most powerful city. There was a charged political atmosphere dividing Athens along conservative and democratic lines. There was disenfranchisement among the lower classes, leading to civic unrest and difficulties in the military.

Pericles' response to these challenges was unified and bold—he would provide more responsibility and participation to Athenians, and in so doing would provide them as well with a sense of their own worth. He would, in other words, extend the range of Athenian democracy and, through this, increase the breadth of Athenian accomplishment, making certain at every step that the Athenians understood that the programs he instituted were reflections of Athens's greatness, not his own.

The most dramatic of the programs Pericles instituted transformed the physical appearance of Athens, notably through the construction of magnificent buildings on the Acropolis. With the Parthenon and other structures, Pericles provided Athenians with visible, permanent proof of both the city-state's aspirations and its ability to achieve those aspirations. A great orator, Pericles understood that oratory alone can go only so far—a lesson that has been learned and relearned for millennia by skilled orators who, having acquired leadership roles, prove to be ineffective leaders.

Pericles knew that if he gave Athens a remarkable physical example through his ambitious construction effort, Athenians would receive constant reminders of their city's purpose and goals as exemplified in architecture. However, at the heart of Pericles' commitment of Athens to art and glory was his brilliance in linking that aesthetic commitment to a practical one: in order for the Parthenon and other edifices to be created, workers had to be hired and paid. While he served the limbic and cortex needs for beauty, he served the very reptilian need for food, clothing, and shelter. Through his efforts, fewer people were starving or worried about starving. Therefore, they could set their sights on thriving instead.

This was very much a conscious decision. "All kinds of enterprises should be created which will provide an inspiration for every art, find employment for every hand," he was recorded as saying. Thus he yoked the long-range (cortex) quest for grandeur and magnificence with the short-term (reptilian) needs of the people who would be employed to create them. He solved a philosophical challenge—how to inspire Athenians to greater pride and achievement—by also solving the pragmatic challenge of unemployment.

While the Parthenon and the physical transformation of Athens are the most striking and visual legacies of Pericles' leadership, it was his transformation of Athenian democracy itself that exerted the largest and most profound effect on the world. It is here that Pericles proves to be a true model for our New Pilots. He understood that the old models of government were no longer sustainable, and he strove to eschew the embedded interests of the privileged (and he was very much a member of the privileged class, having been born rich) for the sake of the future.

Upon assuming leadership, Pericles quickly set about enacting a number of reforms. He changed the judicial and administrative systems to extend the opportunity to serve the government to a far wider range of Athenian citizens. He dismantled much of the hereditary transfer of leadership. He instituted formal salaries for public servants at every level, including those serving on juries. These led to fundamental changes in the way Athens operated as a city, bringing it much more in line with the emerging mind-set of the day.

At the same time, Pericles inspired Athens to continue to think progressively, to continue to look forward rather than backward. He was one of the first Western leaders to champion the rights of women. He spoke out for freedom of speech and freedom to worship as one chose. He expanded programs in education, extolled the value of philosophy, and led an increased appreciation of the arts as a public resource.

Pericles' reforms and innovations were little short of radical; they went against the grain of common practices. He was creating a revolution, but a sublimely practical revolution that served at every step to invite citizen participation in the pursuit of Athenian greatness. He provided even the lowest of citizens with a sense of belonging to something larger than themselves. The result was an Athens transformed, and transformed in ways that we still respect and learn from today.

My First Visit with Pericles

I first encountered Pericles in school, and he has fascinated me ever since. I remember as a young student reading everything I could about the man and his leadership, philosophy, and practice, his wisdom and accomplishments. His thinking on the nature of effective democracy affected my own, and it has continued to influence me throughout my life.

When I first visited Athens many years ago, I was excited to see for myself the greatness that had been created as a result of Pericles' leadership. Yet the Athens I saw was filthy, the traffic horrible, the Acropolis crowded with loud tourists. With the ongoing crises that modern-day Greece experiences, it seems unlikely that such matters will improve until a group of Greeks with an entirely new mind-set leads the way.

This was a sad experience for me, a vivid reminder that even the greatest of civilizations persist into the future only if they constantly renew themselves, their pride, their commitment to participation and growth, their attendance to reptilian basics, and their cultivation of art and philosophy. The Parthenon today, magnificent but crumbling, a touristy attraction exploited as such, is an artifact of a great era long past. There is much to be learned from its example, and many of the lessons are cautionary tales. Great ideas must always be viewed through the prism of one's times. If those ideas aren't reconsidered and revised as the world revolves around them, those ideas become nothing but tourist attractions themselves.

Our Ancient Flight Instructor

In thinking about those who will lead us into the emerging global culture, I realized that Pericles serves as a model for this type of leadership. It is my opinion that Pericles would not have been intimidated by a world where borders are blurry, where cultures pool together, or where information is ubiquitous. He proved in his day that he had an uncanny ability to read his times and adapt accordingly. Meanwhile, he epitomized many of the traits essential to those who will guide us into the future.

For one, he held himself above corruption. In his day, Pericles had quite a few detractors, many who felt the sting of his political ambition, and many who questioned the direction in which he was taking Athens. However, if anyone believed him to be beholden to special interests or open to being swayed by favors, their criticism has not withstood the ages. Our New Pilots need to remain similarly aloof to the temptations of corruption, as those who seek to corrupt them will surely be working toward a personal agenda that will benefit a limited few and therefore be out of sync with the global culture.

Pericles also established his goals in truly inspired fashion. He had one eye on the distant future, establishing structures—both physical and philosophical—meant to stand the test of time. However, he most decidedly had the other eye on the immediate present. Pericles understood that greatness can't come if basic needs aren't being met. Our New Pilots must always remember that achieving their vision always requires a strong and unflagging reptilian dimension. While many things are evolving as our world enters its new day, one thing will never change as long as humans remain human: the reptilian always wins.

Finally, Pericles was the first truly inclusive leader. While the circle he drew his arms around would seem limited by modern standards, it was unimaginably progressive for his time. He extended participation in Athenian achievements to a wide populace, creating a pride and purpose that was shared with the people rather than extended to them. Citizens felt themselves to be part of Athens, not just inhabitants of it. New Pilots need to use this example to the fullest.

A sustainable global culture requires a redefinition of leadership, one that will by its nature include innovative ideas, dramatic reinterpretations, and the synthesis of concepts from disparate sources. Our pilots into the future must embrace the new at unprecedented levels.

At the same time, though, they can seek inspiration from the ancient, at least when those ancient ideas are as timeless as the ideas of Pericles.

NEW DESTINATION, NEW PILOTS

New leaders require new models—and new ways of thinking about those models, and new language for communicating about them. For too long we have viewed leadership through the lens of an inaccurate and in some ways obsolete metaphor.

How often have we heard about the concept of the "ship of state," with its analogy of leaders as captains of seafaring vessels? This is historically understandable—for millennia naval power represented the pinnacle of national and imperial pride. For much of modern history, showing off one's naval prowess was a classic projection of a nation's interests—and, often, its ambitions.

But if we consider the nature of ships and their captains, we see that the metaphor has become dangerously inappropriate for our world. Ships take time—time to travel over distance, time to come up to speed, time to slow down, and above all, time to change course. For all of their charms and ongoing value to world commerce, ships are living reminders of old ways of doing things.

Their captains, however well-equipped their vessels are with ultra-modern equipment, are likewise a bit out of touch with modern realities, at least in terms of leadership of entities other than a ship and its crew.

Onboard a ship, the captain is the complete master. Captains always have the final word, and their judgment is rarely if ever questioned; their command is absolute. This is hardly the sort of inflexibility we seek in our leaders on shore, however effective this approach may be at sea.

Pilot Program

What, then, is a better, more accurate and more appropriate model for our new leaders?

I believe that effective leaders for the modern age will be best served by modeling themselves on aircraft pilots.

Consider the abilities and qualities that a pilot must master, put into practice, and display for his passengers.

Our pilots must be:

- Professional,
- Skilled,
- Able to deal with changing circumstances and situations,
- Concerned above all with safety and security,
- Systematic,
- Committed to constant education and refinement of skills, and
- Dedicated to service.

These abilities, in turn, are applied to one terrifically complex but also very simple and straightforward task: getting the aircraft from its point of origin to its destination, and doing so safely. The pilot's focus on the task at hand must be total, even as he attends to and processes all manner of constantly changing information and input. But above all, the safety and flight-worthiness of his craft is foremost in the pilot's mind from the first moments of preflight inspection to the cheerful farewells to passengers safely delivered to their destination.

In between those two moments—checklist before takeoff, and debarkation of passengers and cargo—the pilot's attention is both focused and on the move. Flight speed, changing weather and traffic conditions, fuel, ground communications, occasional crew and passenger concerns, must be attended to and factored into the overall task of safely piloting the aircraft.

It is important to bear in mind that while aircraft are models of ultramodern technology and computerization, the pilot's chief responsibility is one of the reptilian fundamentals: *survival.*

Checklist for Survival

To ensure that survival, the Pilot's Checklist is essential—a lesson I learned for myself. I know how to pilot helicopters, and long before I was permitted to sit at the controls of a helicopter I was schooled in the importance of the Pilot's Checklist.

From my very first flying lesson in Annemasse, France, in the late seventies I was taught that every possible detail, from structural integrity to adequate fuel, must be reviewed before boarding the helicopter.

These details are itemized on a formal checklist that must be worked through, item-by-item, *each* time you prepare for a flight. More than that, the checklist is then reviewed by the co-pilot for consistency, and then once more by the airport authority. Each step ensures and reinforces the certainty that all of the important elements have indeed been verified as safe and in working order.

This is a basic principle of the reptilian leader/pilot: Check, check, and check again. This vital exercise has been adapted in recent years by a variety of other professions, notably medicine. There is good reason for this—in any complex undertaking, whether sitting at the controls of a helicopter or performing a delicate operation in a surgical theater, the ability to respond to changing conditions instantly and effectively is vital.

By formalizing the fundamentals into a checklist, and ensuring *first* that those fundamentals are in order and correctly attended to, the pilot, or surgeon, or—ideally—leader is better prepared to bring focus to emergency situations and resolve them successfully.

Safe Landing

Think about one of the most famous pilots of recent years, Chesley Sullenberger. On January 15, 2009, "Sully" as he is known (and as you no doubt recall) was piloting an Airbus A320 out of New York's LaGuardia Airport, bound for Charlotte, North Carolina.

Shortly after a routine takeoff—which followed a careful and thorough preflight checklist—the airplane was struck by a flock of birds. The collision disabled the jet's engines, at which point the pilot's skills took over.

Even as he communicated with air traffic control about the location of nearby airports and the feasibility of reaching them without power, Sully was considering another option. That option, he decided quickly and irrevocably, was the only hope for saving the aircraft's passengers.

Sully expertly banked the powerless Airbus through a turn that aligned the crippled jet with the Hudson River. In what appeared to observers to be slow motion, Chesley Sullenberger brought the airplane down onto the surface of the Hudson, raising huge plumes of water as the jet came to rest.

Every passenger and crewmember survived the unexpected landing—and what could have been one of the worst air disasters of recent years became instead an unforgettable and by now legendary example of reptilian survival thinking inextricably linked to complete professionalism, skill, calm and experience.

And it is worth noting that once the jet was in the river. Sully walked the length of the flooding passenger compartment twice, checking and then checking again to ensure that no one had been overlooked.

Distraction-Free Zone

The point of the story of Sully's solution to a potential disaster is clear: even routine situations hold the potential for challenge, crisis and catastrophe. Potential that puts the possibility of survival itself in question. The trained pilot is well prepared to face those potential situations precisely *because* the fundamentals of survival are *always* first and foremost in his thoughts.

Consider the difference between the sorts of performance that pilots demonstrate during thousands of flights a day. The overwhelming majority of those flights proceed from origin to destination without incident. They do so because of a vast array of systems, technologies and protocols, ranging from globally coordinated air traffic control to weather satellites to radio frequencies. But all of those elements exist to serve the flight crew, and particularly the pilot, on whom the ultimate responsibility rests.

Those pilots understand many things, but one quality the best of them share is a deep wariness of distraction. Piloting an aircraft—like effective leadership of any sort—requires a dedicated, trained and educated *concentration*. We have all seen news stories of flights that ended in tragedy not because of mechanical or other system failure, but because the pilots allowed themselves to become distracted.

Good pilots don't become distracted by anything that diverts attention from the task before them—keeping their aircraft safe. The cockpit is a distraction-free zone. Think about this as you consider the world's leaders as they are today.

What Really Matters

How many of our leaders are distracted from the reptilian fundamentals by matters that may attract headlines, voters, or contributors but that have *absolutely nothing to do with the survival of their nation, community or business?* I see this all the time, and so do you.

Leaders should not be wasting time on issues that interfere in people's private lives, such as who can get married to whom or what they are doing in the bedroom. Instead they should be focused on fighting common enemies, and addressing needs such as clean air, clean water, plentiful and safe food, security, a vibrant future.

Yet again and again we see leaders and would-be leaders caught up in such issues, distracted from matters of true import by small, personal, narrow-focus "issues" that may well galvanize "true believers" but that are irrelevant to the larger issues, challenges and crises that threaten a culture's well-being and even its survival.

Suppose for a moment that once his aircraft struck that flock of birds, Sully had given precious time to cursing the environmentalists whose protection of the bird nesting grounds contributed to them being there in the first place.

Or suppose that Sully's preflight checklist and preparations hadn't included maps and other navigational tools that let him know exactly where the Hudson River—and other landmarks—on his route lay. Or that his training and experience hadn't been so deep and complete that he didn't know whether the Airbus was capable of what he would ask of it.

Any of these or other factors could have distracted Captain Sullenberger from ensuring the survival of his precious cargo, his passengers and crew. But faced with an extraordinary situation, the pilot immediately developed and implemented an extraordinary solution.

New Pilots for New Leadership

While the story of Sully's water landing is dramatic and admirable, the real reason our new leaders must become New Pilots has far more to do with those thousands of *un*eventful flights every day. Only by creating a new type of leader—and demanding a new type of leadership of ourselves, our countries, our businesses and institutions—can we have any hope of facing the myriad challenges, threats, and crises that fill our world.

The stately ship's captain whose vessel may take hours to negotiate a turn is no longer an effective leadership model. Rather, it is the New Pilot to whom we must turn. The New Pilot, equipped with a Pilot's Checklist that ensures that reptilian principles of survival are attended to first, will have a clear vision of our point of origin and our new destinations, be prepared and educated to deal with variables and unexpected situations along the way, and possess the discipline to stay free from distractions that have nothing to do with the course being followed—*this* is the most effective model for our new leaders.

It is the pilot, after all, who steers, who guides, who navigates, and who sees to it that we arrive safely. *Arrival* is a key word for pilots. We will be arriving at a very new type of civilization in the near future, a global civilization unlike anything that has come before. The quality of our leaders will help determine what sort of civilization that is. And the quality of our New Pilots will determine whether or not we arrive there safely.

The Future of Leadership Is Feminine

French novelist André Malraux posited that the future will be a feminine one. The Global Code for leadership in the future will depend upon the Global Codes that we have discovered in this book. If the Global Code for women is *transformation,* they are the ideal leaders to change this planet for the better. They know that the priority is to feed and educate their children. This is the wisdom that global leaders will need.

One of the things that we have discovered in studying and following the Satellite Tribe is that this is a matriarchal tribe. This has very important consequences. First we need to accept the original hypothesis that what we called the Global Tribe at the beginning of this book and now the Satellite Tribe is permanently creating and re-creating the Global Code. The fact that this is a matriarchal tribe means that the direction taken by the Global Code has more chances to be feminine. Let's try to understand why this is a matriarchal tribe.

In the Satellite Tribe, rich men are looking for trophy wives. These wives are usually younger (20 or 30 years younger). We already know that women live longer than men. As a result, we find many widows, some who have been married three times and have outlived three husbands. They may now be in their fifties with 40 more years left to enjoy their inherited fortune. They dedicate their time to charities, chair social fundraising events, and socialize. They are the new leaders of the Satellite Tribe.

Of course we have also women who are there by their own doing. International managers, diplomats, professors, artists, lawyers who fit the golden rule of three. In many ways, a new feminine leadership has emerged. It follows the pattern of a U-curve. On one hand, you have religious Islamist extremists who want to send women back to the Middle Ages, killing them for attempting to go to school, and on the other you have the Satellite Tribe, which is developing a higher level of feminine leadership.

We have seen that in the Middle East women want more education, while some men act like spoiled kids who just want to play. By nature, women are more inclusive, while men are more exclusive. More women in global leadership positions might help to pull together people from different cultures, races and religions to fight our common enemies. We should concentrate more energy on the future of our children and on creating a Third Culture global world. We know that mothers are crucial in the imprinting process. Might they help develop a higher level of awareness of the dangers of technosophy and the tyranny of the machine? Hopefully, women leaders can bridge the gap between the two sides of the U-curve. So far, no machine or computer has been able to replace a mother.

Let's summarize why women are crucial to understanding the future. We have seen that in the Middle East, Muslim women want to move ahead, get a higher education, drive cars and give a different future to their children. Women live longer than men, and after a certain age, only women are left. Because of modern science and medicine, they are still active, mobile and play a key role in the education of their grandchildren. Also, many women leaders in the world, including CEOs like Indra Nooyi at PepsiCo, who is Indian, have demonstrated a great ability to promote change and to induce adaptability. They are the new GPS leaders that the world needs.

Let's hope that in the future the feminine side of humanity will re-humanize our species. This is the higher purpose of the women who will lead the Satellite Tribe. We need a global woman initiative. This is the mission of the Satellite Tribe. Let's see how women are the future of our planet and how higher education might be their best tool.

PART FOUR

THE FUTURE OF OUR PLANET

TEN

THE GLOBAL CODE FOR HIGHER EDUCATION

The children of the Satellite Tribe and the Third Culture Kids are the future of this planet. The way they look at education will play a crucial role in shaping the future of the institution. We already know that this planet is in dire need of a new species of leaders with a new understanding of global governance. We have seen the dangers presented by the common enemies.

In April 2011, Georgetown University and the School of Foreign Service in Qatar asked me to discover the Global Code for higher education, and how we could design a program to train future global leaders. Consequently, we launched a project to determine which elements would be attractive to students and their families in specific global markets. Although Georgetown is known around the world as an excellent university, alumni and other sources in China, India, the Middle East and other regions report that few people in their regions are familiar with the university or aware of its programs.

I was particularly interested in Georgetown's mission, as the university has already attracted many world leaders, including some from the Philippines, Saudi Arabia and Qatar, and has campuses in China, India, London and Singapore. Despite the fact that this is a Catholic and Jesuit university, 40 percent of its enrollees are Jewish.

Our purpose was to make specific recommendations about the kinds of messages, phrases and images that are likely to resonate as Georgetown and SFS-Q extend their geographic reach and increase their capacity to enroll the very best students in the future.

As we went through our process of asking people to go back to their first imprints, we realized very quickly that peoples' feelings about higher education had very little to do with its actual components, such as science or the humanities. What became very obvious was that the Satellite Tribe children already knew so much that they were looking for something completely different. They were already in the future; they wanted to be even more ahead of their time. They were time travelers, and they wanted to be with other time travelers. Their number one priority was to be connected with their peers, to create a fraternity or sorority of highly connected glomads. So higher education was more about becoming a member of an elite club of time travelers than getting a prestigious degree in and of itself.

Young people today, who already have an education, are familiar with the new technology and the global library and are not looking specifically for more knowledge, more information, the best lecturer or the most published professor. Even though people in all cultures speak about their aim to gain status and increase their skills through education, the primary function of actual institutions is to connect them with the right people around the world. Georgetown is perfectly positioned to meet this need.

Based on our assessment of other major universities, I was surprised to discover that no one else was using this message of global connection between tribe members to portray their values or programs. Moving first to claim the space with powerful on-code messages would help Georgetown reach its desired global audience at their place of greatest need.

Location became a very good indicator of where the Satellite Tribe children wanted to go to make the best connections. They all want to go to hubs, to city-states—real or symbolic—and they are well aware that these are the places where the other members of the Satellite Tribe are going to be. London, New York, San Francisco, Singapore and Hong Kong were mentioned all the time. But so were famous American universities like Harvard, Stanford, Berkeley, Yale and Columbia. Oxford, though still very prestigious, was perceived as a bubble stuck in the past, where the members of the British Empire were trained. Many Indians prefer London.

"If you had a choice, where would you like to go for higher education?"
"I would love to go to London."
"Why?"
"Because they have the best Indian food."

—Male, 22, Mumbai, India

We see in this example that the reptilian always wins, but there's more to it than food. A connection with your own culture, the possibility to refurbish your cultural sensations, recharge your cultural batteries and increase your Indian network before your next move are all related and fundamental desires.

One dimension that became obvious very soon was that women were already the dominant force behind global education.

Cultures around the world are becoming more "feminized" because women's more inclusive form of leadership is more effective in our new global economy than the exclusive form men often practice. Inclusivity aligns with the biology of women, not men. Even when circumstances are tough or challenging, women push for inclusivity. The United States is actually behind other countries in recognizing the power of this advantage.

We also conducted sessions in Doha, Qatar. We could not mix gender groups, and the women's group was supposed to be led by a woman. The contrast between the two groups was baffling. The women wanted to learn more and travel more. They were already quite advanced, spoke good English and sounded very enthusiastic about getting a higher education. The men, by contrast, did not respect any of the rules, were on their cell phones the whole time and did not care much about higher education. They acted like spoiled kids who didn't want to change anything.

"I would like to go to Paris, not for education, but for shopping, for the girls and for the food."—Male, 21, Qatar

During this discovery we became aware that the Satellite Tribe CEOs have some very interesting traits in common. They speak good English, but with a friendly accent, like the Australians (not the British accent, which is sometimes perceived as pompous). They are also very flexible and adapt easily to various conditions. We found that, while many CEOs of multinational or global companies are Indians (Pepsi, Allianz and so on), very few are Chinese, despite China's outsized role in the global economy. What is it in the Indian culture that makes them a better fit for this role?

The Indian Culture Code is *separate realities.*

I traveled through India in 1964 for the first time. Since then, I've had many experiences in India and studied numerous aspects of Indian culture. The Indian code has never changed, despite great changes and modernizations in recent years. My last visit confirmed the tenacity of the unconscious structure. Very generally speaking, your caste gives you your identity and dictates your behavior. You are not trying to move from one caste to another; you are not trying to change the system. You are just trying to be happy where you are.

Lord Mountbatten used to say that India was characterized by functional chaos. I can certainly confirm that the chaos is incredible. Just driving across India is a cultural experience that nobody can forget. But being trained to survive in such an environment, with so many different realities occurring and with absurd bureaucratic structures, might very well be the best training for dealing with our uncertain planet. We might be making a mistake when we protect our children from danger and crisis. This leaves them unprepared, and the first crisis they have to face on their own will have the ability to destroy them. India is so chaotic that if you can make it there, you can certainly make it anywhere. You can handle whatever the world throws at you.

"I don't know why so many Indians are successful outside India. It is so difficult here. Lots of Indian doctors prefer to start as cab drivers in New York, rather than to stay here. Most of them eventually succeed."—Male student, 19, Dehli

India has a fascinating culture, with more than 3,000 official gods. I was told that it is OK to negotiate with the gods; if one does not give you what you want, you simply go to see another one. Indians are very good at arguing and negotiating. Despite this, however, they are not interested in class warfare, racist conflicts or ideological fights; they are just very practical. We found that the culture inside India might be repressive because of its rigid structures and oppressive bureaucracy, but ironically, it's a good preparation for going global.

This is especially practical for Satellite Tribe members and global CEOs. The training motto of the marines is that you should sweat in peace so you don't have to bleed in war. Conversely, the Indian motto could be that you have to sweat in your culture so you don't have to bleed in another one. Compared to the jungle that is the Indian cultural landscape, New York, Sidney and London seem like nice British gardens, and Singapore is like a paradise of order and discipline.

With this understanding and with models, how can we describe the ideal training for future global leaders? What will they need to help us thrive?

Higher education needs a global dimension. In order to train these Satellite leaders, we need to immerse them in the jet-set mentality, going from Shanghai to Delhi, from New York to London, from Mexico to Moscow, but also Rio and Cape Town. Of course, the priority should be the hubs and city-states, the places they belong to (see Chapter 3—How They Travel). But we might even imagine a time station—a pseudo space station in time, or a fast forward city (we expound on this topic shortly)—already anchored in the future, where the Satellite Tribe could go on a regular basis and see how the future humans are doing and send their children there to graduate. We will develop this concept shortly when we speak of the fast forward city. At one point, this work—going around the world to understand the next evolution of higher education—took us to a a new dimension.

NEW CONCEPTS OF TIME

The Satellite Tribe has a different notion of time and space. It exists in another dimension. In many ways we can say that traveling from a little village in the middle of Africa to Dubai is like traveling through time.

An Iranian woman in Dubai shared with me her very emotional experience:

"When I arrived for the first time from Teheran and discovered Dubai, I cried and cried and could not stop crying. That should be us! We Iranians are more than just a culture; we are a civilization. But the people here, 30 years ago, were just peasants—a group of tribes, eating dirt and drinking camel milk in the desert. What happened to us? The train has stopped at the station and has not moved for 30 years. In the meantime, they have built this incredible city, where you can snow ski in the middle of the desert. It is like traveling in time." We have all experienced how going from one place to another might feel like being transported through time, sometimes to an entirely different century. The first time I went to Afghanistan, in 1964, it felt medieval. When I went to study an Indian tribe in the Amazon, it felt primeval.

Let's explore the different notions of time and how we can look at it through the eyes of the Satellite Tribe.

We have *technological time,* which comes into effect when a certain technology is discovered. Modern cars were created in 1900; airplanes were already used in 1914, but they were not yet available to everyone.

Then we have *sociological time,* which happens when everybody uses and adopts the technology. Today everybody has a cell phone, but it took years to go from a portable phone the size of a suitcase to the iPhone that fits in your pocket.

Then we have *human time,* the time it takes for a baby to become a full-fledged adult. Let's accept the premise that, globally, most humans are considered to reach adulthood at approximately 18 years of age.

We immediately see the tension between on the one hand, technology, which evolves and doubles in capacity every 18 months, and on the other, human beings, which develop over a period of 18 years. We have created technology that develops so much faster than we do, and soon we may be overtaken. But the Satellite Tribe has a different notion of time and space. Third Culture Kids do not really fit into traditional institutions. They are already ahead at two or three years old. "Digital natives"—that is, kids born quite recently—won't have to learn or adapt to the new technology. They *are* the new digital world. Millennials had to learn technology, buy a cell phone, learn how to text. For generation Z this is all second nature, and with that, a quantum leap forward has been accomplished.

Classic education does not work for this new species. If we want to train global leaders, we have to invent a new way, a new environment, where they can connect with other members of the Satellite Tribe. This is when the concept of a time station started taking form. Training people by using case studies that are stuck in the past, like mummified bodies, cannot help you to understand and adapt to the fast-moving future. We are already able to go to outer space and to have space stations; why can't we do the same thing with time and create time stations? For now, this idea lives only in science fiction. But the discovery of the Global Code for higher education has opened up a new perspective, whereby we may soon be able to bridge the gap between technological time and sociological time. This is how *fast forward city* was born.

THE FAST FORWARD CITY

Fast forward city is an idea that came into existence during the discovery on higher education that was done for Georgetown University. It is a place where all of the technology that has just been invented is immediately available to the inhabitants of a totally separate ecosystem. These people are immersed in the most advanced technology that has been invented but is not yet available to the broader public. The inhabitants of this time station already go to work in self-driving cars, have self-cleaning houses, have 3-D printers in their homes and robots that monitor all aspects of their health.

This is a real city, not just an experimental laboratory. People are volunteers who are committed to 12 months in the city, which simulates a reality ten years ahead. Corporations donate new technologies and monitor how it is accepted and how it interferes with others. For the first time, we will explore the interfaces among various technologies and how they impact your evolution as a human creature. Interface means how the impact of one technology, a smartphone, for example, can change your ability to find your way without a GPS. If the basic principal that prosthetics (in this case, a smartphone) atrophies (gradually declines your effectiveness), then it stands to reason that the smarter the phone, the dumber the user.

"People are not present anymore; they are somewhere else, speaking with somebody somewhere else. They are like zombies—they do not even look at you and speak so loud; it is like you don't exist. I hate that. We should have rules against that."—Woman, 45, Berlin

Most people are always texting, are always alone together, are always connected with nothing to say. The Satellite Tribe, however, has a different experience of technology. They are not passive users; they are trendsetters.

This is when the big idea of the time station started taking form. The main challenge is to bridge the gap between technological time and sociological time and, in doing so, accomplish the objective of connecting future leaders. They would have literally experienced the future together, and "graduated" from the future, setting them up to lead the rest of us there.

They would also have established contact with major corporations, not just via ancient case studies, but through current innovations and investments.

Many technologies that were once perceived as indispensable have not lasted. The fax machine was supposed to completely transform our way of working; the hologram was supposed to replace photography. But I know that you do not have a hologram of your grandfather, your children or your dog, and you no longer use a fax machine. The technology exists, but the market never catches up.

What is going to happen to self-driving cars, 3-D printers, Google Glass, robots, home hospitalization, Internet schooling, and the like? What sort of backlash can we expect? What unintended consequences should we anticipate? Studying new technologies with an ecosystem-wide approach has never been done before. Boeing wants to know how people are going to move in a hub and between hubs. Allianz wants to know how people are going to buy insurance (do they need to meet people?). Amex wants to know if money, checks and credit cards are all going to be replaced by mobile money.

But traveling, paying and feeling the need to be protected (insurance) are all related. For the first time, Boeing, Amex and Allianz will work together to decode the future of technology.

SO HOW DO YOU GET TO THE FUTURE?

Collecting all the new technologies available from major global corporations is not the most difficult part. They all realize that this ecosystem is the best way to test and innovate their products, but to take people from the present time and to send them ten years ahead is another problem altogether, even without considering that we might want to bring them back. To make a jump forward in time, we might need to implement stages of depressurization, much like when you dive into the depths of the ocean. So volunteers will need intermediate stations. They will first spend one month in a "three-years-ahead" station, pass some tests, then go into a "six-years-ahead" station, spend another month, pass some tests and then move to a "ten-years-ahead" station, the fast forward city, where they could spend an entire year. This station will be a real city, like an ecosystem, where people work and children go to school. The station will have restaurants and entertainment. Because it is an ecosystem, we can observe the interfaces, the spaces between the different technologies and how they influence each other.

Volunteers will get together in small groups once a week to share their reactions and insights (like the quality circles). They will also brainstorm on how to improve the technologies they are using. The feedback from these sessions will be transmitted to the sponsor companies that provided the technologies in order for them to take it into consideration and improve their products based on real-time user experiences. Their laboratories will be located around the fast forward city, creating satellite cities dedicated to the development of the new technologies.

Of course, we will need a reentry process, to take people back to the present time. The volunteers will go back through the intermediate stations to be tested and to be reacclimatized to the present way of life. They will remain, however, experts on the future, get a master's degree in future studies, and work as facilitators to prepare the new volunteers. They will also become experts working for the sponsors' companies as they have experienced their products in the future.

In summary, the fast forward city is the first *time station*.

THE CONCEPT

1. *The gap:* This is the delay between the technological time (when a technology first exists—like 3-D printers today) and the sociological time (when everybody has one at home).

2. *Time station:* We bridge the gap, as all advanced technologies are now available in the city. (Everybody has a 3-D printer, driverless cars, etc.)

3. It is an *ecosystem* in the future. It is not just a laboratory; it is a real, living environment where interfaces and interactions can be studied.

4. It is *cosponsored* by corporations, which provide the technologies, and by universities, which provide and select the volunteers (students and faculty members).

5. The fast forward city is surrounded by laboratories and start-ups (like a sort of Silicon Valley) where corporations, universities and students can develop their new ideas.

6. Future *circles:* Every week, the inhabitants will share their experiences and their interactions with products. Here, we follow the model of the quality circles (You don't need a hands-free cell phone if you have a driverless car).

7. "Futurenauts" will go through intermediate stations (3 years ahead, 7 years ahead), before going to the time station (10 years ahead) where they will stay for several months (8 to 12) and then go back through the reentry intermediate stations.

WHAT IS IT?

1. The best way to test new technology.

2. The best way to study the interfaces or interactions between technologies, and unintended consequences.

3. The campus of the future where global leaders will be trained.

4. A real city with everything its inhabitants need (restaurants, schools, entertainment). It is a combination of the space station and a college campus.

5. A continuously moving and changing place as new products, technologies and services keep coming all the time.

6. A permanent interaction between technologies, corporations, faculty, students and the global market.

7. A way to anticipate new needs created by the new technologies. (For instance, in 2009, Dubai experienced serious problems with

waste and sewage management as a result of their exploding population.)

WHAT IS IT NOT?

1. A laboratory.
2. A regular campus.
3. A city of the future frozen in time (like those we see in science fiction).
4. Another Epcot or a museum for old futures.

WHERE?

We have explored several possibilities.

This idea was presented to the executive committee of Georgetown University, who have a connection with the Qatar Education Foundation. The goal of this foundation is to connect all its initiatives, train 700 PhDs and get 3 Nobel Prizes.

We think that this project could also be developed by Colombia University. Harvard already has a laboratory of the future, but it's not the same as an ecosystem.

Our goal is to offer to a small group of emerging leaders an opportunity to experience the future, see the interface of several innovations, meet each other and work together to gain critical knowledge to prepare them for global governance.

The location of the fast forward city is crucial. It has to resonate with the Satellite Tribe and their children. It has to be in a city-state or a city that could be perceived as such or become one in the future. Hong Kong, Dubai, Doha and Istanbul, but also New York, London and Washington, D.C. come to mind. Even though Washington is perceived more as a political hub than a city-state, it still qualifies when you need to connect with the right people.

The fact that Georgetown was one of the first meeting places for undergraduates who went on to become the leaders of various governments around the world supports the goal of developing a fast forward city. According to these leaders, their Georgetown interactions provided a foundation for future negotiations and collaborations on cross-national issues during critical times.

Leaders with the potential we seek are becoming more in tune with the worldwide need for higher levels of awareness. Forces like Facebook and Twitter, and the recent Occupy gatherings in spring 2012, are evidence of this need; they show us that awareness is a crucial trait for our leaders in the future. These leaders also need strong links to other global leaders who could join together to develop the world.

We are aware that this program could intersect powerfully with other work on campus—for example, the human development initiative and the global women's leadership project that are in the first stages of development. These intersections could help to elevate the global leadership program through connections with more traditional and authentic academic works.

When people from the areas we studied enroll in American higher education, they are seeking connections to others with shared interests and aspirations from around the world. Acquiring knowledge is not as important as this central goal.

Top leaders seek to address a higher purpose in all they do. In many settings, however, they confront experiences and connections with no content. Some of these experiences are created by the e-world, which fosters many empty situations and encounters.

Global leaders value practical experience and team learning in real-world settings over other forms of training. They welcome and expect engagement in significant locations around the world. The fast forward city gives them an initiation to the future and in turn provides the necessary bonding environment to create this new tribe of global leaders. In the future, global leaders will be trained this way.

At a reptilian level, all around the world, children are the future. We know that the Global Code for the future is *children*. How we educate our children and what kind of tools we give them will dictate the way this planet is going. We need to train a new next generation of pilots if we don't want to crash. Let's explore how the Global Code for higher education and the Millennials predicts our future, and how women are a crucial element of this future.

SUPPORTING WOMEN IN HIGHER EDUCATION

In addition to creating the fast forward city, we should also be working actively to organize a women's initiative that will have the potential to attract significant support from donors around the world, from the Middle East, Asia and the Americas. We hope that a central pillar of this initiative will be to increase the importance of a feminine approach to leadership and to accelerate the critical role that women are playing as world leaders in the years to come.

We have to "think big" for the project.

What would it take to make Georgetown, Harvard, Colombia, Dubai, Berkeley and Doha *the* centers for women's leadership, not just in peacemaking, but in all key initiatives? The goal is to convince hub leaders, members of the Satellite Tribe, that this is crucial.

This has to be a moving platform, a university. It has to have a vision and values based on improving the world through service to others, have incredible access to women of great achievement, and have a body of women students who are eager to learn to lead. There is only one center for women's leadership in the United States, at Rochester University, and it seems limiting to focus only on women in the United States. There exists a wide range of opportunities to leverage in this field.

Such a center would do five interrelated things. First, it would cover three major areas where women's leadership is urgently needed: peacemaking, for which we are already planning; entrepreneurship—that is, women in businesses big and small; and political action—putting women in positions of power wherever they are. Second, it would do research, asking what has worked and how to propel women into positions of leadership. It would also provide training for aspiring women leaders (and some women who don't even realize their leadership capacities).

Third, it would be convenient for women to engage these issues with each other and with men. Fourth, it would partner with universities outside the United States and promote female leadership in places where it is most urgently needed and least addressed. Here is where we can engage with partners in the Gulf and elsewhere. How about partners in Afghanistan? Europe? China? Fifth, it will be a permanent connector for all the members of the Satellite Tribe, constantly evaluating and promoting the best global practices to help society.

We also need to know how to speak about the role of women and when and where those messages will be effective. This complex set of questions foreshadows the coming reality of women's leadership roles. Determining how to speak about women should be a key element of the Satellite Tribe leadership mission.

It is important for this project to be framed and developed as a way to explore and promote the qualities women bring to the table rather than attempting to rehabilitate women in a more masculine environment.

Higher education is crucial for the future of our planet. The next step is to integrate the different elements that have been presented so far: the Satellite Tribe Code, the new Global Codes, the code for higher education, the fast forward city and the global woman initiative.

We need to share this idea with all the leaders, institutions, universities and corporations who have sponsored and supported this work.

If the Global Code for higher education is the *fast forward city*, the women of the Satellite Tribe will become the pioneers of the future, using the fast forward city as a home base to explore and experience what is ahead of us. They will also prepare their children for the next new world, for the changes brought about by technology. Let's see how their children, the Millennials, are dealing with this technology.

ELEVEN

THE GLOBAL CODE
FOR MILLENNIALS

Going around the world to decode this new species was among the most fascinating experiences of my life. In more than 40 years of studying cultures and looking for the commonalities that might transcend them, I had never found such a powerful common code. In fact, it was a thread that linked the members of this new generation together no matter where they were on the planet. It is clear that technology is changing the way that we behave, think, feel and survive—faster than we could ever have imagined.

The first time I flew from Paris to New York and back on the same day using the Concorde, I realized that our collective concept of time and space had changed. When Thomas Jefferson negotiated the Louisiana Purchase, he did not have access to a telephone, and one exchange between Paris and Washington could easily take several months. Jefferson managed, but then, he was exceptional in his ability to plan, take risks and improvise.

When you don't have the type of instant feedback permitted by cell phone technology—the kind we now take for granted—you have to take responsibility and act alone. Today we have a new generation, the Millennials, who were born with cell phones in their hands. My first experience of a computer occurred while I was teaching at Hautes Etudes Commerciales de Paris (HEC) in France. I remember looking through a glass pane at a large machine, which was kept in the only air-conditioned room in the building. The computer took up the whole room and comprised several complex-looking machines and turning wheels. It was very impressive.

We went from COBOL and various programming languages, to PCs, to mobile phones, to tablets and now smartphones. Some mothers tell me that the first word their children learn today is not "Mommy," but rather, "tablet." Technology follows Moore's law and is changing so rapidly that, as one Millennial told me, "When you buy a device, by the time you learn how to use it, it is already obsolete."

NEW TEENS: ARE WE THERE YET?

If we want to take a closer look at how our world is changing and how societies are changing, our best reference point is the next generation.

Three-year-olds master the iPad, six-year-olds can give you a list of the top brands they see on TV commercials and twelve-year-olds know how to complete their homework assignments (without setting foot in a library) with the aid of the vast information powerhouse we call the Internet.

The behavior of teenagers is what I am interested in. Trojan, a popular condom manufacturer, approached me to develop the code for teens. It was not surprising that they wanted to tap into the minds of this group of sexually active individuals, but what *did* come as a surprise was how they did not already know how to market to this demographic that represents such a high percentage of the contraceptives market. If anyone should know teens, it should be a condom manufacturer.

However, Trojan's request revealed to me a much greater concern: today's teens are so different from those of past generations. I couldn't blame Trojan's ignorance because teens today live in a completely different world, which means trying to understand their behavior and their choices is no walk in the park.

What we are seeing is a new species of teens. For centuries, children were considered to be little adults. They wore adult clothing, worked and helped out on the farm, and married at a young age. By the twentieth century, this had completely changed. Before, teens were perceived as rebels against society, rebels without a cause, without direction, easily dismissible. In Victor Hugo's novel *Les Misérables,* the rebel youth were portrayed as disorganized, kids in the barricades, mere actors who were easily manipulated by others. We used to be quick to dismiss childhood and youth as irrelevant and unworthy of any deep analysis.

But childhood is a relatively new concept. In the 1920s and 30s, the developmental psychologist Jean Piaget developed his theory of cognitive development, a new construct of the way we understand early human development. This was a completely new revelation that has helped us discover adolescence as a critical development stage. This transition in thought and how we perceive maturation has led to a cultural shift in the way we treat, and even respect, this special stage of growth.

Why are today's teenagers so different from teenagers of the past? Technology is the principal culprit. It has accelerated their development. Children and teens are the first to understand new technology, adopting it and using it as second nature.

Teens are often the ones teaching their parents how to use modern technologies like Skype or TiVo. This gives teens an unprecedented amount of power. They are one step ahead of the game. Parents no longer have control over their children's access to information as they grow up. This transforms the parent-child relationship completely, whereby parents have less authority and teenagers find it easier to bend the rules thanks to technology, which gives them greater power and legitimacy.

Teenagers are quick learners; they are the first to receive a message, reject it or accept it and then adopt it and adapt it. They define the trends, rejecting what they deem "not cool" and embracing what is "cool." It is no wonder that brands would be so interested in tapping into this market since it is this group of individuals that decides which brands die and which ones survive.

It's a universal fact that we all want to be young, healthy and beautiful. This explains why the world is quick to adopt products that make us feel young. America is an adolescent culture, exporting this to the rest of the world with brands like Coca-Cola, Levi's, Nike and even Michael Jackson. America's adolescent Culture Code is *Peter Pan syndrome*. We don't want to grow up (if we can help it).

In fact, we are so keen on not growing up that adolescence has stretched out well into our 20s and even 30s. Taking a gap year off between high school and college, changing college majors several times and graduating years later than originally planned, hopping from job to job, traveling and backpacking around the world, are behaviors that carry on throughout our 20s. Years ago, this was the decade meant for finding a stable job and career, meeting your spouse, buying a home and settling down. Today, we have delayed adulthood by avoiding responsibilities and maturity. It is still unclear if this will have positive or negative effects on society, but it certainly says a lot about our values as a society as a whole. We live in a new teen world.

THE QUESTIONS BEING ASKED

Several of my clients wanted to discover the code for the Millennials, the idea being that they are the future generation of clients, the customers of tomorrow. It seems that none of our prior knowledge or experience applies to understanding them. Our own memory of adolescence is irrelevant when trying to read and decode their behavior. We had to go deeper and explore the first imprint, their new reference system, their new CNA (Cultural Nucleic Archetype—a concept elaborated upon elsewhere in Chapter 12).

To find out more about Millennials, I interviewed several managers and members of the Satellite Tribe, and, as always, I started by asking, "If I had all of the answers, what would your questions be?" One executive at Trojan confided, "It seems as if nothing we know applies to them; we cannot just remember our own adolescence and think it helps to understand them. They do not see the world in the same way that we do, and it's hard to relate to them."

"Why?" I asked.

"They seem to be very anxious and worried," he replied, "but I don't know why. They don't want to speak to us [the previous generation]. They say that we don't understand anything and that we are obsolete, that we just don't get it. They look at us with a condescending air of superiority. It seems like my generation is stuck somewhere in the past, whereas they've already moved into another dimension." It is clear that this is not just a simple case of adolescent rebellion.

A Boeing executive involved in the project asked me, "What is going to happen to travel in this age where you can go anywhere, at any time, just by sitting at your desk on the computer or phone? What is the incentive to take a plane? Why should you physically move when you can go without moving? They live in a virtual world; does this mean that in the future they will not want to travel in the real world? Do they feel that studying using MOOCs (massive open online courses) is better than spending several years in a dorm on campus? Do they want to live in condensed 'vertical' cities, with buildings and elevators reaching hundreds of stories high and horizontal ground space being navigated on foot or by public transportation?" There is an opposition between the vertical model of going up but staying at the same place and the horizontal model, where you can walk most places, much like Manhattan.

BMW asked me another series of questions: "Do you think these guys are going to want to buy cars in the future? What are their expectations surrounding technology? Do they want cars that drive themselves? Do they want to speak to their cars or vice versa? Do they want to speak through their phones? Is new technology going to replace the chauffeur? The car is so intelligent that you can just tell it where you want to go and it takes you there, during which time you can sit in the back and check your mail, text or make phone calls. If the car chauffeur does all of the work, what is the incentive to learn how to drive?"

In London we met with a marketer from Durex, a manufacturer of condoms, who asked the following questions: "What is love for these people? Do they feel that it is so easy to hook up using the web that they have lost interest in love and romance? Or is it the contrary? So much time with a machine might be creating a new need for more intimacy and emotional contact. Do they still need to touch each other, or are texting and Facebook sufficient? Is sex still a concern for this generation? Do they want safe sex? Do they feel responsible, or do they not care? Today some of them have 'sex friends,' friends with whom the only purpose is to have sex. There is no conversation, no emotional attachment, no drinks before, no cigarette afterward, just 'thanks, see you next time.' Some of them told me that they have three sex friends; others told me 'I'm better—I have five.' So what does this mean for the future of relationships?"

One of my clients at Match.com voiced similar concerns. "What is happening to mating, dating and relationships? Are we seeing a mutation in the way that they operate and the way that they disconnect? Are they losing their ability to communicate with each other because of the prevalence of texting?" Helen Fisher, an anthropologist, human behavior researcher and world-renowned "expert on love" asked me similar questions. "How is this new technology changing the nature of love? Do we still have romance and passion? How is seduction working today? Are love and sex still connected?"

My client at Allianz, a global insurance firm, was interested in how this generation thinks about the future. "Do they plan ahead? Do they want advice, and if so, how do they want to receive it? Are they concerned about risk, and if so, do they want to anticipate and protect themselves? Do they want to buy insurance, and if so, what kind? We are not even sure they want to buy cars or homes anymore."

Firmenich, a perfume company participating in the project, was interested in knowing more about Millennials' relationship with sensuality. "Do they still smell, or care about scents and perfumes? Is this important for them? Do they know how roses smell? In fact, we want to know if they are still reptilian, but also how they relate to each other. Do they offer perfume to their girlfriends? Can they buy perfume on the Internet without smelling it? Do smartphones and tablets have a smell?"

Sephora was more concerned about the future viability of their current successful model. "What do they want in a store? Are stores even still relevant to them, and will they go there to shop? Is the Amazon.com generation still going to go shopping, and if they do, what kind of shopping experience do they want? We have revolutionized the way that people shop for perfumes and cosmetics; is it already obsolete, and if so, what's next?"

THE DISCOVERY

So after speaking to Boeing, Trojan, Allianz, BMW, Durex, Firmenich and Sephora, we decided to go around the world to apply our unique approach for decoding the Millennials. We started in New York, Paris, Berlin,

London and Munich, and already we were surprised by the consistency of the structure we were encountering. So we pressed on to San Francisco, Seoul, Shanghai, Singapore, Mumbai and Istanbul. After visiting these cities, we really started to become convinced that these young people had a lot in common all over the globe. There was a lot more in common than just a mere cell phone; they had a new cosmogony and a new philosophy, but the same CNA. They were a new species. And they were in another dimension.

We then headed south to Recife, Rio de Janeiro, Bogotá and Mexico City. In the near future we will go to Africa, where we already know that a large portion of the population is using cell phones to make purchases; it is already a more prevalent form of transaction than checks and credit cards. In today's world, Africa is ahead of us in adopting mobile money.

During our first breakout meeting in New York, we reviewed several insights. The observation that "the number of transistors in a dense integrated circuit doubles approximately every two years" existent in Moore's law can be applied to Millennials. They are hyper-connected and have thousands of friends, but the gap or abyss between them and the previous generation (parents, teachers and adults) is more than dramatic; it is irreconcilable. In New York, London, Paris and Berlin we heard, "My parents—they just don't get it. I don't even speak to them anymore. They don't understand anything; they don't understand what I am speaking about. It's as if we don't speak the same language. They want me to be with them for dinner, so I sit with them at the table. In five minutes I am bored, nothing they say interests me, so I use my cell phone under the table."

Because Millennials are not in the real world, the technology they use does not prepare them to move out of their family environment. Being unable to function after leaving home, they would rather stay home as long as they can. Home becomes a very practical hotel where your reptilian needs, such as cleaning, food and shelter, are taken care of. But you don't really communicate with your parents, whom you consider more like hotel employees. You are too busy in the virtual world communicating (i.e., texting) with your friends.

This disconnect might also go the other way very soon. In San Francisco, a 20-year-old man told us, "My little brother, he's six years old. He was born with a cell phone in his hands. It is instinctive; he just knows . . .

he doesn't have to learn, and he's already ahead of me." Not only are Millennials disconnected from their parents, but they also sense that very soon they will lose connection with the younger generation as they become "old." The next generation is coming soon and already pushing them over the cliff. Their anxiety is increased by their acute awareness.

Thus the Millennial generation lives in total uncertainty; they don't know what the world will be like tomorrow. They have no sense of continuity, no feeling of stability, no vision of the future. Technology keeps creating new instruments that they must learn how use, yet those could be superseded by others at any moment. At the same time, they know too much. Infinite information equals total uncertainty. Time is measured by how long it takes for a Snapchat to disappear; communication is reduced to 140 characters. The code for infinite information is *total insecurity*.

This total insecurity is the price we pay for the infinite availability of information. If everything is free (like MOOC) and available, then the choices are infinite. This leads to a fear of making the wrong choice, as you might be missing out on a better opportunity in the process. Millennials live in constant anxiety, and they often prefer not to choose anything in order to keep all of their options open until the last second, even if it means they might miss everything. The code for planning is *missed opportunities*.

In Seoul, I asked a group of Millennials if they had plans for the night. The answer was a resounding, "Not yet. In an hour, when the session will be finished, I will check my phone and see what's going on." In Istanbul, they told us, "We are never late anymore, because I can just text my friends to let them know that I'm on my way or how long I'm going to take. Because I'm always connected I am never late." Choosing means less choice.

THE NEW PHILOSOPHY

The code for smartphone is *new philosophy*. Technology is the new philosophy. It has no morals, no logic, no metaphysics, no ethics, no content, no ideology, no higher purpose and no God. Technology is the dictator; it makes and imposes its rules, its definition of time, space and energy. In 1950, David Riesman wrote *The Lonely Crowd,* where he describes three trends in the socialization of humans. According to his analyses, we were first influenced by tradition, or were "tradition oriented." This means that tradition was telling us what to do. Then we began internalizing values and became "inner-directed." This translates to, for example, someone being honest because they *feel* that this is a good value and orientation. Riesman felt, at the time, that outside pressure (from, say, the media, peer groups, fashion and ideological conformism) made us "outer-directed." Rather than listening to their inner selves, people succumbed to group pressure or popular fashion.

Today, I feel that people are experiencing a fourth level of influence: we are becoming "technology-directed." Contrary to what we may think, our friends are not the influencers. It is not peer pressure that we are experiencing now; it is *technological* pressure. Let's explore the notion of time: technology is in a time frame of the instantaneous, the instinctive, one of reflexes. Like the medulla reflex, it does not even reach the brain. If your hand touches fire, you immediately retract it without having to think about it. This is Millennials' reaction to almost everything, starting with texts. They are not impatient; they just have a different notion of time. Their code for time is the *next, now.*

They receive a text, and instinctively they feel the need to respond right away. If you don't feel that way, something is wrong with you. You risk being rejected, ostracized or ridiculed, which is devastating. "I text, therefore I am" and "I receive a notification, therefore I am alive"—these are mottos that define Millennials' sense of identity.

The cell phone is becoming an appendage of the body. You don't look at the world directly anymore; you see it through your cell phone. Technology is the filter, the transformer. It is your new reality. Your face, your reputation and your status are not generated by your physicality or actions in the real world; they are generated virtually.

THE GREAT EQUALIZER

Technology has no hierarchy, and the Internet is the great equalizer. Everything has the same value; everyone is at the same level. A lie has the same value as the truth, since there is no obvious context in which to immediately know it's a lie. So whatever people say about you, good or bad, has the same impact, be it a lie or the truth. The absence of hierarchy translates into an absence of priorities, and technological imperatives fill the void. The last text is the priority.

NO CONTENT

The code for the technological brain is *no content*. Technology has no content, no morals, no ethics, no higher purpose. You need to be connected because everybody else is connected, not because you have something important to share. You are not the Dalai Lama trying to send a message or Hillary Clinton trying to change someone's vote or BMW trying to get someone to buy a new convertible. You are just connected because other people are, so you have to be too if you want to exist. You are on your cell phone, nothing else, nothing more. You are your cell phone. "When I lost my cell phone, I thought I was dead, that was terrible. I panic when my cell phone is dead. It's as if I were dead," reported an 18-year-old girl from London.

Let me explain what I mean by "no content." No content means that technology by itself is only a series of electromagnetic connections. A telephone line connects people, but it does not tell these people what they should say. The same line can transmit love, hate or even indifference. Two people might even be connected without having anything to say. This is what I mean when I say "no content."

No content also helps to illustrate the concept of technosophy, a philosophy that has no content. It contains no values, no hierarchy, no beliefs, no higher purpose, no metaphysics and no morals. This is why the Occupy movement didn't get anywhere. They had great connections, but no content. After a while this technosophic tribe, in a desperate search for meaning and content, turned to the best providers thereof: the church and the army.

Both of these structures have a higher purpose, a hierarchy, answers to all of your questions and an explanation for the meaning of life and death. In both the army and the church, when you die, you know why. The reward structure is also very clear: honor, respect, eternal life, virgins waiting for you in heaven, etc. The net does not provide any of this.

NO ELECTRICITY MEANS FREEDOM

The code for electricity is *addiction*. Going around the world, I asked Millennials what would happen if all of the sudden there was no more electricity, no Internet, no cell phone service, no light and no cars. The answer was unanimous: "Then we would be free. If nobody has a cell phone, then

I have no obligations and I am free." They are aware that they are all addicted to technology, the superpower organizing their lives and dictating what they should and should not do.

TECHNOLOGY IS LIKE A BODILY FUNCTION

The code for checking your mail is *bodily function*. The first thing Millennials do in the morning is check their mail/smartphones; they do this even before going to the bathroom. It is also the last thing they do at night before going to bed. They even do it in bed, right before falling asleep. They keep the phone on all night, just in case. Their intellectual alibi, of course, is, "Just in case there is an emergency." They keep the phone on during concerts, at the movies, during dinner, in church or at the doctor's. Parents are now asking teachers to let kids use their cell phones during class in case of an emergency. Airlines are asking themselves whether or not they should allow cell phone service inside planes.

This new species does not want to speak; they want to text! Of course this is not new, and a lot of older people also became subject to the same addiction. But what we found very interesting was that the Satellite Tribe, if they are familiar with e-technology, use it as a means to expand their contact with reality rather than as a means to escape it. We can see the beginning of the great divide here, the opposition between the e-world or virtual world of texting, and the r-world, or real world of hands, touching and reptilian needs.

DON'T SPEAK, PLEASE, TEXTING ONLY!

The code for communication is *text*. Millennials have a clear preference for how they want to use their technology.

First, they want to text. It is simple and efficient; they can see when people receive their texts and how long it takes for them to answer. They also can correct and change their texts before they send them, not for spelling and grammar (which they don't seem to care about), but to make sure they're saying what they want to say.

Second best is email, which, for them, is more formal. They are not used to communicating so formally: A 21-year-old man in San Francisco explained, "With my friends, I text all of the time. I maybe get 1,000 texts a day, but with my boss, I email. Email is for work, texting is for friends."

Least popular is speaking on the phone. "I text so I don't have to call . . . I don't like to speak on the phone; if I say something and I suddenly regret it, it is too late. I am too emotional on the phone," said a 19-year-old Korean male from Seoul.

A LETTER, WHAT IS A LETTER?

When I asked Millennials in New York, Shanghai and Seoul when the last time was that they wrote a letter, they looked at me as if I was really from another planet. "A letter? Ha, ha, I've never written a letter." They simply don't write. They are completely losing the ability to correspond via letter, and they think it is obsolete, not unlike riding a horse from New York to Boston. You just don't do it anymore.

PROSTHETIC ATROPHY

The code for "smart" is *atrophy:* the smarter the phone, the dumber the user. Millennials are aware that they are losing something. They are not simply "unlearning"; they are losing their ability to survive without their cell phones. When asked if they could find their way without a GPS or map-enabled device, the majority answer was, "No, I can't, and I've never had to do it, so why bother? Without my cell, it's like having to light a fire by striking two stones together. It's like going back to the Stone Age." GPS, spell check, Google, Wikipedia—you don't need to know anything anymore; the technology does it for you. Technology is like a big monster that is sucking all of the knowledge out of your brain and replacing it with a device, a sort of implant. At this stage, technology begins to control you. It is more than an addiction; it becomes a lobotomy followed by an implant that controls you.

Millennials are familiar with artificial intelligence; they know that machines and technology will progressively take over every aspect of their lives. Are they afraid? Yes. And they are very anxious as well. Yet they do not see what they can do about it. Because technology keeps changing all the time, they do not see how they can anticipate or prepare. They have no choice, as they see it, but to be dominated by their cell phones.

"WE ARE ALONE TOGETHER"

Can you remember a time when people were busy in conversation, entranced by a book they were reading or distracted by the scene outside the bus window? You surely won't see this picture when stepping onto the bus or metro in today's world. You're more likely to see a scene of zombie-like individuals with their eyes glued to a small screen they grasp in their hands. How bizarre would this image look to an alien visiting our planet or even to someone teleporting from 20 years ago?

Today's state of technology has reached unimaginable heights. Just ten years ago we had simple cell phones that allowed us to make phone calls, text message and receive voicemails. Maybe we even had a few games (do you remember Snake?). Now our cell phones allow us to access our email accounts, browse the Internet, pay the telephone bill, listen to music, and record videos. We can even download applications that monitor our bowel movements, tune our guitars and tell us our horoscopes. We can find anything we need or want in this tiny device that fits into the palm of our hands.

TECHNOLOGICAL CHANGE

Before I can share with you the Global Code for technology and the ways in which the Satellite Tribe uses modern technology differently from the rest of the public, I need to paint a picture of why technology is so important. I need to show you how in today's globalized and interconnected world, technology has infiltrated nearly every aspect of our lives. Hence, it is imperative that we understand it and use it wisely.

> *"We've arranged a civilization in which most crucial elements profoundly depend on science and technology."*
>
> —Carl Sagan

Technology has changed at an exponential rate. Since the beginning of the twentieth century, every decade has seen more and more technological advances in a cumulative fashion.

If we look at the timeline of innovation, in the first decade of the twentieth century, we had the invention of the zeppelin, the radio, and the first

Ford Model T. From 1910 to 1919, we invented the first motorized movie camera; from 1920 to 1929, the first robot and loudspeaker; from 1930 to 1939, the first jet engine, Polaroid camera and photocopier; from 1940 to 1949, color television, the microwave oven and the atomic bomb. Then, in the second half of the century, we had the invention of credit cards, oral contraceptives, floppy disks, laser printers, magnetic resonance imaging, personal computers, digital cellular phones and the World Wide Web.

We have come a long way in just 100 years. What's more, from a historical perspective, access to technology has been significantly reduced. While we are impressed to see how many people in cosmopolitan cities own a smartphone—and some even own several phones as well as other high-tech devices—there are still many people around the world who don't have access to a basic cell phone or Internet service.

Money is one of the barriers to adopting new technologies; time is another factor. I've categorized three different notions of time for technology: technological time, social time, and psychological time.

Technological time is very straightforward; it's the moment when a technology is invented, developed and available for the public to use. When the first personal computer was invented, it existed and then became available to the market for purchase. Social time is the moment when everyone in society is able to understand and adopt a new technology. Cell phones, for instance, are now in social time in most developed countries and urban cities.

Psychological time, however, is the gap between technological time and social time. It's when people around the world are still wrapping their minds around the new technology and are still learning how to become familiarized with it. For example, solar panels are still in psychological time because most people are cautious, still dubious of the true costs and benefits of putting solar panels on their roofs. Also, since not enough people have done it yet, they still think solar panels look rather ugly because we are so used to the traditional way roofs should look.

CHANGE IS NOT THE SAME AS PROGRESS

The problem with technology is that our minds do not change as fast as technology does. Some things are easier to adopt than others, like transitioning from black-and-white television to color television. It doesn't take much mental effort to make the switch. But for some, like moving from operating a PC to operating a Mac, the switch is not as intuitive as we'd hope.

As I've mentioned before, teenagers are experts at closing the gap between technological time and psychological time. They are quick at adapting to new technologies because they were bred to do so from the very beginning; ever since childhood they've been exposed to technology. They are problem solvers. Instead of children looking to their parents for answers, parents are asking their children for help with the computer or other electronic devices. Even if you hand a 10-year-old an electronic device he's never seen before, chances are he can figure out how to use it by fiddling around for a few minutes. In less than a minute a child can take a picture and set it as the background for her grandmother's phone.

Members of the Satellite Tribe are also not afraid to take on the challenge of learning how to use new technology. If the rest of the world is using it, they want to find out what's the charm and give it a try too. Since they are great at adapting and being flexible to change, they too are quick at bridging the technological and psychological time gap.

> *"It has become appallingly obvious that our technology has exceeded our humanity."*
>
> —Albert Einstein

Technology has severely changed the way we experience our world and our relationships. People don't talk face-to-face anymore; they text, email, Snapchat, or post on social media.

Rather than enjoying a concert, we often observe a sea of cell phone screens. People are forgetting to live the experience because they are too busy documenting it. Similar to the time of the Wild West when cowboys would leave their gun by the side of their plate during mealtime, now we quickly whip out our cell phones and place them on the table, screen facing upward, just in case we receive notifications outside of our immediate experience. You've probably noticed it too—at a restaurant you'll see more people fiddling on their phones than actually conversing with the people they are dining with.

Not only has technology changed the nature of our interpersonal relationships and social experiences; it has also changed our power dynamics. Technology has given unprecedented power to governments and corporations, changing the way companies market products and services to us and the way governments watch over and protect their citizens.

Information is power. It is not folly that fascist regimes throughout history burned truckloads of books that contained ideas they deemed as threatening to the ideals of the ruling power. The Internet has given people access to information that we would have never otherwise known existed. We have direct access to information about our history, other societies far away, live updates from the news and millions of opinions and differing perspectives. This is huge.

We've seen the impact of technology on social movements. Social media played a pivotal role in the Arab Spring uprisings that began in late 2010. Facebook and Twitter enabled activists to communicate and organize collective action against the state and mobilize citizens. Digital technology like cell phones and video cameras helped document what was happening directly on the field, serving as great visual material for the international media to disseminate to expose the civilians' reality of the situation.

PRIVACY IS DEAD

Thanks to companies like Google and Facebook, the Internet has managed to collect a wealth of information about people. Through our search activity and what we share online, these companies capture quantitative data concerning our tastes, preferences, behavior and interests, even our secrets. They can tap into our private emails and Skype conversations and gather information we thought no one had access to.

This information is the jackpot. Corporations pay big money to the Googles, Facebooks and Twitters of our time to have access to information that will help them know what products and services will make them more money. They pay even more money to use these Internet platforms to market their products to the people who are most likely to purchase it.

But companies aren't the only ones who have recognized the power of the Internet; governments have capitalized on this resource as well. The

Chinese government has put in place more than 60 countrywide laws that regulate, restrict and monitor Internet user activity within Chinese borders. Many other countries in the Western world have also censored the Internet to varying degrees, for instance, blocking child pornography or hate speech. The motives behind online censorship vary from national security to public interest; however, it's still debatable if the public supports such invasive practices, regardless if the intentions are noble.

"Relying on the government to protect your privacy is like asking a peeping tom to install your window blinds."

—John Perry Barlow

But beyond mere censorship, the Internet has also permitted governments to monitor and essentially spy on citizens. In 2013, computer specialist Edward Snowden leaked classified documents to the press that uncovered the existence of various global surveillance programs run by U.S. government intelligence units. These programs gave the U.S. government access to an exceptional quantity of information via observing and recording online activity of not only U.S. citizens, but people abroad as well. This situation brought about a public debate over the balance between national security and individual privacy. In a world where technology gives certain individuals great knowledge and information, and hence great power, who is to decide who can use it and how?

If we look back in history, the game of war was very different. Our ancestors fought with their bare hands, then sticks and stones, then weapons made of bronze, iron and steel; then we developed gunpowder and used canons, guns and heavy artillery. Eventually, we developed the weapon of all weapons: the atomic bomb. Never before had we developed a weapon that could cause such mass destruction. The Cold War was the beginning of a new era in which power struggles between nations no longer required on-the-ground combat. That's not to say that we are seeing an end to face-to-face conflict; however. Since the Cold War, the traditional nature of warfare no longer depends on military strength; rather, we now give greater weight to diplomacy, negotiation and strategic international interference.

Similarly, in the twenty-first century, we are seeing a rise in the use of drones for warfare. These unmanned aerial vehicles (UAVs) can be operated remotely via satellite or be preprogrammed to complete a specific mission. The concern with drones is that they essentially give the operator an advantage to target and kill individuals with essentially no human risk on their end. Technology has allowed us to let robots fight battles that can have alarming consequences for victims.

> *"If we continue to develop our technology without wisdom or prudence, our servant may prove to be our executer."*
>
> —Omar N. Bradley

You may have deduced by now that modern technology has huge implications. In a positive sense, technology has given us greater access to information, facilitated communication and transparency, increased our life expectancy and unburdened us of trivial and mundane tasks that take up our time. However, technology has also facilitated the complete opposite—it has controlled freedom of speech through censorship, reduced our privacy, devalued real-life experiences, undermined our interpersonal relationships and amplified the way in which we harm and kill each other. How can we reconcile this tension? How can we live fulfilled lives in an age when modern technology reigns? Let's see how the Satellite Tribe is doing it.

EXHIBITIONISM: AVATARS AND SELFIES

Technology breeds chaos; it challenges our sense of identity and our relationship to time, space and energy. Despite being more connected than ever, we are still experiencing a sense of alienation. How can this be? How is it possible to feel so alone while being so connected? The feeling of being in constant communication with others through technology like social media in essence makes us more alienated because it lacks the authenticity of genuine face-to-face human contact.

In order to compensate for this feeling of loneliness, we try even harder to connect through multiple means of communication. We use technology to reaffirm our existence. We post photos of ourselves, of what we are eating, what we are doing and whom we are with. We share songs, quotes, stories and articles that display our desperate attempt to share with the world who we are, what we like and what we believe in. We join multiple social platforms where we can expose ourselves and reach out to an even greater network of people. Essentially, we are trying to confirm our identity.

> *"The representation of human beings by means of an apparatus has made possible a highly productive use of the human being's self-alienation."*
>
> —Walter Benjamin

The Internet is a fascinating tool that has given us two very distinct forms of self-expression: anonymity and exhibitionism. These expressions of self are polar opposites—on the one hand, we are able to hide our identity online, and, on the other, we are able to share everything about ourselves. What a dichotomy!

An older man can pose as a teenage girl in a chat room; a young woman can create a fake Facebook profile to spy on her boyfriend; a boy can create a fake IP address to download music and video games illegally. People create fake personalities online for all sorts of reasons. The anonymity of the Internet helps us hide parts of ourselves that we are perhaps ashamed of being identified with in our real lives.

In forums or for online games, people can create an avatar of themselves, a graphic representation of how they want to appear to the rest of the online world, rather than using their actual photograph. Avatars and screen names like "cougarlover69" or "needforspeed666" allow us to present ourselves to online communities in ways that are relevant to the online forum and untraceable to the real you. You are by no means pressured to reveal your authenticity. Sherry Turkle, an MIT Social Studies of Science and Technology Professor, refers to this phenomenon as an "emerging culture of simulation that substitutes representations of reality for the real world." We are living our lives through a screen, a facade.

At the same time that we have anonymity, we also have the *selfie* culture. A selfie is a photo someone takes of him- or herself and then shares. The selfie represents a greater cultural phenomenon whereby we are becoming accustomed to oversharing every aspect of our lives online. It is technology reinforcing the ego. When teenagers enter puberty and adulthood they are desperate to find out who they really are—the selfie culture has made us all teenagers again.

"It's a matter of adolescents and teens constantly trying to define themselves. They crave positive feedback to help them see how their identity fits into their world. Social media offers an opportunity to garner immediate information.

"The problem is they are looking in a dangerous place."

—Dr. Robyn Silverman

This culture is a childish one. It regresses us to a point in time when we were dependent on others for survival, for self-confirmation. In childhood, our sense of identity is still immature. When we were little, our mother would constantly pester us and ask, "What did you eat today, darling? Did you eat enough? Did you eat something healthy? You need to eat more; you're so skinny!" Now we take that feeling of dependence on our mother's supervision and take photos of our meals and share them with the rest of the online world.

Celebrities are also using the selfie as a means to stay relevant and get the roles they want in upcoming blockbuster films. Actors, musicians and socialites are creating Instagram, Facebook and Twitter accounts and sharing moments in their lives that range from the insignificant to the extravagant. They are showing us that, on the one hand, they are just like us—they shop, walk their dogs, go to the gym and cook dinner like ordinary people do. But they also want to prove to us that they should not be mistaken for a member of the hoi polloi—they attend red-carpet events, grab drinks with other celebrities and fly on private jets to exotic destinations on a whim.

The selfie represents a search for identity. We become so concerned with garnering acceptance that we need others to boost our self-confidence and validate that we are special, attractive, smart and likeable.

"If you want to stay in connection with the world, it's not because you are over connected, that you are well connected."

—Karl Lagerfeld

But the selfie culture does not mean that we are sharing our real self; rather we are sharing a *manufactured* self. We are the curators of our self-representations. We will take dozens of photos of ourselves before we find the perfect one that captures who we want to be and then we share it with everyone else. The selfie culture is disingenuous because we fabricate and control our image online.

What's more, selfies glorify narcissism. They tell us that physical appearance is very important and your looks speak more about who you are than your values, experiences, ideas and beliefs. The Satellite Tribe is not part of this selfie culture because its members don't need it for self-validation. They are so comfortable and confident in who they are that they don't need to put themselves on display for the rest of the world to see. Rather than being anonymous curators of their online identities, they much prefer being invisible. They'd rather be the curators of their *real* lives. They keep their identity separate from their technology.

Indeed, we live in an age of exhibitionism. We exhibit our pains, our joys and our life experiences for the world to see and judge. Exhibitionism is not only paramount to teen culture but also inherent to American culture. From celebrity culture to school shootings, the United States fosters this culture of needing to appear different and unique through self-confirmation.

The fascination surrounding the Kardashian family in their reality show *Keeping Up with the Kardashians* highlights the ultimate display of exhibitionism. They are famous for being famous rather than being famous for any particular accomplishment. Just like "stars" on other reality television programs that are so popular in the United States, the Kardashian family invite the cameras into their private lives and want everyone to see what they are doing—they want to show the world how they are just like your average American family that goes through highs and lows, but at the same time they want to prove that they are extraordinary, wealthy and not like you and me.

Exhibitionism requires that we make up an alibi, an excuse to share too much information. Even though it's cold outside, someone with tattoos on his body will buy clothing that reveals those specific body parts so everyone can see his tattoos. He might argue, however, that he purchased those clothes because they are more "fashionable." For him, each tattoo says something specific about his personality. Whether it is a saying, someone's name, a date, a graphic image or symbol, tattoos are people's way of exhibiting those aspects that say something about who they are or what their values are. It's a permanent walking billboard of self-promotion.

The American culture of exhibitionism expresses a frustration. It's the frustration of a need to belong. As I've mentioned earlier, the American culture is a very teenage culture—Americans are stuck in a Peter Pan syndrome. Social media like Facebook give us an outlet to temporarily hide the frustration of loneliness and our need for confirmation. But the comfort we receive from the online community is superficial. There is a reason why Facebook's button says "like" and not "love"; it is completely noncommittal. It's a world where we don't want to commit too much or interact on an intimate and physical level; we would much rather not get too involved and stick to the surface.

This is completely reptilian. It's the need to instantly satisfy a need the quickest and easiest way possible. Many decades ago, before we had phones and the Internet, we had to wait weeks or months before receiving a well-thought-out love letter. We were forced to be patient, take our time, and make an effort if we wanted to foster our relationships.

"Technology changes, people don't."

—Deb Schultz

OUT OF SYNC WITH THE REPTILIAN

Today, we are so connected through different mediums that we spread our relationships around but never work hard enough to create a deeper connection and more meaningful content. We are constantly disappointed and frustrated if someone doesn't reach out to us even with so many possible paths of communication. There is no room for patience.

We need contact now. Since the reptilian is all about immediate satisfaction, modern technology is also completely in the realm of our reptilian brain. We don't like to think of technology as being slow; we want high-speed Internet, quick access, fast solutions and immediate answers to our questions. Our cell phone apps eliminate the wait for finding a date for the evening, making a restaurant reservation or hailing a cab. If we take a look at the names of some social media products like Instagram or Snapchat, you'll see that even their names reflect this reptilian immediacy. Technology is all about being in the now, in the reptilian realm, and leaves little room for the cortex to think things through in a rational and high-content manner.

The reptilian brain is great for responding to instinctual needs or immediate threats; however, it's not our best ally when it comes to long-term planning. I compare it to a more mob-like mentality. It's disorganized and reactionary rather than a carefully thought-out strategy. The problem with this kind of reptilian thinking is that its lack of order gives religion and the state an excuse to intervene.

The Occupy movement that took place all over the world in 2011 was a reptilian movement because it was highly reactionary and impulsive. Social media managed to disseminate a collective call to action at an alarmingly quick rate. Within hours, people around the world gathered in town squares and city centers to voice their discontent with the global financial system, among other sociopolitical messages.

New York Times columnist Thomas Friedman referred to them as "the square people," or individuals virtually or physically connecting en masse "united less by a common program and more by a shared direction they want their societies to go." These square people maintained communication through social media and organized their localized movements through the same outlets. They gathered in city centers around the world, from Istanbul to Cairo, Kiev to New York City, Moscow to Rio, and each group had a unique set of views and concerns they wanted to express relevant to the local concerns or frustrations.

Few if any of these groups have managed to have any sort of impact on political decision making. Rather than recognizing the square people as representative of the general population who have real concerns that need addressing, those in power have easily dismissed their cries. Why is this, if so many are causing such mayhem and more and more people are expressing that they feel the same way? Because, as Friedman puts it, they are too focused on "disruption" and not enough on "construction."

Their message and energy were so scattered, erratic and reptilian that no one really wanted to invite them to the table to discuss changes. Their demands were too broad and intangible, not concrete enough to even attempt to implement. Their energy and behavior disrupted the daily order of things and gave them less authority. They did not come across as a respectable and organized group that should be heard out.

"Violent movements attract thugs and firebrands who enjoy the mayhem. Violent tactics provide a pretext for retaliation by the enemy and alienate third parties who might otherwise support the movement."

—Steven Pinker

When we use technology and social media in an exhibitionist, narcissistic and quantity-centered fashion, we are less likely to be taken seriously. We all experience a deep-rooted frustration of loneliness and need for self-validation—after all, loneliness is the human condition. However, using technology as a means to define our sense of self is not the direction we should be taking. With such incredible innovations and technology at our fingertips, we could be taking much greater advantage of our modern world.

TECHNOLOGY IS DESTINY

The Global Code for technology is *empty*. When we share information about ourselves online, when we chat on the phone or text message, the content is ultimately empty. It is pure blabber, pure noise. Meaningful content arises from human interactions, from being face-to-face.

The tension that arises from technology is lack of emotion. We are in a generation of "like," not "love." This is because technology is ultimately about quantity—how many friends we have on Facebook, how many people we are texting at once and how many people "retweet" or like what we post. Just because we have *more* information doesn't necessarily mean we have *greater* information.

"Technology over technique produces emotionless design."

—Daniel Mall

With more technology, the more we need emotions. Our reptilian brain demands we think about instinctual needs like sex, food, sleep, and so on. Technology ultimately robs us of these very human, very animalistic needs. We can have virtual sex using a web camera, but we all know that it is most definitely not the same thing.

In Japan, the relationship between men and women is very complicated. If you ever have the chance to visit Japan, observe the interaction between genders in public spaces. In restaurants, women and men sit apart, barely interacting and barely touching.

Through studying the unconscious with peer groups in Japan, I've come to understand Japanese culture and how they perceive love and sex. For the Japanese, love is like a temporary disease; it's a state of insanity that is not conducive to long-term planning. Respect between two partners is what is really needed to keep a relationship strong.

For obvious reasons, this has implications on romantic and sexual dynamics. So when I found out that Japan is now the world leader in developing sex robots, I was not surprised in the slightest. It makes complete sense that sex for pleasurable purposes would be separate from the institution of marriage and family. They have used technology as a way to deal with emotions.

Love, sex and mate selection have now entered the technology realm. With applications like Tinder or Grindr, we can browse through hundreds of photos of potential dates with the swipe of a finger. With a mere photo and tagline, you are encouraged to quickly judge if a person is suitable for a potential encounter. You can open chats with dozens of people simultaneously and have conversations that are ultimately empty. It is speed dating 2.0. If you had met any of these people in real life, say, and asked them for directions on the street or had casual conversation at the bar, maybe you would have a different opinion of them and perhaps exchange numbers. The virtual will never replace the real thing.

Technology completely changes the way our emotional relationships work. Birth control, for instance, brought about a new age whereby women gained control over their bodies and over their sexuality and their pleasure. Women no longer had to abstain from pleasure in order to avoid getting pregnant. This impacts a society emotionally and affects how we deal with our reptilian needs.

Emotions are real and necessary for survival. We need to be able to feel—if not, what would make us any different from the robots we are building? This is a matter of quality versus quantity. Technology comes in waves of quantity—more efficiency, more contact, more gadgets, more connected. But with more quantity we quickly forget about quality, about creating content.

Freud said that biology was destiny, which was a good argument in Vienna at the beginning of the twentieth century. Today we know that biology is not destiny—transgendered individuals, surrogate mothers and hormone therapy have changed all of that. No, the new motto is *technology is destiny*. The Millennials know that technology will dictate their future; it will create the new class system, the new race. The gap between the techno-savvy and the masses will grow wider and wider, to the point that they will be living in two separate dimensions. It might even be possible that these two different species will never meet in the future.

ONE-WAY MIRROR

The code for Millennials is *coma*. They are prisoners behind a one-way mirror.

Millennials are prisoners of the web, like Spider-Man (a repressed adolescent who gains superpowers) or Peter Pan, looking at themselves in a one-way mirror, not seeing the crowd that lies behind it. They are permanently checking their faces (Facebook) and taking pictures of themselves (selfies) and are permanently anxious about their own insecure image.

A lot of people are behind the one-way mirror, but they are all looking at themselves. Nobody goes through the mirror anymore. In some myths, the mirror is a door; in this case, it is a wall. Millennials are alone together, each one looking at him- or herself in this farce of communication.

Millennials are a transition tribe. They may very well represent the next phase of human evolution. Their reality may become the reality of all humankind. Just like cars have replaced horses and become ubiquitous, technosophy will become universal. Millennials are followed by Generation Z, or the "Swipe Generation," which is already ahead of them. They are born in a world of ever-changing technology, and adoption has become almost second nature. Millennials live in complete anxiety when it comes to this technology, whereas Generation Z are like fish in the water. The mother of a one-year-old recently told me, "My son was given a book and he tried to swipe the pages! The first word that came out of his mouth was not Mommy but tablet!"

Yet every revolution has a counterrevolution. Is technology going to dominate our lives and will robots take over? Or are we going to dominate and control technology to create a better world for our children? We will see that if the Satellite Tribe can generate new integrative global leaders (or pilots), we might achieve a positive vision of progress for humanity and for our planet. But in order to create a more integrative world, we first have to face the reality of the world becoming more and more fragmented. We will see in the next chapter that technology divides the world more than it unifies it.

TWELVE

THE GREAT DIVIDE
THE U-CURVE

I do believe that a very simple way to look at the new grouping of human population that I describe in this book has to do with the way these two groups relate to technology.

What I call the E-Group (or, as I like to say, *E-diots*) is made up of individuals who are transferring their intelligence, sense of orientation, memory and identity to a smartphone. They have less and less content and suffer from prosthetic atrophy. Their life is dictated by the tyranny of technology.

On the other side, we have the R-Group. They are the ones who are anchored in the real world—they are the Satellite Tribe. Their world is not local, territorial or national. They can enjoy the reptilian pleasure of the real world (handmade luxury, for example) because they master more than just technology.

The E-Group is composed of technological slaves. The R-Group is composed of people who are not prisoners of any local restrictions and at the same time who master modern technology.

The relationship between the two groups resembles a U-curve. The U-curve is shaped, as the name suggests, like an inverted Gauss (or bell) curve where the two opposing sides grow exponentially apart. The U-curve is essentially an analogy that I have invented to better visualize the evolution of the planet from the perspective of society. It follows a Darwinian approach and takes into account societal evolution in terms of psychosociology, anthropology and politics. There are a few implications of this U-curve.

Technology is accelerating the division between the *Manchine* (an amalgamation of man and machine) and the Satellite Tribe. Third Culture Kids can become billionaires at 15, whereas low-skilled and poorly educated men might lose their jobs and drop out of college. At the same time, the virtual *Manchine* still has to eat, sleep and go to the bathroom. They might spend 90 percent of their waking time in the virtual world, but they still need to be in the real world sometimes in order to survive.

On the other hand, the Satellite Tribe enjoys the real world. Sometimes, this enjoyment comes precisely from the way they manage the E-World. They are able to navigate the E-World with ease, but they are not enslaved by it. The Satellite Tribe members are content creators. They pick and choose the best of each culture and in doing so create the Global Code and a Global Culture. They give content to the *Manchine*. Hopefully, because the Satellite Tribe is multicultural, the content provided will be aspirational. It will create and enhance the core of the Global Culture, which is still in the process of being created. The exponential development of the *Manchine* has deeply challenged most of our nineteenth-century values (such as equality, progress and democracy) and created the Great Divide, thus increasing the anxiety around an eventual robot takeover.

EQUALITY IS DEAD

Equality is quickly becoming a quaint and irrelevant notion. The phrase "all men are created equal," despite its popularity during the French and American revolutions, was coined at a time when Thomas Jefferson owned slaves and Napoleon re-established slavery in the French colonies. Today, many places on Earth have something much closer to the ideal of equality, at least under the law, but other nations and cultures (representing over a billion people) do not.

Certainly this is true of predominantly Muslim countries. Many foreign executives in Chinese companies also report feeling as though they are not being treated equally. Russia and most of the remaining communist-influenced nations (Cuba, Venezuela, Peru and Argentina etc.) have the same problem. It is clear this notion of "equality" dating from the eighteenth century is becoming increasingly less relevant with the passage of time.

The Global Code for women is that they are not equal. This is ironic, since, in terms of survival of the species, they are definitely more important than men—indispensable, in fact. Life cannot be reproduced without a woman's womb. We might be able to freeze semen, and with a large enough stock we may not need men anymore, but we still need women to be biological mothers.

The new code for equality, in reality, is *biology*. The Global Code for life is *death*; we are all going to age, suffer and die, but some of us will live longer. In fact, for the first time in human history we are going to have more than one million people over the age of 100. We keep challenging this "destiny." Nowadays, women are able to freeze their eggs and have children when they are 80 with the help of a surrogate mother. Recently, a child was born from his own grandmother, as his mother was not physiologically able to become pregnant. The mother's fertilized eggs were implanted in the grandmother's womb, and she subsequently became pregnant with her daughter's child. An inequality due to biology has been reduced. With anti-aging drugs, sexual reassignment procedures and oocyte cryopreservation (the ability to "freeze your eggs"), we will keep bringing more equal opportunities to everybody, independent of their biology. But on the other hand, not everybody will have access to these biological innovations. The U-curve creates a gap, a void in between the two major inhabitants that group this planet. The R-Group keeps challenging biology while the E-Group is enslaved by technology.

DEMOCRACY IS DEAD

Recently in the United States, many believed that Obamacare passed Congress only because voters had been manipulated, and that the Obama administration was hiding facts from the public. Congresswoman Nancy Pelosi was quoted as saying, "We need to pass the bill so that you can find out what's in it." The political elite minority in America has long imposed legislation and regulations on the rest of society without their explicit consent. To make matters worse, some legislation is becoming so complicated that people would rather not do anything than try to comprehend its implications.

But one of the key problems with democracy as we know it is that the qualities required to be elected have nothing to do with the qualities required to govern. So we elect incompetent leaders, and on top of that, in America, we don't even need a majority to elect them. Ask Al Gore how he feels about that.

Let's suppose you take a representative sample of 100 citizens. You can already assume that 20 percent of these people are not going to be eligible to vote, either because they do not have the right (too young or possessing a criminal record). Fifty percent of the 80 remaining are not even going to make it to the polling station, and this is due to a variety of factors, ranging from indifference to inconvenience. So now we are down to 40 people; out of those people, only 21 votes are required in order to secure a win and pass the law in question. Thus, out of 100 people, only a minority (21) makes the decision for the rest and imposes their will on the majority. This is what is called the tyranny of the minority.

In many cultures, mobilization and manipulation of the masses are what really matter. Our modern politics lack a sense of duty or higher purpose, and as a result, Western democracy has completely lost its appeal. Washington, D.C., is a perfect example of dysfunctional governance. More and more people want to elect a Santa Claus rather than an actual leader. Hollande in France and Obama in the United States are both examples of candidates who proposed unrealistic goals in order to be elected. Hollande essentially gave his electorate the impression that, were he elected, they would not have to work and that the state would take care of them.

In France, out of roughly 66 million citizens, approximately 15 million are retired and receiving pensions. What's more, roughly 11 percent of the population is unemployed and receiving benefits. It was recently discovered that thousands of educators were receiving a full salary even though they were not teaching any classes and had no students. In England, the navy has fewer sailors than it has bureaucrats.

It's fairly clear that almost nobody likes politicians, and that politics is often a despairing subject for many people. Today a new Global Code for democracy is emerging, and it is totally disconnected from politics and politicians. The cell phone generation knows too much; they have access to all of the information at any given time, and they are increasingly harder to lie to and deceive. Whatever trust we once had in the "system" is now gone.

In many parts of the world, people are distancing themselves from politicians, associating them only with short-term manipulation, corruption and power-mongering. Instead, these same people are moving back to two institutions that provide pure content: the church and the army. In times of *flash mob, no content, occupy* and *anonymous,* the answer to chaos is too often these two archetypal structures, which connote hierarchy and discipline and still have the respect of the population. We can see around the world the constant fight between these two structures. In Egypt, for instance, once the Arab Spring lost its steam, the church took over and imposed a clear inequality between men and women; it essentially imposed a return to medieval standards, thus generating another rebellion. Then, of course, the army took over. Whereas the church serves the purpose of instilling moral justice in the minds of citizens, the army imposes rule of law (however draconian).

Turkey is another example of a cultural revolution. Its independence was won by Mustafa Kemal Atatürk, a military man, and has now been taken over by the church. It can be argued that Istanbul, with its secular and Western value systems, is not representative of Turkey as a whole. The majority of the Turkish population lives in Anatolia, which is deeply religious and underdeveloped. It is these people who voted for Erdogan, Turkey's current president, who publicly endorses his wife's use of the veil. The return of the church (Turkey) and the return of the army (Egypt) can be seen as the end of democracy as we know it. The dysfunctional state of Washington, D.C., and the general resentment that permeates the American population (as witnessed by Congress's extremely low approval rating) mark the decline of this system of governance.

This is why the U-curve is an interesting model to view governance. On the one hand, we have a return to medieval times with the church (most notably in the form of Sharia law) guiding faith and the army imposing order. On the other hand, the Satellite Tribe is becoming increasingly secular as it separates from the masses. These Platinum Gypsies are bound by no ideology and no nationality; their philosophy is practical and based on what works.

But with the failure of government, who is in charge? The rule of law is necessary. You cannot play a game if the rules are unclear and ever-changing.

Uncertainty is bad for business. Platinum Gypsies are becoming the de facto pilots of the spaceship we call planet Earth. Two elements are key to understanding the evolution of the Anthropocene. This small group of people wield enormous power, and they can choose to vote with their feet. In doing so, they are showing the way forward for the others.

If Beijing keeps swallowing Hong Kong, the Platinum Gypsies living there will simply move to Singapore. If France continues in its destructive path, young entrepreneurs will keep moving to London. Glomads, by nature, live out of a suitcase. They have no special attachment to a nation, church or state: they are free. Free-thinkers, free-movers, free-adaptors. Modern technology enables their lifestyle. You can run your business from a smartphone or tablet from almost anywhere. With the help of technology, your office can be run from almost anywhere you go with almost no overhead cost. This is the new Cultural Nucleic Archetype—the CNA— of the Satellite Tribe and the new Global Code.

What I call the Cultural Nucleic Archetype is the core or center of a culture. The CNA is to a culture what the DNA is to a species. It assumes the permanence and survival of the culture. The three basic elements of the CNA are time, space, and energy.

PROGRESS

Today communication is almost free. Technologies like the Internet, Wi-Fi, Skype and What's App are becoming so ubiquitous that you don't need the expenses of an office. Your team can be with you all of the time, anywhere. Whereas the E-Group side of the U-curve is still stuck in one location, one time zone and lots of overhead, the other side has liberated itself from location, time zones and administrative expenses.

This is not even really a class division—more like two different species who are functioning in completely different dimensions. We have to add one dimension to the classic CNA model of time, space and energy. This dimension is "direction," or *sens* (the French word for direction, which is also synonymous with meaning). What is the direction of the movement? The salient question of identity is no longer "Who are you?" but rather, "Where are you going? What are you becoming?"

Are you moving up, or down? Are you expanding and growing, or slowing down and regressing? The notion of progress has to be reconsidered. We know that in the last few decades, millions of people in China have been lifted from poverty. Are they happier? Is the measure of GDP correlated with happiness? How do we measure progress when it is such a relative notion? Let's learn from the Platinum Gypsies. For them, progress translates to "one step." In fact, *one step* is the Global Code for progress. When companies create products with countless buttons and complicated instructions that require time, energy and frustration in order to be able to use them, this is the opposite of progress.

When you need to take a week-long class on how to operate the radio on your new BMW 7 Series, this is not progress. When the U.S. tax code comprises so many thousands of pages, countless complicated rules and a myriad of scenarios that not even the IRS understands, this is not progress. When you spend more time in the car and in the airport than it actually takes you to fly to your destination, this is not progress.

If more regulation, more steps and more bureaucracy do not equal progress, then what is progress? Progress is one step, no airport, flat-tax, one button, on or off, no waiting, no cables. This is progress.

We need to revise our notion of progress. After the Berlin Wall came down, a lot of people spoke about the end of history, the world being flat and a New World Order. But this was approached with a nineteenth-century mind-set and overlooked the transformational impact of new technology.

What we have discovered by going around the world and exploring the collective unconscious is that, contrary to the post–Iron Curtain dream of unity, we are going to be more and more separated. Simply put, the forces that separate us seem a lot stronger than those that unify us. In this universe of isolation, some of us are turning toward machines to experience closeness and intimacy.

ROBOT CONSPIRACY

"It seems like machines and robots are taking over every aspect of our lives, becoming more intelligent than we are. Look at all these coffee machines; it looks like they are programed to train us to become dumber and dumber. The same with the GPS; without a GPS, we cannot find our way anymore."—21-year-old male, Mumbai

"One day, they might not need us anymore."—19-year-old female, Mumbai

I would like to share the following story I created not long ago. It is about an anthropologist visiting from outer space on a mission to observe life on Earth. This anthropologist diligently collected notes, films and pictures, then went back to his planet and described life on planet Earth as follows:

This planet is inhabited by very intelligent individuals called CARS. They have two eyes in front, which project light, and four wheels. They are divided into several races and have to wear the name of their race on their body. Some belong to the Chevrolet race, others to the Mercedes race, etc.

They start moving in the morning, leave their home that they call garage, and go to places where they meet other cars. Most of the time the meetings last all day and are held in places called parking lots. In the meantime, their servants, also called humans, go to work to be able to buy the liquid that the cars need. They also wash them.

The servants work, go shopping, and take them back home at the end of the day. Sometimes they (the CARS) have a companion waiting for them in the garage. They usually spend the night with their companion. We have observed "ménage a trois," when they live in a three-car garage, but this is relatively rare. Life on this planet is completely organized for the best functioning of their inhabitants, the CARS. The planet is covered with what they call highways where the human slaves are not allowed to walk.

They have also developed a higher intelligence, which makes them independent of the human slaves. They are going to be able to go to their everyday meetings without the help of the human slaves, so the latter would be able to work more and produce more for the cars. The humans will also have more time to search on the ground for more food for their masters. From the distance it looks like there are more and more cars, as their rate of reproduction is very high. Considering that some places on this planet are seeing less and less human slaves being born, and the CARS becoming more and more independent, we might consider that the human species might soon be extinct.

There is also another group of inhabitants; they are called *dogs*. Each *dog* has at least one human slave. They pull them around in a leash and force them to pick up their body excrements. The human slaves feed them every day. The dogs don't work. Sometimes they yell at their slaves and even bite them. But it looks like the humans are too weak to rebel.

This observation might suggest that we have reached a breaking point in human history. Like the sorcerer's apprentice, we cannot understand or control our own creations. If machines double their capacity and intelligence every 18 months, when it takes 18 years to create a new generation of humans, then time is not in our favor. If machines can learn and adapt faster than we do, who is going to lead whom? In an interview with the BBC, Stephen Hawking sent an alarming message when he said, "The development of full artificial intelligence could spell the end of the human race." One of the top engineers at Google, Ray Kurzweil, reinforced this view when he predicted that digital immortality—that is, the ability to upload one's brain to a computer—was a not-so-distant reality. The future of mankind is now dictated by machines.

If you're looking for examples of the way robots are taking over our human life and our human interaction, there is no better place to look than Japan. In Kawasaki, Yahui and Tatso Matsui met, as many Americans do, because of their dogs. We know that walking your dog at night is one of the best ways to meet strangers. Their dogs' names were Ai and Doggy. When they got married, their two dogs were at the wedding, dressed as a traditional Japanese bride and groom and seated at the head of the table. That was in 2004. Now the two dogs are old and can barely move. When Doggy meets Ai, he tries to communicate with her but she does not respond. She cannot even move her head.

The problem is that Matsui cannot take the dogs to the vet because they are not real animals. They are robots—toy dogs called Aibos, made by Sony. According to an article by Takashi Mochizuki and Eric Pfanner in the *Wall Street Journal,* an estimated total of 150,000 Aibos were sold by Sony.[1]

But in order to cut costs, Sony stopped producing spare parts and providing maintenance service. To try to find a solution, the pet owners have created a support group. "Aibos owners' attachment to the dogs reflects Japan's attitude toward robots, which are often seen here as man's best friend, rather than Hollywood-style monsters," says Takashi.

In one of the meetings, Sumie Maikawa said that she and her husband, who have no children, see their Aibo as a daughter. Miss Maikawa, who is 72, talks to her Aibo every day, travels with it and makes clothes for it. Mr. Maikawa does not want to take any risk repairing his dog. "I can't risk my precious dogs because they are important members of our family and they are the reason my wife and I met," he says. Miss Maikawa agreed that whoever of the two lives longer should be cremated with the dog. They expect to be reunited in the afterlife.

Anthropomorphism is not new. Little children treat their teddy bears as if they were alive, but they know they are not. The robot conspiracy represents another dimension of the evolution of the *Manchine.* After a while, the robots are treated like humans. They are not toys anymore. When a little girl in America plays with a doll, it is OK that she treats her like her child. But when the little girl becomes an adult, she usually does not take her doll everywhere anymore. She usually relates to real humans and sometimes even has a real daughter.

This is an obvious slippery slope—a force that is taking the human away from humanity into *manchinity.* Once the robots learn how to repair themselves and reproduce themselves, they might not need humans anymore. I remember reading a story many years ago in a comic book for children in France. A woman is preparing a lunch box for her husband. He is going to work. She accompanies him to the door, kisses him goodbye and waves at him as she watches him walk away toward the bus. As he goes toward the bus, a car hidden by the bus drives by at full speed and kills him. The woman slowly goes toward the dead body, picks up a tag that he was wearing and goes back into her home. She takes her phone and calls the central operation system. "Hi, my number 56X24 has been terminated. I need another one." The next day, a new husband is there looking at his wife. She decided to go out to for a walk to get some fresh air, but she did not see the bus coming. She was crushed and killed. The husband goes slowly toward the dead body. He picks up her tag, goes back to his house, picks up the phone and calls the central operation system. "Hi, my number XX7876 is terminated. I need a new one."

The robot conspiracy could be compared to the automobile conspiracy. When cars were first produced more than 100 years ago, only some crazy elitists could afford—mentally and financially—to drive an automobile. The law in England at the time was that anyone traveling by automobile should employ a man to wave a red flag and blow a horn to warn pedestrians and other users of the road. The idea was to warn the inhabitants of the village of the arrival of this monster and to make sure that they were not hurt or afraid. Many people at the time anticipated that this ugly moving engine would never replace the beauty and the elegance of a horse and would never become popular. Some people advanced an idea that came to be called the automobile conspiracy. They described a world completely dedicated to automobiles, with highways, garages, gas stations and pollution and people stuck in traffic for hours. Of course, at that time, people said that this was absurd and would never happen. My warning here is that we might be in the same situation with the robot conspiracy.

In keeping with this trend, the Japanese, to stick with a theme, have also created the perfect robot sex partner, with artificial skin much like what's used in plastic surgery and various programs for all of the positions you might need. Their commercials call it the perfect wife—a lot cheaper than a real wife. You also don't need to divorce her; you just trade her in for a new model.

The robot conspiracy further increases the risk of the great divide. After all, as we've seen, the Satellite Tribe moves in the opposite direction: more hand and less machine, more human contact and fewer robots. The Satellite Tribe is ahead of time, thanks to the fast forward city. They are not following the machines; they are ahead of them. We will see later that this split could, in fact, speed up the cessation of the human race.

CONCLUSION

THE SATELLITE TRIBE

We have seen that the Satellite Tribe lives in hubs, that the future of cities is city-states, that old-fashioned universities should be replaced by fast forward ecosystems and that robots might soon take over the planet. But the overarching Global Code that we have discovered is *the Great Divide*.

The time of unity is over. The European Union is in shambles; the Chinese want to take revenge against the Japanese, who are ready to re-arm; the Middle East is a permanent tribal battle field where artificial nations created after World War I are melting like snow in the sun. At the same time, nationalism and fascism are making a comeback, and religious warfare, led by Islamist terrorists, is dissolving any sense of security. The de-uniting or fragmentation of the planet is the unconscious force in action. Technology and its "technosophy" have created a hyper-connected world with no content. We are alone together. We are more connected and more isolated than ever before; we have access to all the information in the world, but we have less and less ability to make clear judgments.

But on the other end of the spectrum, we have the Global Tribe, the Satellite Tribe. They have the NASA point of view. Whereas Millennials do not exist in a real dimension of space (they are never here, and space is the missing dimension), the Satellite Tribe masters space. They do not depend on any special location; they are at home wherever they are. Whereas

Earthlings are moving backward in time toward medieval values, the Satellite Tribe is ahead, never thinking about the past, always using any new situation as a new starting point. They recalculate, as opposed to wasting their time on blaming.

The U-curve should serve as a new pair of glasses; it offers a new way to look at planet Earth. Our current mental tools, left over from the eighteenth and nineteenth centuries, are obviously obsolete. Equality was a dream whose time has passed, as reality takes over. Biology does not understand equality—men cannot get pregnant, aging creates a second diaper generation and genetic heredity is destiny.

It is clear that the United Nations' declaration that all men and women are equal and should be treated as such is nonnegotiable. However, even though they "agree" with it on paper, many national cultures blatantly reject this notion in practice. In my book *Move Up,* I present the countries where women are still not treated equally and why this is not acceptable. The fact that the United States still considers Saudi Arabia as a respectable ally is baffling, especially when all signs are pointing to a future in which renewable energy sources will become the norm.

In other part of the world, people feel differently. The Brahman does not want to be equal to the Dalit, the Sunni to the Shiite, the general to the foot soldier. Confucius, who is regarded as the master thinker and great philosopher in large parts of Asia, does not care much about equality. Confucians value filial piety (respect of your parents), social hierarchy, leadership and harmonious relations—these are deemed more important than your individuality. The role and status of women are clear indicators of how evolved any culture is, and the medieval treatment of women worldwide should not be accepted, but rather systematically challenged.

Our new, multipolar world needs a multipolar philosophy and vision. Today, the West is perceived as both a model to aspire to and a decadent enemy. But when those critics come from countries that still practice female genital mutilation and honor killing, the real sign of decadence is the West's willingness to stand by and watch.

The Satellite Tribe does not belong to any of these centers of influence. They navigate easily between all of them and can see what works and what does not. They know Voltaire and Confucius, the Quran and the Bible, the West and the Far East, but they are not partisan. Women of the Satellite

Tribe are more than equal. They are aware of their unique contributions, and they are aware that the new global world needs inclusive leadership.

The fact that they are out there, in a symbolic space, permanently navigating around the globe, gives them a freedom that goes beyond modernity.

THE GREAT DIVIDE

The key issue is the Great Divide between the E-Group and the R-Group. These two groups are pulling apart, like the universe that is always expanding. We are not going toward greater unity, but rather great disconnection. In the future, these two groups might even become two separate species: people on Earth will be dominated by robots, while the Satellite Tribe will achieve higher human connection by giving priority to physical human contact, the reinforcement of tribal rituals and the sharing of common symbols. The Great Divide means that *Manchines* will have less and less content and meaning in their lives, and consequently will regress to medieval behaviors and mentality.

Religious wars and extreme violence will become the norm, while the Satellite Tribe, feminine and integrative, will become symbol creators with a planetary vision and mission. On the one hand, the character of our society will be determined by engineers who have no clue what the consequences of their innovations will be on those humans who will be adopting them. Technology is always being used before it is completely understood. On the other hand, we will have a feminine tribe, free from the machines but using this technology as a domesticated tool, giving reptilian importance to the hand, to touching, to rituals of pleasure and living in the real world.

There is always a *lag* between the arrival of "innovation" and the appreciation of its consequences. We are living in that *lag*: Robots and *Manchines* are reducing the human condition. The Satellite Tribe are the dissenters, the new refuge for the humanists. By choosing reality over the virtual, they challenge the engineers' world; by choosing humanities over robotics, they are the *divergents*. Rebellion starts by saying *no* to cell phones at dinner, then during a meeting and then at the club. Look up and see the real world. Free yourself from being enslaved by the machines.

Never mind the texting, the millions of breaking news stories, the total pollution of infinite information. Your solemn responsibility should be to create *substance*.

SUBSTANCE

We are in deep need of new philosophers. The posthumanist world, created by the new technology, *technosophy*, and *googlesophy*, clearly states that there will be no distinction between humans and machines. Well, we need dissenters. Those dissenters will come from the Global Satellite Tribe, the Third Culture Kids, the rebels who will fight the tyranny of technology. After all, processing information is not the highest aim of the human species.

THE NEW PHILOSOPHERS

We had philosophers, real philosophers, who were behind the Enlightenment of the eighteenth century, and who fought against obscurantism. Light was pitted against darkness during this age of reason. Then we had the nineteenth century and the revolutionary philosophers, who were more motivated by passion than they were by reason. This was a century in which the French gave us many words that we still use today: terrorism (*La Terreur*), communism (*La commune de Paris, 1870*), sabotage (putting your wooden shoe, or sabot, in a machine in order to break it), sadism (the famous Marquis de Sade who was jailed in the Bastille) and bureaucracy (comes from the word *bureau,* which means both a desk and an office).

The twentieth century became a labor of deconstruction, with philosophers like Derrida, Foucault, and many others, but in the twenty-first century, we have a new kind of philosopher: the journalist "philosopher." The French even invented the term *nouveau philosophes*; one such example is Bernard Henri Levy, a famous French public intellectual. If you are good on TV and followed by many very-nice-looking girls, then you are considered a "philosopher." But in fact they are just good journalists, adept at controlling the media and promoting their books. Catchy titles like *The World Is Flat* and *The Tipping Point* get published as bestsellers. But these authors are no Voltaire, Kierkegaard or Schopenhauer. They are just journalists pleasing the *Manchines.* They are the mirrors of the posthuman society, not the leaders, not the dissenters or the rebels that we need to challenge the tyranny of the robots.

Now we also have the engineer philosophers. Their goal is to make you a slave to new technology, as we have seen when we studied the Millennials. The engineers are being taken over by their own creations. Technology is the new philosophy of the masses. It dictates values, behaviors, imposes its time frame, and transforms people who are unaware of their surroundings into zombies. It is taking them to a virtual world where machines and robots rule.

On one hand you have the missing dimension, space; on the other hand, you have a total mastery of space. The Millennials are in a biological coma, stuck physically in one place while traveling in a virtual world. The Satellite Tribe is always moving in the real world, selecting the best human and handmade experiences. The disconnection is getting worse and worse. The *Manchines* are unlearning basic elements of dealing with the real world, losing all social skills, replacing any communications with texting. They are the Global Texting Tribe. I text, therefore I am. On the other side, the Third Culture Kids are more creative, can adapt to very different situations, enjoy constant change, and have a global group of friends.

WHAT MIGHT HAPPEN?

On the positive front, we can expect that the Satellite Tribe and the Third Culture Individuals are going to become the trendsetters, the dissenters, the new philosophers; they will create an aspirational world. They might promote very simple universal values, such as safety and security, as opposed to chaos and terrorism, life as opposed to death, respecting your parents, taking care of your children, rewarding hard work, valuing beauty (0.7), luxury (hand), pleasure (rituals and talent) and other feminine values that resonate throughout the desirable cultures on this planet.

At the same time, however, the Satellite Tribe is pro-freedom and choices, which might be in conflict with different religious and cultural beliefs. Most people will agree that we should pull together, forget our differences to fight the common enemies, *ignorance* being one among them. The first mission of the Satellite Tribe should be to rally the world to get *prepared* to follow the Global Code for survival and the Swiss model.

On the negative side, we have to be aware of the hidden forces of obscurantism, of obsolete dogma and manipulation of the masses by a new technology at the service of sadistic thugs whose only interest is accumulating and maintaining power. The journalists have to become journalists again, to do an honest job of checking and reporting facts and to stop thinking of themselves as philosophers. If they don't change their attitudes, they will increase the dangers of radicalizing young people lost in a virtual world with no content, and only false promises. (Seventy-two virgins, oh really? And a free chocolate sundae?)

The fact that so many thousands of young people are so easily radicalized and become criminals is baffling. The rules of the game have changed. Your enemy does not want to win and then to have peace. You never end a war against terrorism; there is no peace treaty at the end, because there is no end. Suicide bombers do not care if they die. Terrorism is a social cancer, and the idea that you can negotiate with cancer is a dangerous illusion. The Satellite Tribe knows all that.

JOINING THE TRIBE

If you want to change the world, be a leader and experience success. One of your first obligations is to join the tribe. This is not just being with the wealthy, as many rich people don't belong to the tribe and many young average people who are not wealthy definitively belong to the tribe. Remember, this is an attitude, not a bank account.

How do you join the tribe?

Learn, learn, learn. Never stop learning; at any age, wherever you are, learn. But it is not just about how many languages you speak; it is also about developing your feminine side, your integrative attitude, your two sides which complement each other. The more the merrier! Take languages, for example—how many do you speak, two? It's time for a third one. How many musical instruments do you play, none? It's time to buy into the Suzuki method. Immerse yourself in other cultures; go work on a farm in Africa, in a vineyard in the south of France, in a school for the deaf in inner-city Washington.

Speak, speak, speak and always speak to people. Get to know them; ask for their names, where they are from, what they do, what they like.

I was in a taxi the other day in Washington, and I noticed that my cab driver was from Africa. So I started speaking with him.

Me: "Hello, how are you; where are you from?"
Ahmed: "Somalia."
Me: "Interesting! I was born in France, but I am an American today."
Ahmed: "Well, I want to become an American too."
Me: "What do you do besides driving a cab?"
Ahmed: "Well, I am an engineer, but I did not get a job as an engineer here yet, so I drive a cab, work as a gardener in the morning, and go to school at night to get an MBA."
Me: "Do you have children?"
Ahmed: "Yes, three." He shows me the picture with his wife.
"They are going to school. They are good kids; they are learning English and starting to play softball. I am Ahmed."
He shakes my hand as we have arrived at my destination.
Me: "I am Clotaire; it's nice to meet you."

I am sure he is going to make it. He already has some elements of the Satellite Tribe: he speaks several languages, has had several cultural experiences and has Third Culture Kids. And at the same time, I learned a little bit about Somalia and the attitude of the immigrants from this African country.

Move, move, move and never stop moving. Now you know that you don't need a suitcase, just friends (remember Jeffrey?). But even if you cannot take a plane, walk or take a bike and discover. Follow the saying that you should look at the world you know as if you had never seen it before, and the things you have never seen before as if they are the most familiar. As Marcel Proust said, "The real voyage of discovery consists not in seeking new landscapes but in having new eyes." The Satellite Tribe has developed a new way to look at things; these tribe members have new eyes.

Get the right attitude. Knowledge is easy to acquire, whereas attitudes are difficult to change. Remember, do not dress for the job you have; dress for the job you want to have. So do not think, dress or function for the local tribe you belong to. Dress for the tribe you want to join: Speak Satellite

Tribe, think Satellite Tribe, dress Satellite Tribe. Look at the Court and the Courtesans; they are the trendsetters. You are not a tourist on this planet; you function at a higher level of awareness. You have different glasses, different motivations and different goals. Get to identify the members of the Satellite Tribe, and get to know them. Soon you might become a member of the global family and be *invited!*

At the end of the journey, the big question remains: does the Global Code exist? Do we possess a simple word to summarize and explain our future? Or do we have a dual mind, tyrannized by opposite forces—one side going away from modernity and back into medieval times, with a dominance of *Manchines* dominated by robots, and, at the opposite end of the spectrum, a new species of multicultural satellite individuals, who manage to use machines but at the same time free themselves from the dictatorship of the engineers.

Our planet has a new brain; this is clear and unquestionable. The global brain is made of unlimited connections. But don't forget that cows and elephants have big brains, although we do not see them flying to the moon. So the global brain is the infrastructure that could lead to the appearance of a Global Mind. What we have discovered is that the fast development of the brain has not been followed by the same development of the mind. We have a hyperactive global cortex, and at the same time an empty mind. As we have seen, Millennials are always texting and have nothing to say. The code for this Global Mind at the cortex level is *no content.*

NO CONTENT

People are constantly connected with nothing to say. Texting is the new drug; even in public safety campaigns, "don't drink and drive" has been replaced by "don't text and drive." At the limbic level we have a resurgence of anxiety. The Global Code at this level is not "peace of mind," but rather, "only the paranoids survive." The Swiss, the Koreans and the Singaporeans have paid a price for their accomplishments: they are permanently worried, constantly anxious, always expecting the worst. The technosophy, of course, thrives on chaos and disasters, and thanks to 24/7, always-catastrophic breaking news, we have plenty of them. If a suicide bomber kills ten people anywhere in the world, the whole planet is going to know it and see the dead bodies immediately multiplied thousands of times by social media. So at the limbic emotional level, the Global Code is *hyper anxiety*.

HYPER ANXIETY

But when we move to the third brain or reptilian level—and we know that the reptilian always wins—what do we see?

We see a gap, a huge vacuum between two extremes. On one hand the technosophy, Moore's law, has created a generation with a missing dimension. *Manchines* do not exist in real space; they are taken over by "smart" machines. For the first time in human history, the evolution of smart machines is leaving the evolution of the human species in the dust. Because of the basic principle that prosthetics atrophy, we can see that "the smarter the machine, the dumber the human." Cars don't need drivers, planes don't need pilots, wars don't need warriors, and friends are replaced by robots. So we will lose the ability to drive, pilot, fight, or care for other humans. Smart is now an adjective that we use for machines: smartphone, smart cars, smart bombs. As we see intelligence moving away from humans, are we following the fate of the dinosaurs?

But on the other side of the gap, we see a small group of people (actually, not so small) who might change the evolution of our planet. They are the dissenters. They are the Satellite Tribe. They benchmark everything and can tell us what is best. Today, if you don't know something, it is because you choose not to know. If 80 percent of the world population has a cell phone, then 80 percent of the population has access to all of the knowledge available.

But the next step is not more information, which only creates more anxiety. Saturation brings immobility. Too much is worse than not enough.

TO SIMPLIFY

If you speak another language, nobody can steal it from you. If you have two suitcases, somebody might steal one from you. If you know many rituals of pleasure, you are rich inside. If you have a large family, you have biological bonds and reptilian connections around the world. And if you follow Confucius's recommendation that you should respect your family (your reptilian connections), you have more chances to survive and thrive. These are some of the values brought by the Satellite Tribe that will influence the future of our planet.

If we follow the Satellite Tribe and let them show the way we might be able to bridge the gap and end the Great Divide, and if we all agree that life is better than death and succeed in uniting against common enemies, then we might end up as being a united human tribe.

But in order to move in that direction, we need an Integrative Leader. The masculine principle is exclusion, separation, segregation, "you are either with us or against us." No gray area.

The feminine principle, based in biology, is integrative. Women need to take something inside themselves to transform it and create life. Men just take something out of their bodies. "Done, next," is their motto.

When men are asked to make a definition, they always do it by exclusion. "This is not it, this is not that and not that," until they consider the remaining possibilities and say, "That's it, this is that." (By the way, this is how we make diagnostics in medicine.)

Research has proven that women operate in the opposite way. When asked to make a definition, they will proceed by inclusion: "This is it and that also and this as well." They will keep adding. Men will ask, "When is it done?" Women will answer, "It's never done," which, of course, men cannot stand. We can understand this as women are the (biological) experts of constant transformation. And as the world is constantly evolving and changing, who is better prepared to deal with these changes?

It is time for our species to move away from men's principles to female principles. I am not advocating discrimination of gender differences. For the record, I know a lot of men who are more feminine than most women and, vice versa, women who are more masculine. I am speaking of a switch in principles. Christina Kirchner in Argentina and Dilma Rousseff in Brazil are not the best examples of feminine leadership and of the feminine principle of integration.

We have to acknowledge that we still cannot create a human being without a woman's womb, the feminine capacity of integration and motherly love. The wisdom of the feminine Global Code is to keep adding. Keep moving, and never stop. It is time for the human species to stop the blame game and to adopt the GPS philosophy of permanently recalculating.

We saw earlier that the ideal leader could be a hybrid between Lee Kuan Yew, Pericles, Al Maktoum and Mustafa Kemal. Up until now, these leaders have mostly been men. But the Satellite Tribe is going to be the one to change that, and it is women who will take the reins of our planetary spaceship. The structure of the Satellite Tribe is already a matriarchal one. We have seen that women are more educated and that a higher percentage of women go into higher education than men. Women live longer and are going to be in higher positions than men. It is clear that women are the game changers of the future. They are going to lead the Satellite Tribe and hopefully the planet. The female principal is integrative and predetermined by biology. We need global connectors who can go beyond culture, beyond differences to create a common global culture that will fight common enemies. *The Da Vinci Code* expressed a fundamental idea rooted in archetypes: Human creation comes from the Holy Grail, which is an analogy for the woman's womb, where we all come from. Maybe, after all, André Malraux was right: "the future will be feminine or will not be." In the end, the Global Code is *women*.

GLOBAL BRANDS, GLOBAL LEADERS AND A GLOBAL WORLD

I would like to summarize some of the findings, answer some of the questions that you may be having as a reader and provide you with a checklist of what can be done with these findings:

HOW TO CREATE A GLOBAL BRAND

1. You need a "village of origin." When we studied Jack Daniel's in Russia, young men who hated the United States told us that Jack Daniel's is not American; he is Tennessee.
2. You need a reptilian hot button. The reptilian is not influenced by cultures. Pantene is not in the shampoo business, but in the food business. Women worldwide want to feed (feeding is loving), and they want their children to grow. So Pantene is food for your hair to grow. This is a global reptilian hot button.
3. You don't buy a brand; you *join* a brand. One example of this is Laphroaig whiskey, which offers clients a piece of land in Scotland and a chance to become a member of the clan when they buy a bottle.

4. You need to have a global archetypal logic of emotion. One example that resonates with Jeep owners is the following: "I don't need a road; I make my own road."

5. You need to be the best at what you do; permanently benchmark your competitors and follow the indications of the Satellite Tribe. Paris lost the number one ranking for tourists' destination to London. The Carlyle in New York City did not adapt and is now losing its clientele to the St. Regis.

6. Money is not the goal; it is a consequence of your *passion* and *commitment*.

7. A global brand is a *signature*. Ralph Lauren, Rolls-Royce, Veuve Clicquot, Marriott and Coco Chanel are all great examples of signature artists who have passion and commitment.

8. You need to follow the Satellite Tribe and anticipate their needs: one step, no luggage, renting vs. owning, real vs. virtual, etc.

9. Your brand should always be growing, changing, adapting and following the GPS philosophy.

10. You should decide where you belong on the U-curve. E or R.

HOW TO CREATE A GLOBAL LEADER

1. I believe that companies need global leaders, and they should choose them from the Satellite Tribe; this gives them the bird's-eye view of the planet they so desperately need to lead. We need our politicians to benefit from the same view.

2. Global leaders should bring *content*. Moses asked his people to follow him, as he had seen the promised land, but it's not enough to say "let's do it" when you don't communicate what you want to do.

3. Global leaders should symbolize the aspirations of the people they want to lead by liberating women from their daily chores and creating an environment with no pollution (Tesla).

4. Global leaders should be members of the Satellite Tribe and ideally part of the Court.

5. Global leaders should always have a higher purpose. Shareholder value is not a higher purpose; it is a consequence of doing the right things.

6. Global leaders should have a village of origin and be proud of it, yet at the same time they should have a feminine, integrative approach to problem solving. Each culture has a contribution to make to the world; it's just a matter of selecting the best ones.

7. Global leaders should not only speak several languages; they should speak several cultures by being aware and trained to understand cultural and global codes.

8. They should be champions of fighting the common enemies.

9. Finally, they should be consistent in their higher purpose and long-term vision.

HOW TO CREATE A GLOBAL WORLD

Today, piloting our planet is too important to be left up to robots and engineers who have no idea of the unintended consequences of what they are doing. So here are some suggestions to create a better world for our children.

1. Planet Earth needs a *pilot,* a leading philosopher, a modern Pericles, a Lee Kuan Yew to create a new global culture.

2. We all need the NASA point of view that the Satellite Tribe can provide. When you are in space and see this little ball called Earth, you realize that this is our unique home, that it is fragile and that we are in this together.

3. Let's learn from other cultures; let's benchmark and promote the best education, health care, pleasure, safety and security. Let the Satellite Tribe tell us.

4. If democracy and equality sound like old, obsolete ideas from the nineteenth century, we need to go further, recalculate and create better institutions, create better separation of power, create more respect for gender and age differences, create better opportunities and create better education and health care.

5. The world does not need nation-building (nineteenth-century concept) but to move tribes to create collective culture (culture-building).

6. Finally, the United Nations, which has proven to be completely useless and inefficient, should be replaced by the United Cultures of the world, whose mission would be to unify and integrate the best of each culture to create a global culture.[1]

ACKNOWLEDGMENTS

For the better part of the last decade, this literary endeavor has dominated my life. The extraordinary research and hours of traveling it took to write this book demanded constant intellectual, financial and, most importantly, moral support. In this respect I have been most fortunate to have so many friends and colleagues willing and able to assist me.

First off I would like to give many thanks to the ROC Family, my network of colleagues, affiliates and friends who support me, host me and work with me around the world. I would like to give a special thanks to Mustafa Kelekçi in Istanbul, Dico Tostes in Rio de Janeiro, Jean François Hautot in Paris, Hans Arnold in London, Carlos Gutierrez in Bogotá, Mr. Cho in Seoul, Jacky Cheung in Hong Kong and Shanghai, Parag and Aisha Khanna in Singapore and Nandita Kaushik in New Delhi.

Special thanks to Dr. Andres Roemer in Mexico for introducing me to so many great intellectuals and inviting me to speak at La Ciudad de las Ideas, where I met Richard Dawkins, Steven Pinker, Alain De Botton and Helen Fisher. Their brilliant minds have stimulated me beyond recognition. Thanks to Ricardo Salinas for inviting us all to his beautiful hacienda to brainstorm our "Dangerous Ideas."

I want to thank Dr. De Gioia, the president of Georgetown University in Washington, D.C., for giving me the opportunity to discover the Global Code for higher education in Doha, Oxford, Istanbul and Dubai. Thanks also to Susan Frost and Anne Aufort, who traveled the world with us for this project.

Of course this book would not have been possible without the financial support of my loyal clients: special thanks to Blake Emery and Ralph Heinz at Boeing; to Armand de Viloutrey, Olivier de Lisles and Debra Butler at Firmenich; to my good friends Dr. Christian Deuringer and Folker Michaelsen at Allianz in Munich, Sophia Skinner and Lisa Gregg at American Express in London, Anne Delliere at Richemont Paris, Johann Rupper at Richemont in Cape Town and William Lauder in New York who gave me the opportunity to discover the code for China and Martin Riley at Pernod Ricard in Paris. Many thanks to Gerd Nonneman and Amol Dani at the School of Social Service in Doha.

I'd also like to express my gratitude to Lou Aronica, who helped me to draft the proposal and Keith Ferrell who inspired the chapter on Pericles. I'm grateful to Veronica French, who now has helped me with two books. With her ingenuity and experience, she has helped me a great deal in structuring my ideas and finding creative illustrations. I'd also like to thank James Richard Erwin, who did an excellent job with research and creating the bibliography, and Jesse Steele, my friend and personal assistant, for his constant and demanding positive criticism, as well as his informative multicultural perspective. Without these special individuals, this book might not have been possible.

A special thank you goes out to Emily Carlton, my editor at St. Martin's Press, who trusted me and gave me unconditional support.

Finally, I'd like to dedicate this book to my dear wife, Missy de Bellis, who traveled with me around the world, helping me to collect and analyze data. She put up with my nocturnal writing stints for several months while finishing this book with grace, and I would never have been able to navigate the insane travel marathon we put ourselves through without her on my side.

Ultimately, it was her insights, patience and support that were most invaluable.

Finally I would like to thank all my dear friends from the Satellite Tribe for your inspiration and support.

You know who you are, even though you choose to remain anonymous!

HOMEWORK FOR THE SATELLITE TRIBE

GENERAL REFERENCES

Ahonen, T., and A. Moore. *Communities Dominate Brands.* (London: Futuretext, 2005).

Aronczyk, M. *Branding the Nation.* (New York: Oxford University Press, 2013).

Bamyeh, M. *The Ends of Globalization.* (Minneapolis: University of Minnesota Press, 2000).

Berreby, D. *Us and Them.* (New York: Little, Brown and Co., 2005).

Chudacoff, H. *The Evolution of American Urban Society.* (Englewood Cliffs, New Jersey: Prentice-Hall, 1981).

Dayan, S. *Subliminally Exposed.* (New York: Morgan James Publishing, 2013).

Diamond, J. *Guns, Germs and Steel.* (London [u.a.]: Vintage, 2005).

Friedman, T. *The World Is Flat.* (New York: Farrar, Straus and Giroux, 2005).

Fromm, J., and C. Garton. *Marketing to Millennials.* (New York: AMACOM, American Management Association, 2013).

Fukuyama, F. *The End of History and the Last Man.* (New York: Free Press, 1992).

Godin, S. *Tribes.* (New York: Portfolio, 2008).

Gordinier, J. *X Saves the World.* (New York: Viking, 2008).

Greenberg, E., and K. Weber. *Generation We.* (Emeryville, California: Pachatusan, 2008).

Greer, J. *The Long Descent.* (Gabriola Island, British Columbia: New Society Publishers, 2008).

Guthrie, D. *China and Globalization.* (New York: Routledge, 2009).

Heinberg, R. *The End of Growth.* (Gabriola Island, British Columbia: New Society Publishers, 2011).

Hoersting, R. C. "No Place to Call Home: Cultural Homelessness, Self-Esteem, and Cross-Cultural Identities." Denton, Texas. UNT Digital Library. http://digital.library.unt.edu/ark:/67531/metadc10991/.

Hollis, N. *The Global Brand.* (New York: Palgrave Macmillan, 2008).

Houle, D. *Entering the Shift Age.* (Naperville: Sourcebooks, 2012).

Howe, N., and W. Strauss. *Millennials Rising.* (New York: Vintage Books, 2000).

Huntington, S. *The Clash of Civilizations and the Remaking of World Order.* (New York: Simon & Schuster, 1996).

Jia, W. *The Remaking of the Chinese Character and Identity in the 21st Century.* (Westport, Connecticut: Ablex Pub, 2001).

Kahn, B. *Global Brand Power.* (New York: Wharton Digital Press, 2013).

Kapferer, J., and V. Bastien. *The Luxury Strategy.* (London: Kogan Page, 2009).

Lyttle, A.D., G. G. Baker, and T. L. Cornwell. "Adept through Adaptation: Third Culture Individuals Interpersonal Sensitivity," *International Journal of Intercutural Relations,* 35 (5), (2011), 686–694.

Melles, E.A., and J. Schwartz. (2013) "Does the Third Culture Kid Experience the Predicted Levels of Prejudice?" *International Journal of Intercutural Relations,* 37 (2), 260–267.

Morley, M. *The Global Corporate Brand Book.* (Basingstoke: Palgrave Macmillan, 2009).

Pollock, D. C., and R. E. Van Reken. *Third Culture Kids: The Experience of Growing Up Among Worlds.* (Boston: Nicholas Brealy, 2009).

Rein, S. *The End of Cheap China.* (Hoboken, New Jersey: John Wiley & Sons, Inc., 2012).

Richerson, P., and R. Boyd. *Not by Genes Alone.* (Chicago: University of Chicago Press, 2005).

Rodrik, D. *The Globalization Paradox.* (New York: W. W. Norton & Co., 2011).

Rozenblit, B. *Us Against Them.* (Kansas City, MO: Transcendent Publications, 2008).

Shenkar, O. *The Chinese Century.* (Upper Saddle River, New Jersey: Wharton School Pub., 2005).

Singh, D. *Adaptive Significance of Female Physical Attractiveness: Role of Waist-to-Hip Ratio.* (1993), http://www.femininebeauty.info/i/singh.pdf (Washington D.C.: American Psychological Association Inc.). Web. June 11, 2014.

Stam, R., and G. Smith. (2010). *Almost Our Time.* (Holland, Michigan: Black Lake Press, 2010).

Stiglitz, J. *Globalization and Its Discontents.* (New York: W. W. Norton, 2002).

Strauss, W., and N. Howe. *The Fourth Turning.* (New York: Broadway Books, 1997).

Tuschman, A. *Our Political Nature.* (Amherst, New York: Prometheus Books, 2013).

Useem, J., and R. Useem. (1967). "The Interface of a Binational Third Culture: A Study of the American Community in India." *Journal of Social Issues* 23 (1), (2009), 130–143.

Von Teese, D. *Burlesque and the Art of the Teese/Fetish and the Art of the Teese.* (New York: Regan Books, 2006).

Wang, J. *Shaping China's Global Imagination.* (Basingstoke, UK: Palgrave Macmillan, 2013).

Yarrow, K. *Decoding the New Consumer Mind.* (San Francisco, California: Jossey-Bass, 2014).

LUXURY

Berghaus, B. *The Management of Luxury: A Practitioner's Handbook.* (n.d.).

Chevalier, M., and G. Mazzalovo. *Pro Logo: Brands as a Factor of Progress.* (New York: Palgrave Macmillan, 2004).

Chevalier, M., and M. Gutsatz. *Luxury Retail Management: How the World's Top Brands Provide Quality Product and Service Support.* (Singapore: Wiley, 2012).

Gutsatz, M., and G. Auguste. *Luxury Talent Management Leading and Managing a Luxury Brand.* (Houndmills, Basingstoke, Hampshire: Palgrave Macmillan, 2013).

Tungate, M. *Branded Male: Marketing to Men.* (London: Kogan Page, 2008).

BEAUTY

Dixson, Dr. Barnaby, New Zealand University.

Dove Campaign for Real Beauty Case Study: Innovative Marketing Strategies in the Beauty Industry. (Indiana: Datamonitor Plc., 2005).

Jerome, Burn. "Health: What a Man Can't Resist: The Perfect Hip-Waist Ratio," *The Independent,* Oct. 1994–Dec. 2014.

Lehnert, G. *A History of Fashion in the 20th Century.* (Cologne, Germany: Konemann, 2000).

Rhode, D. *The Beauty Bias: The Injustice of Appearance in Life and Law.* (New York: Oxford University Press, 2010).

Scarry, E. *On Beauty and Being Just.* (Princeton, New Jersey: Princeton University Press, 1999).

Singh, D. *Adaptive Significance of Female Physical Attractiveness: Role of Waist to Hip Ratio.* (Austin: University of Texas, 1993).

Tungate, M. *Branded Beauty: How Marketing Changed the Way We Look.* (Philadelphia, Pennsylvania: Kogan Page, 2011).

Von Teese, D. *Burlesque and the Art of the Teese.* (New York: Regan Books, 2006).

LEADERSHIP

Argyris, C. *Organizational Traps: Leadership, Culture, Organizational Design.* (Oxford: Oxford University Press, 2012).

Burtis, J., and P. Turman. *Leadership Communication as Citizenship: Give Direction to Your Team, Organization, or Community as a Doer, Follower, Guide, Manager, or Leader.* (Thousand Oaks, California: SAGE, 2010).

Goleman, D., and R. Boyatzis. *Primal Leadership: Realizing the Power of Emotional Intelligence.* (Boston, Massachusetts: Harvard Business School Press, 2002).

Kouzes, J., and B. Posner. *The Leadership Challenge: How to Get Extraordinary Things Done in Organizations.* (San Francisco: Jossey-Bass, 1987).

Liff, S. *Managing Government Employees: How to Motivate Your People, Deal with Difficult Issues, and Achieve Tangible Results.* (New York: American Management Association, 2007).

Phillips, D. *Lincoln on Leadership: Executive Strategies for Tough Times.* (New York: Warner Books, 1992).

WOMEN LEADERSHIP AND CEO

Dean, D. *Women in Academic Leadership Professional Strategies, Personal Choices.* (Sterling, Virginia: Stylus Pub, 2009).

Kellerman, B. *Women and Leadership: The State of Play and Strategies for Change.* (San Francisco, California: Jossey-Bass, a Wiley Imprint, 2007).

Nohria, N. "Women and Leadership." In *Handbook of Leadership Theory and Practice: An HBS Centennial Colloquium on Advancing Leadership.* (Boston, Massachusetts: Harvard Business Press, 2010).

MILLENNIALS

Cooper, A. *The Inmates Are Running the Asylum: Why High-Tech Products Drive Us Crazy and How to Restore the Sanity.* (Indianapolis, Indiana: Sams, 1999).

Fromm, J., and C. Garton. *Marketing to Millennials: Reach the Largest and Most Influential Generation of Consumers Ever.* (New York: AMACOM, 2013).

Howe, N., and W. Strauss. *Millennials Rising: The Next Great Generation*. (New York: Vintage Books, 2000).

Taylor, P. *The Next America: Boomers, Millennials, and the Looming Generational Showdown*. (New York: PublicAffairs, 2014).

Thead, R. *Millennials Speak: Essays on the 21st Century*. (New York: R. P. Thead, 2013).

Winograd, M., and M. Hais. *Millennial Momentum: How a New Generation Is Remaking America*. (New Brunswick, New Jersey: Rutgers University Press, 2011).

ROBOTS

DeSouza, G., and H. Duan. *Robotic Rehabilitation and Assistive Technologies*. (Bradford: Emerald Group Publishing Limited, 2014).

Lura, D. *The Creation of a Robotics Based Human Upper Body Model for Predictive Simulation of Prostheses Performance*. (Tampa: University of South Florida, 2012).

Mohri, M., and A. Rostamizadeh. *Foundations of Machine Learning*. (Cambridge, Massachusetts: MIT Press, 2012).

Moravec, H. *Mind Children: The Future of Robot and Human Intelligence*. (Cambridge, Massachusetts: Harvard University Press, 1990).

Tan, D. *Brain-Computer Interfaces*. (London: Springer-Verlag London, 2010).

CELL PHONES

Carr, N. *The Shallows: What the Internet Is Doing to Our Brains*. (New York: W. W. Norton, 2010).

Edens, A. *Cell Phone Investigations: Search Warrants, Cell Sites and Evidence Recovery*. (Police Publishing, 2014).

Hanson, J. *24/7 How Cell Phones and the Internet Change the Way We Live, Work, and Play*. (Westport, Connecticut: Praeger, 2007).

Horst, H., and D. Miller. *The Cell Phone: An Anthropology of Communication*. (Oxford: Berg, 2006).

Kent, C. *Catering to Addictions: Stealth Marketing in the Age of Web 2.0. Cell Phones, Text Messaging, and Social Networks*. (C. Kent, 2014).

Ling, R. *The Mobile Connection: The Cell Phone's Impact on Society*. (San Francisco, California: Morgan Kaufmann, 2004).

Thulin, H., and S. Gustafsson. *Mobile Phone Use While Driving: Conclusions from Four Investigations*. (Linköping, Sweden: Swedish National Road and Transport Research Institute, 2004).

HIGHER EDUCATION

Duderstadt, J., and D. Atkins. *Higher Education in the Digital Age: Technology Issues and Strategies for American Colleges and Universities*. (Westport, Connecticut: Greenwood Press, 2002).

Smart, J. *Higher Education Handbook of Theory and Research*. (Dordrecht: Springer, 2010).

Smith, W. *The Racial Crisis in American Higher Education: Continuing Challenges for the Twenty-First Century* (rev. ed.). (Albany: State University of New York Press, 2002).

Stambach, A. *Confucius and Crisis in American Universities Culture, Capital, and Diplomacy in U.S. Public Higher Education*. (London: Routledge, 2014).

PREDICTING THE FUTURE

Friedman, G. *The Next 100 Years: A Forecast for the 21st Century.* (New York: Doubleday, 2009).

Greenspan, A. *The Age of Turbulence: Adventures in a New World.* (New York: Penguin Press, 2007).

Kaku, M. *Physics of the Future: How Science Will Shape Human Destiny and Our Daily Lives by the Year 2100.* (New York: Doubleday, 2011).

Lee, K., and G. Allison. *Lee Kuan Yew: the Grand Master's Insights on China, the United States, and the World.* (Cambridge, Massachusetts: MIT Press, 2013).

Reich, R. *Aftershock: The Next Economy and America's Future.* (New York: Alfred A. Knopf, 2010).

COCO CHANEL

Brown, S., and I. Publishing. *Fashion: The Definitive History of Costume and Style.* (New York: DK Publishing, 2012).

Garelick, R. *Mademoiselle: Coco Chanel and the Pulse of History.* (New York: Random House, 2014).

Simon, L. *Coco Chanel.* (London: Reaktion Books, 2011).

BUCKMINISTER FULLER

Bibliography and Chronology of Richard Buckminister Fuller. (Los Angeles, California: Buckminster Fuller Institute, 1983).

Early Postmodernism: Foundational Essays. (Durham, North Carolina: Duke University Press, 1995).

CONFUCIUS INSTITUTE

Confucious Institute. *A Good Man in China.* (London: Singing Dragon, 2012).

Harper, D. *Discover China.* (Footscray, Victoria: Lonely Planet, 2011).

Vance, S. *Confucius Institutes and China's Evolving Foreign Policy.* (Saarbrucken, Germany: LAP Lambert Academic Publishing, 2010).

DOWNTON ABBEY

Fellowes, J. *Chronicles of Downtown Abbey: A New Era for Family, Friends, Lovers and Staff.* (London: St. Martin's, 2012).

Henry, D. *An Historical Description of Westminster Abbey, Its Monuments and Curiosities.* (London: Printed for J. Newbery, at the Bible and Sun in St. Paul's Church-Yard, 1767).

Perks, L. *Media Marathoning: Immersions in Morality.* (Lanham, Maryland: Lexington Books, 2014).

GLOBAL CULTURE

Anheier, H. *Encyclopedia of Global Studies.* (London: SAGE Publications, 2012).

Hirsch, E., and J. Kett. *The New Dictionary of Cultural Literacy* (completely rev. and updated, 3rd ed.). (Boston: Houghton Mifflin, 2002).

Livermore, D. *Cultural Intelligence: Improving Your CQ to Engage Our Multicultural World.* (Grand Rapids, Michigan: Baker Academic, 2009).

Meyer, E. *The Culture Map: Breaking Through the Invisible Boundaries of Global Business.* (New York: PublicAffairs, 2014).

Morrison, T., and W. Conaway. *Kiss, Bow, or Shake Hands: The Bestselling Guide to Doing Business in More Than 60 Countries* (2nd ed.). (Avon, Massachusetts: Adams Media, 2006).

MACHINES TAKING OVER OUR LIVES

Goodman, M. *Future Crimes: Everything Is Connected, Everyone Is Vulnerable, and What We Can Do about It.* (New York: Doubleday, 2015).

Lopes, L. *Progress in Artificial Intelligence: 14th Portuguese Conference on Artificial Intelligence, EPIA 2009, Aveiro, Portugal, October 12–15, 2009.* Proceedings. (Berlin: Springer-Verlag, 2009).

Singer, P. *Cybersecurity and Cyberwar: What Everybody Needs to Know.* (New York: Oxford University Press, 2013).

Turkle, S. *Alone Together: Why We Expect More from Technology and Less from Each Other.* (New York, Basic Books, 2011).

HUMAN SPARE PARTS

Dyens, O. *Metal and Flesh: The Evolution of Man: Technology Takes Over.* (Cambridge, Massachusetts: MIT Press, 2001).

Ferber, S. *The Body Divided: Human Beings and Human "Material" in Modern Medical History.* (Farnham, Surrey: Ashgate, 2011).

Gawande, A. *Being Mortal: Medicine and What Matters in the End.* (New York: Henry Holt & Company, 2014).

Lusardi, M. *Orthotics and Prosthetics in Rehabilitation* (2nd ed.). (St. Louis, Missouri: Saunders Elsevier, 2007).

Mesko, D. *The Guide to the Future of Medicine: Technology and the Human Touch.* (Webicina Kft, 2014).

Skurzynski, G., and F. Schwarz. *Bionic Parts for People: The Real Story of Artificial Organs and Replacement Parts.* (New York: Four Winds Press, 1978).

Smith, M. (2006). *The Prosthetic Impulse: From a Posthuman Present to a Biocultural Future.* (Cambridge, Massachusetts: MIT Press, 2006).

BRANDS

Buckingham, I. *Brand Engagement: How Employees Make or Break Brands.* (Houndmills, Basingstoke, Hampshire: Palgrave Macmillan, 2008).

Collins, J. *Good to Great: Why Some Companies Make the Leap—and Others Don't.* (New York: HarperBusiness, 2001).

Wheeler, A. *Designing Brand Identity: An Essential Guide for the Entire Branding Team* (3rd ed.). (Hoboken, New Jersey: John Wiley & Sons, 2009).

HUBS AND CITY-STATES

Black Book Lists. (n.d.). Retrieved August 16, 2014, from http://tcbmag.com/Lists-and -Research/BIG-Book?djoPage=view_html&djoPid=18824.

Carmona, M., and F. Wunderlich. *Capital Spaces: The Multiple Complex Public Spaces of a Global City.* (Abingdon, Oxon: Routledge, 2012).

Zhang, A. *An Analysis of Fortress Hubs in Airline Networks.* (Hong Kong: City University of Hong Kong, Faculty of Business, Dept. of Economics and Finance, 1996).

AIRPORTS

Ashford, N., and S. Mumayiz. *Airport Engineering Design, Planning, and Development of 21st Century Airports* (4th ed.). (Hoboken, New Jersey: Wiley, 2011).

Botton, A. *A Week at the Airport.* (New York: Vintage International, 2010).

Neufville, R., and A. Odoni. *Airport Systems: Planning, Design, and Management.* (New York: McGraw-Hill, 2003).

ADAPTABILITY

Cabrera, A., and G. Unruh. *Being Global: How to Think, Act, and Lead in a Transformed World.* (Boston, Massachusetts: Harvard Business Review Press, 2012).

Doidge, N. *The Brain's Way of Healing: Remarkable Discoveries and Recoveries from the Frontiers of Neuroplasticity.* (New York: Viking, 2015).

Martin, L. *Reproductive Tourism in the United States: Creating Family in the Mother Country.* (Hoboken: Taylor and Francis, 2014).

CHANGE

Caligiuri, P. *Cultural Agility Building: A Pipeline of Successful Global Professionals.* (San Francisco: Jossey-Bass, 2012).

Gleick, J. *Faster: The Acceleration of Just About Everything.* (New York: Pantheon Books, 1999).

Kaku, M. *The Future of the Mind: The Scientific Quest to Understand, Enhance, and Empower the Mind.* (New York: Ballantine Books, 2014).

Mlodinow, L. *The Drunkard's Walk: How Randomness Rules Our Lives.* (New York: Pantheon Books, 2008).

Mlodinow, L. *Subliminal: How Your Unconscious Mind Rules Your Behavior.* (New York: Pantheon Books, 2012).

INEQUALITY

Dadush, U. *Inequality in America: Facts, Trends, and International Perspective.* (Washington, D.C.: Brookings Institution Press, 2012).

Flannery, K., and J. Marcus. *The Creation of Inequality: How Our Prehistoric Ancestors Set the Stage for Monarchy, Slavery, and Empire.* (Cambridge, Massachusetts: Harvard University Press, 2012).

Grusky, D. *The Inequality Reader: Contemporary and Foundational Readings in Race, Class, and Gender.* (Boulder, Colorado: Westview Press, 2007).

Mason, P. *Encyclopedia of Race and Racism* (2nd ed.). (Detroit: Macmillan Reference USA, 2013).

Stiglitz, J. *The Price of Inequality: How Today's Divided Society Endangers Our Future.* (New York: W. W. Norton & Co., 2012).

Takaki, R. *A Different Mirror: A History of Multicultural America*. (Boston: Little, Brown & Co., 1993).

ATOMIC WEAPONS PROLIFERATION

Croddy, E. *Weapons of Mass Destruction: An Encyclopedia of Worldwide Policy, Technology, and History*. (Santa Barbara, California: ABC-CLIO, 2005).

Schwartz, S. *Atomic Audit: The Costs and Consequences of U.S. Nuclear Weapons Since 1940*. (Washington, D.C.: Brookings Institution Press, 1998).

PANDEMICS

Aberth, J. *Plagues in World History*. (Lanham, Maryland: Rowman & Littlefield, 2011).

Crosby, A. *America's Forgotten Pandemic: The Influenza of 1918* (2nd ed.). (Cambridge: Cambridge University Press, 2003).

Karlen, A. *Man and Microbes: Disease and Plagues in History and Modern Times*. (New York: Putnam, 1995).

BUREAUCRACY

Aldrich, J. *Why Parties? The Origin and Transformation of Political Parties in America*. (Chicago: University of Chicago Press, 1995).

Cicero, Q., and P. Freeman. *How to Win an Election: An Ancient Guide for Modern Politicians*. (Princeton, New Jersey: Princeton University Press, 2012).

Epstein, L., and J. Knight. *The Choices Justices Make*. (Washington, D.C.: CQ Press, 1998).

Wilson, J. *Bureaucracy: What Government Agencies Do and Why They Do It*. (New York: Basic Books, 1989).

TERRORISM

Buckley, M. *The Bush Doctrine and the War on Terrorism: Global Responses, Global Consequences*. (London: Routledge, 2006).

Freedman, D. *Media and Terrorism: Global Perspectives*. (Los Angeles: SAGE, 2012).

Kushner, H. (2003). *Encyclopedia of Terrorism*. (Thousand Oaks, California: SAGE, 2006).

Spaaij, R. *Understanding Lone Wolf Terrorism: Global Patterns, Motivations and Prevention*. (Dordrecht: Springer, 2012).

RETURN OF RELIGION

Collins, F. *The Language of God: A Scientist Presents Evidence for Belief*. (New York: Free Press, 2006).

Dawkins, R. *The God Delusion*. (Boston: Houghton Mifflin, 2006).

Russell, G. *Heirs to Forgotten Kingdoms: Journeys into the Disappearing Religions of the Middle East*. (New York: Basic Books, 2014).

Sharpe, M., and D. Nickelson. *Secularisations and Their Debates: Perspectives on the Return of Religion in the Contemporary West*. (Dordrecht: Springer Netherlands, 2014).

RETURN OF MEDIEVAL MENTALITY

Bauer, S. *The History of The Medieval World: From the Conversion of Constantine to the First Crusade.* (New York: W. W. Norton, 2010).

Russell, G. *Heirs to Forgotten Kingdoms: Journeys into the Disappearing Religions of the Middle East.* (New York: Basic Books, 2014).

Siewers, A. *Strange Beauty: Ecocritical Approaches to Early Medieval Landscape.* (New York: Palgrave Macmillan, 2009).

JET SET SOCIETY

Botton, A. *The Art of Travel.* (New York: Pantheon, 2002).

Stadiem, W. *Jet Set: The People, the Planes, the Glamour, and the Romance in Aviation's Glory Years.* (New York: Ballantine Books, 2014).

THE 1 PERCENT

Brands, H. *Masters of Enterprise: Giants of American Business from John Jacob Astor and J.P. Morgan to Bill Gates and Oprah Winfrey.* (New York: Free Press, 1999).

Suskind, R. *The One Percent Doctrine: Deep Inside America's Pursuit of Its Enemies Since 9/11.* (New York: Simon & Schuster, 2006).

Wartofsky, M. *The Occupiers.* (Oxford: Oxford University Press, 2014).

KOREAN CULTURE

Storey, R., and E. Park. *Korea* (5th ed.). (Hawthorn, Victoria: Lonely Planet, 2001).

Swaine, M. (2011). *America's Challenge: Engaging a Rising China in the Twenty-First Century.* (Washington, D.C.: Carnegie Endowment for International Peace, 2011).

SINGAPORE

Lee, K. *From Third World to First: The Singapore Story, 1965–2000.* (New York: Harper-Collins, 2000).

Lee, K. *The Essentials of Economic Growth.* (Singapore: Ministry of Culture, 1968).

Lee, K., and F. Han. *Lee Kuan Yew: Hard Truths to Keep Singapore Going.* (Singapore: Straits Times Press, 2011).

Oakley, M. *Singapore* (7th ed.). (Footscray, Victoria: Lonely Planet, 2006).

LEE KUAN YEW

Ang, C. *Lee Kuan Yew's Strategic Thought.* (London: Routledge, 2013).

Barr, M. *Lee Kuan Yew: The Beliefs Behind the Man.* (Washington, D.C.: Georgetown University Press, 2000).

Lee, K. *The Papers of Lee Kuan Yew: Speeches, Interviews and Dialogues.* (Singapore: Gale Asia, 2012).

DR. RAPAILLE'S BIOGRAPHY

Dr. G. Clotaire Rapaille is an internationally known expert in archetypal marketing, creativity and innovation. His unique approach to marketing combines a psychoanalyst's depth of analysis with a businessman's attention to practical concerns.

He has written more than fourteen books. His most popular book, *The Culture Code,* was #9 on the bestseller list of *Businessweek* and has been translated into twelve languages.

Dr. Rapaille's technique for market research has grown out of his work in the areas of psychology, social psychology, psychoanalysis and cultural anthropology. His work is an extension of the work done by many of the great scholars of the twentieth century, including Jung, Laing, Levi-Strauss and Ruth Benedict.

Dr. Rapaille's work for the past 20 years led him to develop a new process for understanding how we are imprinted for the first time by what he calls the "logic of emotion," which is the code for each cultural archetype within the collective unconscious of a given culture.

Dr. Rapaille's world travels, a term in the diplomatic corps and extensive marketing research on product and brand archetypes for international corporations have given him a fresh perspective on American and global business and the interactions among the Americas, Europe, the Middle East and Asia.

He is fluent in English, French and Spanish. Dr. Rapaille is a sought-after lecturer on creativity, communication and cultural literacy.

BIBLIOGRAPHY OF DR. G. CLOTAIRE RAPAILLE

El Verbo De Las Culturas. Mexico City: Taurus, March 2015. A humorous look at 26 different cultures as explained through their code "verb."

Move Up (in English). London: Penguin, 2015.

Dr. G. Clotaire Rapaille and Dr. Andres Roemer, *Move Up* (in Spanish). Mexico City: Taurus, 2013. An explanation of upward social mobility from a biological and cultural perspective.

The Culture Code: An Ingenious Way to Understand Why People Around the World Live and Buy as They Do (in English, German, French, Portuguese, Spanish, Japanese, Korean, Chinese [Mandarin and Cantonese], Italian, Russian). New York: Broadway Books, 2006.

Social Cancer: The Code for Terrorism (in English). New York: Tuxedo Productions, 2003.

7 Secrets of Marketing in a Multi-Cultural World, First Edition. (in English). Provo, Utah: Executive Excellence, 2001.

7 Secrets of Marketing in a Multi-Cultural World, Second Edition. (in English). Provo, Utah: Executive Excellence, 2001.

Versteh' Deine Eltern (in German). Munich: Bucher, 1984.

Comprendre Ses Parents et Ses Grands Parents (in French). Paris: Marabout, 1982.

Escuchelo: Es Su Hijo (in Spanish). Barcelona: Pomaire, Coleccion Libre, 1981.

Le Trouple (in French). Paris: Editions Menges, 1980.

Si Vous Ecoutiez Vos Enfants (in French). Paris: Editions Menges, 1978.

Comprendre Ses Parents (in French). Paris: Editions Menges, 1978.

La Communication Creatrice (in French). Paris: Editions Dialogues, 1976.

Wisdom of Madness (in English). Grand Rapids, Michigan: Thomas Jefferson College, Grand Valley State University, 1975.

La Relazion Creatrice (in Italian). Assissi: Cittadella Editrice, 1975.

Dr. Michele C. Barzach, Je T'aime, Je Ne T'aime Pas (in French). Paris: Editions Universitaires, 1974.

La Relation Creatrice (in French). Paris: Editions Universitaires, 1973.

Laing (in French). Paris: Editions Universitaries, 1972.

Analyse des Pratiques Medicales et des Croyances Liees a la Maladie et aux Soins dans Quinze Communautes Nicaraguayennes (in French). Paris: Sorbonne, 1969.

NOTES

CHAPTER 1

1. A. D. Lyttle, G. G. Baker, and T. L. Cornwell, "Adept through adaptation: Third culture individuals interpersonal sensitivity," *International Journal of Intercutural Relations,* 35 (5), 2011, 686–694; E. A. Melles, and J. Schwartz, "Does the third culture kid experience the predicted levels of prejudice?" *International Journal of Intercutural Relations,* 37 (2), 2013, 260–267; D. C. Pollock and R. E. Van Reken, *Third Culture Kids: The Experience of Growing Up Among Worlds* (Boston: Nicholas Brealy, 2009).

CHAPTER 12

1. http://www.wsj.com/articles/in-japan-dog-owners-feel-abandoned-as-sony-stops-su pporting-aibo-1423609536

GLOBAL BRANDS, GLOBAL LEADERS AND A GLOBAL WORLD

1. G. Clotaire Rapaille, *7 Secrets of Marketing in a Multi-Cultural World,* Second Edition (Provo, Utah: Executive Excellence, 2001), 274.

INDEX